# Jules Michelet

# Jules Michelet
*A Study of Mind and Sensibility*

Stephen A. Kippur

*State University of New York Press*
ALBANY

Published by
State University of New York Press, Albany

© 1981 State University of New York

For information, address State University of New York
Press, State University Plaza, Albany, N.Y., 12246

*Library of Congress Cataloging in Publication Data*

Kippur, Stephen A 1947-
  Jules Michelet, a study of mind and sensibility.

  Bibliography: p.
  Includes index.
  1. Michelet, Jules, 1789-1874. 2. Historians—France—Biography. I. Title.
DC3698.M5K56 944.0072'02'4 [B] 80-14750
ISBN 0-87395-430-0
ISBN 0-87395-431-9 (pbk.)

*In Memoriam*

Shirley Kippur
1921–1973

# Contents

# Acknowledgments

Much as Michelet brought to life neglected documents of the past, Oscar Haac and Michela Magó, two eminent Michelet scholars, discovered this work when it was a dissertation gathering dust in New York City, and encouraged me to revise and to publish it. To them I am deeply grateful.

My research was done primarily in Paris. I wish to express my gratitude to the librarians and archivists of the Archives Nationales, Bibliothèque de l'Arsenal, Bibliothèque historique de la ville de Paris, Bibliothèque de l'Institut, Bibliothèque Nationale, and Collège de France.

I owe special gratitude to M. Paul Viallaneix for inviting me to the university in Clermont-Ferrand to read typescripts of notes taken by Michelet's students at his courses given at the Ecole Normale and the Collège de France. All Michelet scholars will always be indebted to M. Viallaneix for preparing the *Journal* and for his current editing of a new *Œuvres complètes*.

I would also like to thank the following individuals who helped me in various ways: Frank E. Manuel for the scholarly advice as well as enthusiasm for intellectual history he imparted to me over a period of five years; Mark Senn for his many useful comments on style; my father for his love and support; Robert Mandel, my editor, for his encouragement, and last, but certainly not least, the center of my life, my wife, Susan.

I have used the available English translations whenever possible, but with revisions. All other translations are my own.

# Introduction

This is the first full-length biography of Jules Michelet in the English language. Yet his ideas are not unknown and his importance and influence in history is assured. His multitude of ideas and many, creative works have led to his continued use and mention in the last hundred years from a wide spectrum of sources—Charles de Gaulle quoted him; Edmund Wilson focused on him in the first part of *To The Finland Station*; and Lucien Febvre, one of the founders of perhaps the most dominant school of historiography today, the Annales School, acknowledged him to be the guiding force of modern historical writing.

As a historian, Michelet was one of the truly unique stylists of the art. Is there anyone before or since who has given to the reader such a sense of involvement in the French Revolution? He used the word "Renaissance" to apply to a particular period of history before anyone else; he wrote the first modern work on witchcraft; and he discovered the writings of the early eighteenth-century Neapolitan genius, Giambattista Vico, for the Western world. In Michelet's romantic translation of the *New Science*, Marx recognized the idea of class conflict, and James Joyce found the philosophy of *corso, ricorsi* which permeated his novels. Most of all, Michelet was *the* historian of France—officially recognized as such during the Third Republic. It took him almost four decades to write the history of his beloved France. His conception of France and her history influenced generations of French schoolchildren.

And still there was much more to Michelet. He wrote "bestsellers" on women, nature, and religious controversies. After deciding that he loved "the people"—a concept with wide-ranging resonances throughout the last two centuries—he wrote *Le Peuple*, one of his most revelatory books.

No subject of importance in nineteenth-century France escaped his pen. All of the big issues—social class conflicts, race, education, and moral concerns—received significant treatment. As a lecturer at the Collège de France, the highest appointment a French professor could have, his course was the most well attended in the history of the country. Plainclothes police spied on his class, and many pointed to Michelet for helping to bring about the February 1848 Revolution. In sheer quantity his complete works contain dozens of books, thousands of letters, and thousands of pages of diaries. In sheer diversity he spoke to all the issues of his day.

Until recently, it has been impossible to analyze and interpret Michelet fully, because of the fate of his manuscripts. After his death in 1874 his widow received all his papers, including thousands of unpublished pages of correspondence and diaries. From these personal documents Mme Michelet periodically edited a few books under her husband's name. The most important of these works, *Ma Jeunesse* and *Mon Journal*, published in 1884 and 1888, respectively, were purportedly compilations of key excerpts from Michelet's autobiography. However, recent evidence collected by Paul Viallaneix has shown that these volumes were largely inaccurate, beset primarily by careless editing and frequent citations that turned out to be Mme Michelet's own thoughts, instead of those of her famous husband.[1]

In 1899, the year of her death, Mme Michelet asked that all of Michelet's historical works and notes (many of them unedited) be deposited in the Bibliothèque historique de la ville de Paris and that the personal papers be given to Gabriel Monod.[2] Inadvertently, Michelet's intimate writings from 1820 to 1828, containing the manuscript upon which *Mon Journal* had been fabricated, were included among the unedited writings at the Bibliothèque historique de la ville de Paris. The revelatory information from these diaries of Michelet's early years was only edited and published in 1959.[3]

Although Michelet's personal documents for the years 1828 to 1874 were entrusted to Monod, the first biographer of Michelet, Mme Michelet stipulated that he could not publish these materials. In 1911, in accordance with Mme Michelet's wishes, Monod had the *Journal* deposited at the Bibliothèque de l'Institut with the instructions that it remain locked and sealed until 1950.[4] Only in 1951 did a commission under the supervision of the Secretary of the Académie des Sciences morales et politiques allow the *Journal* to be opened for preparation and publication by Paul Viallaneix and Claude Digeon.[5] Thus, the personal documents of Michelet have become available only within the last twenty years. Their importance is paramount to any work on Michelet's life and ideas.

Gabriel Monod's magisterial two-volume study of Michelet, which only covers two-thirds of Michelet's life, was published posthumously from his notes in 1923.[6] This book set the tone for Michelet scholarship.[7] Nearly everyone has noted, like Monod, that Michelet was a man of feeling, who loved "the people" and France. He has also been seen variously as a precursor of totalitarianism, democracy, socialism, liberalism, nationalism, republicanism, Gaullism, or any other "ism."[8]

The present study attempts to portray Michelet as an extremely complex figure, whose voluminous writings reveal values and assumptions on many levels. His ideas and preconceptions defy a single unified interpretation, and are, instead, charged with tensions and replete with ambiguities that appear to be part and parcel of any individual's psychic nature and of any dynamic society. I have chosen, while proceeding chronologically, what I consider to be the main problems or topics for each period of Michelet's life. Examined are his childhood, class identity, social status, intellectual development, philosophy of history, geographical preconceptions, psychology of human nature, religious ideas, social theory, educational theory, idea of "the people," theories on man and society, and his multifaceted attitudes toward his country. Furthermore, Michelet's historical works are discussed along with his roles as archivist, educator, and historian; his idea of a genius and a hero; his varied assumptions on the movement of history and of time and history; and his theories on women and nature. A note on the fortunes of Michelet during the century following his death concludes the work.

The elucidation of Michelet's ideas manifest his social and philosophical preconceptions. In this work it is assumed that the unconscious can shed light on the thoughts and actions of any individual. Therefore, personal biographical details are mentioned and analyzed primarily to illuminate his ideas and preconceptions. For example, he had an overwhelming need for unity and harmony in his ideas and life, yet he never found this harmony—not in his family, not in his childhood, not in his ideas, such as "humanity," "the people," or even in "*la patrie*." Analysis of his diary helps explain this orientation—the reasons for its existence and for his inability to achieve permanent realization of this need. His own personal tensions commingled with the tensions of the society.

Hence, this is a study of "mind and sensibility"—what Michelet thought and felt recast in twentieth-century language and terminology—and not a quest for quantitative comprehensiveness of all intellectual and biographical details. In terms of quality of thought, he can be seen at various times as a tremendously creative figure or a rather shallow thinker full of delusions. Yet, Michelet happened to be an extremely prolific writer with antennae into all currents of French thought, both philosophical and popular. This propensity to write on every pressing issue and problem in French society, infusing each with meaning and ambiguity, makes Michelet an ideal figure for revealing both his manner of thinking and believing and the orientation of the society he inhabited.

# 1

## *Remorse and Admiration*

In Paris fifteen months before the 18th Brumaire, Jules Michelet, who became the great romantic, philosophical historian and the revealer of France's unitary soul, was born.

His parents, Jean François Furcy Michelet and the former Angélique Constance Millet, had recently arrived from the provinces, and Jules, their only child, entered the world "as a blade of grass without sun between two cobblestones of Paris" on August 21, 1798.[1] Fittingly, this later polemicist against Christianity was delivered in a deconsecrated church owned by the nuns of Saint-Chaumont at 16 rue de Tracy at the corner of rue Saint-Denis. Years later, Michelet would recall an early independence, apparently enhanced by his father's linking him with the goddess of love. "I had the enormous advantage of being born free. My father named me Jules and said, 'That will serve him always, since Pope Jules or Julien descended from Venus.'"[2]

Michelet took his Parisian origins seriously. As a historian, he would reveal repeatedly his indebtedness to this city as a central formative element in his personal life, philosophy, and profession:

> This city has been everything for me. I was born here. I have lived here,
> I will pass all my days here . . . All my emotions, all my traditions are tied
> to it, as are my past and my future. Others have sensed the awakening of
> their genius in the midst of the countryside, in romantic sites, in poetic
> solitudes; myself in the grime of the street corners. One is born Spanish,
> another English, another German, I was born faubourg Saint-Denis . . .
> All the solemn moments of my life are associated with such or such a place

*1*

of this great city. I passed my childhood in the humid and somber center, my youth in the distant faubourgs. I have dreamt for ten years on the roads of Père Lachaise and Vincennes. This cohabitation with such a city, has without doubt contributed to the awakening of history in myself.[3]

Association and identification with Paris were of paramount importance to Michelet, but he also liked to claim geographical idiosyncrasies from the native regions of his parents. He thought that he had inherited the Picardy "choleric" of his father's family and the Ardennes "serious and critical spirit" of the maternal side. In addition to acknowledging these northern France origins, he occasionally asserted that the Michelets had descended from the Normans and the Millets from the Walloons. "The Michelets: Picards, Irish-Walloons, Normans; Millets: Champagne-Lorraine, Walloons."[4] By the 1820s, a steady correspondence had developed between Michelet and various aunts and cousins on his mother's side of the family. Although he visited them for the first time in 1817, he would often exclaim, as he did to the local notary after his Aunt Hyacinthe's death in 1849, that "I am and remain Ardennais."[5]

Michelet's famous introduction to *Le Peuple* is and will remain the major source of information on the Millets of Renwez in the Ardennes during the eighteenth century, since the archives for the pre-Revolutionary years in Mézières were destroyed in the early months of World War II before any scholar had explored them thoroughly. In his 1845 introduction Michelet painted a bleak picture of the economic hardships faced by the resourceful Millets. Thierry Millet and Jeanne Micheaux Millet, Michelet's grandparents, had nineteen children, but only seven survived childhood.[6] Michelet, characterizing the family as "peasant in origin," described how they all worked extremely hard and made extraordinary sacrifices for each other. The five sisters, "economical, serious, and austere," neglected their own needs and saved their meager earnings in order "to contribute to the education" of their two brothers.[7]

The few documents available on the Millets after the French Revolution indicate that they were not at the bottom of the socio-economic scale as Michelet had suggested. In the local registers in Renwez, it was noted upon the death of Hyacinthe on August 3, 1849, that she "was the daughter of Thierry Millet and Jeanne Micheaux" who were "proprietors."[8] Although "proprietors" could have been poor peasants in French social classification terminology, other factors dispel this possibility for the Millets. When the house of Michelet's grandparents was sold in 1821, the bill of sale mentioned the socially important phrase that it was located on *"la Grande Rue."*[9] This ability to own property by the family was confirmed after the death of Jeanne Micheaux Millet on May 8, 1810, when she left an estate valued at 99,473 francs to her children.[10] During the nineteenth century there was social mobility within the family structure. The registers showed the three celibate sisters rising from "proprietors" to "stockholders," while a fourth sister married Jean Nicolas Lefebvre, who was in commerce and who became mayor of Renwez.[11] The children's finances helped sustain the poverty stricken Michelets in the nation's capital.

Félix Michelet and Marie Barbe Lecart Michelet, the paternal grandparents of Michelet, were married, as recorded in the parish register of Semilly-sous-Laon, on April 11, 1769. Twenty-one years old at the time, Félix soon became choirmaster in Laon, remaining in that position until the Revolution. According to Michelet's account in his *Histoire de la Révolution française*, eighteenth-century Laon was controlled by priests operating out of the enormously wealthy monastery of Chartreux. The financially and politically dominant priests irked the poor community, causing public opinion to be "not only indifferent, but rather hostile."[12]

Although Michelet's grandparents "spoke poorly of religion, because . . . the priests, being the richest men, continually aroused the envy of the poor," they still pressured their son, Furcy, to become a priest or a monk.[13] In his *Histoire de la Révolution française*, Michelet remarked that his father, born in 1770, little desired to fulfill his family's wishes, even less so after coming across some dangerous writings of Voltaire:

> He was presented to the abbé de Bourbon, son of Louis XV and of mademoiselle de Romans, who had a half million in income from a benefice. This twenty-year old prince, good-looking, amiable and worldly, received my father admirably, spoke for a moment with him, found him a man of the world, without any ecclesiastical vocation, tapped him amicably on the shoulder: "Very well, my friend, very well. I like you; I will make you a canon!" Fortunately for my father, the Revolution followed shortly thereafter.[14]

3

Furcy Michelet came to Paris from Laon in October 1792 and went to work for a printing firm. As a printer he became attuned to the various political intrigues and machinations around him, which later made him a living source of information for his son's *Histoire de la Révolution française*. Furcy's own career was one of frustrations and failures. For twenty years after his arrival in Paris he operated a printing press, initially under other companies and then his own small shop, only to be closed by one of Napoleon's many decrees against the press. Finding himself in the center of the Revolution, Furcy started printing assignats then moved to the Sourds-Muets printing office during the Terror. With Robespierre's henchmen in his midst, jailing and executing men whose articles he had printed, Furcy prudently decided to escape while it was still possible:

> On 9 Thermidor, when Hébert perished with the commune, my father protected himself wisely by failing to show up at the suspected printing press of the Sourds-Muets. Fortunately, he did not return there. But on the advice of his friends, at this moment when a new freedom exploded onto the horizon and gave an incredible boost to printing, he undertook with some cash that my grandfather had given him, to start his own printing press. That was the beginning of the misfortunes which nearly made the family perish and which associated him with the changing cycles through which France passed, breathing by moments, then deflated and finally cruelly asphyxiated during the Empire.
>
> The great eruption of printing presses in '94-'95, did not last. In '96 it was already dampened. But my father, as a former employee of the Sourds-Muets, inspired, without having in the least merited it, the confidence of Jacobins, at a time when prison had united them with their former enemy, Babeuf, and when the Robespierristes had reconciled themselves to his ideas on agrarian law.
>
> A Jacobin from Lyon, Revol, carried to my father a manuscript to print. Was it their 'Manifesto of '96' for the insurrection of the Directory? I believe it was. Because my father often said that his death was certain if this would have been discovered.[15]

In his son's eyes, Furcy had a way of rubbing elbows with history.

While trying to survive financially, Furcy had to contend continually with the consequences from political mistakes in revolutionary Paris.

The first of several seals on his press in October 1795 (18 Vendémiaire year IV) closed the daily *Portefeuille politique et littéraire*, because the publisher, Lamiral, was arrested. In a letter to the "Citizens composing the Committee of Public Safety," clearing himself of any improper action, Furcy emphasized that he was just the printer and had no personal involvement in "what the paper says."[16]

On March 27, 1795 (7 Germinal year III), the twenty-five-year-old struggling artisan, Furcy Michelet, married thirty-four-year-old Angélique Millet, daughter of a peasant landholding family. The age differential would be similar in Jules's first marriage. In *Le Peuple* Michelet viewed both sides of his familial heritage as "peasants," but their social origins, at least as of the mid-eighteenth century, did not coincide with this label. These social class disparities will be further complicated when Michelet emerges from this world into the Parisian intellectual world of the 1840s. The one link that Michelet always stressed was that between his father's occupation, printer, and his vocation, historian. Before writing history, he had learned from Furcy how to "compose" books.[17]

In the fourteen years between Jules's birth and the closing of his father's press, the Michelets moved five times, generally in the vicinity of the Marais, to find economic betterment and probably also to avoid creditors. The quest was entirely futile. Two months after Brumaire on January 17, 1800 (27 Nivôse year VIII), a decree limited the number of presses in the Department of the Seine to thirteen; Furcy's *Courrier des armées* was not among the unlucky number. "They only permitted my father to print an ecclesiastical journal; and after this undertaking had been begun at considerable expense, the sanction was bruskly stopped and the authorization was given to a priest whom Napoleon thought safe, but who soon betrayed him."[18] Unemployment led to debts, for which Furcy was arrested in 1808, incarcerated for nearly a year. Freed, he managed to print a few books, while living on money coming in from Renwez. However, "Bonaparte, who now wanted to undertake bigger things, felt the need to control the very instrument of revolution, the press . . . we were sacrificed, . . . and we lost our only resource."[19] As Michelet related in *Le Peuple*, Napoleon "struck with sixteen decrees in two years," and one day a government agent informed the Michelets that the Emperor "had reduced the number of printers to sixty; the big ones were kept, *the little ones were shut up*."[20] Before the decrees of February 5, 1810 and February 2, 1811, the police department compiled a list of 156 printers in the city of Paris. Under the name Michelet, the report quickly detailed the general failure of Furcy in the printing business, ending with the judgment: "*Wretch*: he doesn't even pay for licensing."[21]

The collapse of his father's occupation, precipitated by dictates from the Emperor, engendered in Michelet a hatred and scorn for Napoleon and the Empire. The periodic romantic revival of Napoleonic sentiment would never engulf nor enrapture Michelet. His father had been struck down from the hand of the Emperor and sentiments for Napoleon and later for the nephew only initiated further bitter epithets. In his last work, *Histoire du XIXᵉ siècle*, Michelet continued to spew forth the vitriolic opinions inculcated during his childhood:

> History, here, it appears, has fallen into an abyss. From great subjects, . . . from ideas, and popular movements, it has fallen to the individual, to pure biography . . . The human spirit appears to have forgotten everything, all theory, all language. One word alone has replaced everything, one word alone that cripples and which is not even French: *Buonoparté* . . . It is interesting both to witness the decline of intelligence as the world lowered and also to observe how the great miracle-worker, the clever conjurer, who made miracles of illusion and of blindness, was prepared for his astonishing career—Adieu science, ideas, nation, adieu *Patrie*! . . . all is adjourned. I have to occupy myself with a man.[22]

Michelet's disdain for Napoleon branched out into a psychological and emotive characterization of the whole historical period. Men could neither think nor feel during this epoch:

> Me, my infancy and the end of the Empire . . . the waiting without hope, without desire, if not that of death . . . all was dark. Dark was France! Light only shined on the army, outside of France, on such or such barbarian name. . . . Read the papers of the Revolution all shining with ideas; among the rhetoric and the harangue you felt yourself in the light. But read the *Moniteur*, the *Debates* under the Empire. What dryness! What poverty! . . . intellectual death within, and no principle on which one would want to sacrifice himself. . . . No hope.[23]

Michelet would hardly have believed that anyone could have been happy living or growing up in the constrictive atmosphere of the Empire that he described. This somber mood gradually spread through all of France; there was no escape from the darkness, for one man stifled all possibilities of development and of hope.

During his youth, Michelet abhorred the government which persecuted his father and made his family suffer. There were, moreover, in addition to Napoleon's printing sanctions, other family problems and tensions recognized by Michelet and referred to in his youthful writings.

There are two major sources on Michelet's family life and childhood: his autobiographical *Mémorial* begun on June 4, 1820, continued to at least November 30, 1820, only to be set aside until March 31, 1822 and finished shortly thereafter; and the introduction to *Le Peuple*, written twenty-three years later. The *Mémorial* was initially falsified by Mme Michelet and published as *Ma jeunesse*, but the correct transcription first appeared in 1959 as part of Michelet's *Ecrits de jeunesse*.[24] The contrast between the *Mémorial* and *Le Peuple* is striking. With only ten pages on his childhood, the introduction to *Le Peuple* is shorter, briefer, and less revealing than the earlier autobiography. In *Le Peuple*, written in 1845, preoccupation with religious controversies and class problems permeated Michelet's revised summary of childhood. His portrayal of a united and devoted family, part of "the people," replaced the less harmonized and less polemical version presented in the *Mémorial*.

The very personal *Mémorial* focused directly on Michelet and his immediate family. Contained in this pristine document, locked up during his lifetime, were Michelet's earliest and purest revelations of himself, his family, and his world. Before any of his major writings, Michelet had composed this complex view of the world—the autobiography of a Parisian written between the ages of twenty-one and twenty-three. Like many of his contemporaries, the young Michelet had imbibed the writings of the great revealer of the eighteenth century, Jean-Jacques Rousseau. The opening passage of the *Mémorial* acknowledged this inspiration, in words recalling the powerful first page of the *Confessions*, by boldly proclaiming that "Rousseau will not be the only man who was known."[25] The passionate tale of a solitary youth growing up in poverty during the Empire followed. Michelet never traveled during these years, remaining in the area of the Marais until 1812 when he crossed the river to the Jardin des Plantes.

The dominant childhood problem presented in the *Mémorial* was economic deprivation affection all aspects of his life. "For nourishment, I was accustomed to such frugality that often it was sensuous for me to eat some green beans."[26] The economic plight of the Michelets pervaded the whole atmosphere of the household. Materially only "the money from Renwez continued to sustain us"; emotionally it was very "sad"; physically it was extremely cold during the winters.[27]

No refuge awaited Michelet outside of his home. In the 1850s he reflected: "Why was my somber childhood so tardy? Why stunted for such a long time? Because it lacked festivals, society."[28] The climate of life was hostile, the societal and national structures being equally forbidding. "For eight to twelve years I remained without study, without amusement, without friends my age, seeing only from nature the Jardin des Plantes."[29] Alone in the world, as Rousseau before him, Michelet's only reprieve was walking in Père Lachaise. In 1869 he recalled: "I had a wonderful sickness which clouded my youth, but was worthy of a historian. I loved death. I lived nine years near the gates of Père Lachaise, my only walking place."[30]

Michelet's favorite pastime as a child became strolling hour after hour in that famous cemetery where people from another society and another historical time lay. What kind of personality developed under such joylessness and duress? According to Michelet, he became extremely "timid" with other people and passed the time "imagining" happier circumstances as an escape from his predicament.[31] As a middle-aged man, Michelet indicated the double-edged nature of his timidity: "Timid by habit from a solitary life, I never took pleasure in great gatherings of men; absent, I envied them more, regretted them, desired them."[32]

Historical as well as revelatory value must be ascribed to the *Mémorial*. Not only is this Michelet's personal version of his mental and psychic state, but it also contains the greatest amount of factual and psychological evidence available both on his childhood and on his parents. Otherwise, there are virtually no other documents on his mother and father. Angélique died in 1814 while Furcy lived on until 1846. He saw his son become famous, but there were only a handful of letters exchanged between them, since they lived in the same house. Occasionally Michelet remarked that he was fortunate to have "the best father and best mother that one could possibly hope for."[33] He always praised Furcy, but rarely elaborated on his personality. From Furcy's small correspondence, it appears that there was a certain simplicity to him. His few letters were straightforward, honest, humble, and practically devoid of adjectives and adverbs, quite opposite to the style Michelet developed. In addition, Furcy had a dreamy quality, termed by Michelet as "his credulous hopes" which might have aided Furcy in blotting out the unpleasant realities of his continual vocational failures.[34] Above all, Furcy Michelet was a warm and good-hearted man, totally devoted to his family. In his last twenty years, Furcy found his most rewarding pleasures in fervently assisting Jules with his research.

While his father was frequently engaged in naïve dreams, his mother instilled "reasonableness" into the family and, from Michelet's viewpoint, into his own character.[35] Her death on February 9, 1815, understandably grieved her son as the apparent unity of the family had been forever ended.

Beneath the surface, key passages in the *Mémorial* undercut the pre-1815 harmony. In a section on his father, Michelet lauded Furcy as "a true practical *philosophe*," but who had been "deceived every time he had trusted other men," and then had been forced to confine his abundant love and compassion only to those "who immediately surrounded him." Even then, Michelet added, "Why should he have found in his family such harsh natures, ones so contrary to his own?"[36]

Furcy's qualities of altruism and concern for others apparently were not reciprocated by his wife. In the central familial sketch of the *Mémorial* the pain of the author appears clearly, amplifying the phrase, "such harsh natures":

What aggravated our position was mother's irritable character; she was exasperated by so much sorrow and privation and attributed all of this to father's negligence. There were some agonizing scenes. My father listened with a goodness and patience worthy of Epictetus. I should have been quiet; but my impetuous character made me side first with one and then the other, and I further irritated the dispute. It is certain that my poor mother found little consolation in me. Imagine a spoiled child, hard, given to violence when contradicted, reasoning incorrectly but with a strange subtlety. I must cite an example which makes me blush while writing it. I was looking for a pretext for disobedience and I recited to my mother two lines of Voltaire that I had heard; "Mortals are equal, it is not at all a question of birth." And so I distressed my poor mother to the point of tears, she who was already so depressed by our other misfortunes. I was immediately touched, but I was too proud to return. I've said enough for now but promise to relate later on the wrongs I did to her and which always left me the most poignant remorse.[37]

This was the only time Michelet ever described his mother's personality, other than the few instances during his life when he attributed her realism and "reasonableness" to his own character. Michelet, the future advocate of the unity and harmony of families and nations, seems to have come from a divided family himself. While he felt that his mother's "irritable character" had "aggravated" the situation, she had "attributed" the family problems to her husband's "negligence." For her, apparently, Furcy's vocational inaptitude and failures had caused the misfortunes of the family.

A second area of discord among the Michelets, in addition to parental conflict, was the mother and son relationship, which left young Jules with the "most poignant remorse." Although he promised "to relate later on the wrongs" that he had done towards his mother, there are no known documents containing this information. However, Michelet never forgot his mother and referred frequently to their unfulfilled relationship:

I lost her thirty years ago and nevertheless, always living, she follows me from age to age. She had some bad times from me and she was not able to profit from my best. Young, I saddened her, and I will not console her . . . I owe her much . . . I sense myself profoundly her son. Each instant, in my ideas, in my words—without speaking of gestures and of traits—I find again my mother in me. It is the blood of the woman, the sympathy which I have for past ages, this tender memory of all that is no more.[38]

When Michelet mentioned in this revelatory section of the *Mémorial* that in the family disputes "my impetuous character made me side first with one and then the other," it was no idle phrase, because, according to Michelet, his parents constantly reinforced the image that he was the center and the most important member of the family. Therefore, he received continual attention from them and his attention was coveted by them. "Frequently, when I was little, papa and mama would take me into their bed in the morning, and place me between them; and papa loved to sing me this song: 'I am so happy to be a father / My son is my consolation / Until my dying hour / My dear son will make my happiness.'"[39] Furcy and Angélique placed all their hopes in their son, which, years later, Michelet still recalled with "astonishment"; their "effort" despite the "misery of those awful years, in order to get me to respond to this hope, was so great, so heroic, that it still remains inexplicable to me."[40]

Michelet was taught not to be like his parents, but rather to succeed where they had failed. One senses that he was treated as a near equal at an early age. As is common among great thinkers, Michelet the child seemed to sense his future greatness. Referring to his family life, he remembered, "Everywhere I was feted, admired; sometimes I was to become one great man and sometimes another; the largeness of my head portended well for my future. . . . This admiration of all those who surrounded me gave me a fantastic idea of my powers."[41] Buoyed by his parents from an early age, as they prophesied his future superiority, Michelet never filled the role of the son who would imitate the father. Instead he was the mature young man who "mediated" between his parents during quarrels and who consoled them during despondency, while slowly preparing to pass beyond them and bring to fruition all that had been lacking in their lives and in his childhood. When he attempted to play with little children his age, such as Titine and her brother Coco, he did not enjoy it; "I was a man in comparison."[42]

Michelet conceived and imagined many "great projects," as he termed them, during his childhood.[43] The longest lasting fantasy was "a chateau in Spain." While this wish for a chateau was not uncommon among French children, the details Michelet added in his *Mémorial* were unique. There "it was not only a question of civilizing a savage people. I made provisions for everything; the number of those that I admitted into this new society, the sharing of the land, the grandeur of the city, the number of doors."[44] In this chateau he installed and implemented his vision of the world. Through dreams, such as this one, Michelet could temporarily escape from the tensions and unhappiness of his childhood, and create an ideal world, where perhaps the whole family and the whole society would be united under *his* direction—if only for a moment—in total harmony and bliss.

# 2

## *Nothing Personal*

In his *Histoire du XIX$^e$ siècle* Michelet rhapsodized over the increasing importance of education in France beginning under the Directory:

> . . . the Ecole Normale summons from everywhere in France all those who already teach or will teach tomorrow.
>
> Twelve chairs are inaugurated at the Ecole Normale, twelve chairs at the Museum of Natural History. On December 4 the three schools of medicine. Finally the Ecoles centrales (or lycées) on February 25, '95.
>
> Stupendous creations, astounding in their grandeur, but even more in the spirit of life, the heart which one feels beating everywhere . . .
>
> Teaching, until then disdained, appears in its true worth as a magistracy. One sees the Convention summon all the geniuses of the age to its schools. At the Ecole Normale, one sees the Lagranges and Laplaces teaching mathematics. Men like Bernardin de St. Pierre, Volney, etc., were called to teach morals, literary, and historical studies.[1]

More than a comment solely on the Directory, the continuation of this tremendous thrust in the prominence of education catapulted men born three years later, such as Michelet and Auguste Comte, into careers and worlds which would have been far less attainable before the Revolution. For Michelet, education became the "way out" from a dreary childhood, an escape which he clearly recognized, leading him to always intone the miraculous powers of education. Freed by books, he always felt that others could be freed in the same manner.

Furcy Michelet had realized and had communicated to his son the power of words with the true power residing in those who write the texts instead of those who merely "compose" them. It was primarily he, along with his wife's whole-hearted support, who made the decision to have young Jules educated properly. At the age of twelve, Michelet "knew nothing, except four words of Latin."[2] Shortly thereafter a publishing friend of Furcy's suggested an apprentice opening for Jules in a large publishing house. Despite this enticing offer, Michelet's parents decided that he "should study, regardless of what might happen."[3]

In his *Mémorial* Michelet declared that "this is perhaps the most important period of my life. I begin my studies and I will soon no longer be alone."[4] In October 1810, Furcy sent Jules to learn Latin with M. Mélot, a former bookseller, now managing a *pension* or boarding house on rue Saint-Thomas-du-Louvre. The future educator and philosophical historian recognized immediately that his first tutor "knew all the grammarians, knew all the rules . . . but he had no philosophical view and spoke vaguely and inaccurately."[5] Two years later, urged on by his parents, he began his formal schooling at the Collège Charlemagne now named Lycée Charlemagne, housed in a former Jesuit teaching center. Although starting slowly and having to repeat his initial year of secondary school, Michelet gained confidence the next year, studied diligently, and finished first in his class for the academic year, 1813-14. After this success, others followed rapidly: August 1816, first prize in French oration and Latin translation at the general competition held at the Institut; May 1817, secondary school diploma; July 1818, bachelor of arts; July 1819, defended doctoral dissertation successfully at the Sorbonne; September 1821, accepted for the first doctoral written comprehensive examination (*agrégation*), in which he placed third. One of his professors whom he most impressed was Abel-François Villemain. Villemain had established himself quickly, teaching at the Collège Charlemagne by twenty-one; assisting Guizot in his chair of modern history at the Sorbonne five years later; and eventually becoming minister of public education, at which time he aided and supported his former pupil in his conflicts with the Jesuits.

Michelet's educational accomplishments began to fulfill his father's early desires to have his son attain a higher position in life than himself. Periodically unemployed, Furcy finally managed in October 1815, to find employment in the small sanitarium of Dr. Duchemin on rue de Buffon. Although Furcy was able to earn an income there for the next three years, interest in his own fate had long since passed. Every hope, desire, and affection were now riveted onto his son. In a touching entry in his diary written three days after his father's death on November 18, 1846, Michelet caught the spirit of this intensely close relationship:

> To my father, printer-bookseller from 1794 to 1812 . . . I had to bury him who loved only me . . . My father had been my father, my cause, and my reason for being . . . From the time of my birth, with neither reason nor motive, he had a faith in me that was so naïve and so strong that it gave me faith in myself. Without restriction, with the most indulgent and even the weakest of educations, I was forced by this faith of my father to make my destiny such as he had imagined it . . . . He never demanded any work of me . . . the less he demanded the more I did . . . He never understood the man of work I was. This work, constant, solitary, often unsociable, kept me separated from him. I lived near him, with him, and nevertheless only saw him for moments . . . . He had seen the *ancien régime*, the Revolution, the Empire, the Restoration and July, and the ruin of July. He was tradition. Especially for the eighteenth century and for the Revolution. He was born before the death of Voltaire; he was 20 in '90. His best years were those of the last years of the Republic from '94-'98. During '98, which is the year of my birth, began the decline, the death of the press, the ruin of the printers, annihilated under Napoleon. I am able to say that after 1800 my father began to die in himself, to live in me, in the faith of my future . . . The most terrible catastrophes, private and public, even his personal ruin, did not at all alter his serenity . . . . People never understood the reason. It was that he no longer lived in himself, nor in the present, but in the future, in me.[6]

For Michelet, his father "no longer lived in himself," but rather in his son. Furcy was wholly immersed in his son's career and wholly committed to the advancement of that career. In a letter to his nephew, Xavier-Félix Millet, dated January 17, 1820, Furcy told him, after reviewing Jules's work, that "as you can see, my son is rather fortunate, truthfully, he deserves it."[7] Two years later he informed Xavier-Félix that "Jules is presently studying philosophy, especially English authors who have written on these subjects, and who have not yet been translated; he analyzes them and, in short, he works immensely hard . . . . He always gives me the greatest satisfaction possible."[8] In addition to fatherly pride, Furcy aided Michelet's research by searching daily for books in the libraries and bookstores of Paris. Victor Duruy, a former student of Michelet's and later minster of public education, remembered, in an 1880s letter, that he and several friends went to Michelet's home every day, arriving "at seven in the morning and found him already at work. He gave to each his task for the day, a work that M. Michelet *père* had found the night before at the Bibliothèque Royale or at that of the Arsenal."[9] After Michelet completed a book, Furcy would take copies to each of the important newspapers and journals in order to receive commitments for reviews. Having failed with his own press, he succeeded in getting his son's words commented on and printed by other firms.

Despite scholastic ambitions, Michelet acknowledged personal difficulties with his peers at the lycée. Prior to his life as a student he had had no friends at all, by his own admission. Now most of his contacts became dreaded encounters, often sending him home in tears. The atmosphere of the school, upon his initial visit in 1812, was "somber."[10] His first oral lessons were met with howls of laughter. To such a child, having previously felt the hostility of the social world, the mocking of his schoolmates in this more intimate setting, had to diminish his already slim confidence in personal relations. Michelet attributed this laughter to his general "awkwardness."[11] He was a bit clumsy physically, and his lack of playmates as a child had left him uncertain and unknowing in the more competitive school world. After the laughter and derision started, Michelet's performances in class were further aggravated by understandably increasing nervousness. "I was already a little disconcerted when M. Andrieu asked me to read my theme. I began in a voice so trembling . . . that a universal laugh rose from all corners of the room. This cruel laughter increased my problems and made my reading even more ridiculous."[12] After a few days of this, the newly initiated student surmised that "the most embarrassing place to be scoffed at is in a classroom. While one person gives you a compliment, another throws your book or notebook onto the ground; frequently, with closed fists, they make fun of you."[13] Rejected from the beginning, Michelet became their "playtoy." It was not one or two belligerent youths, but the entire class, which surrounded him day after day from the moment he entered the classroom. He was "alone against all."[14] Frequently, the physically short

Michelet was beaten by the tall boys, Jouffrey and Pouchard, "nearly men by their size and force."[15]

Michelet did not try to skip quickly through his peer problems in his *Mémorial*. The sections on them constitute the longest part of the autobiography. It was a tale of scorn and of rejection. While attributing his failure to his "awkwardness" and nervousness in the *Mémorial*, in his heavily oriented social class analysis of *Le Peuple* he imputed the ridicule of others to his financial poverty. The youths were motivated by egoism rather than by love, sympathy, and unselfishness, qualities which Michelet saw in himself and always searched for in other people.[16] Unable to cope with or to solve these personal problems directly, he sought ways around them. He diverted his energies into his studies, feeling that this was his method for finding gratification and power. Finishing first in scholarship "reconciled me with the lycée."[17] This success could be used not only for his personal advancement but also as a means of revenge. "I did all that it was humanly possible to do in order to succeed and I was determined to crush these other students if I ever had the least advantage over them."[18]

The one major exception to Michelet's want of comrades was Paul Benoist Poinsot. Born in the same year and same city as Michelet, Poinsot was the son of a wine merchant, formerly from Vermenton. Neglected by his father and eventually placed under the educational direction of Michelet's first tutor, M. Mélot, the two twelve-year old boys met in early 1811 and began perhaps the most intimate friendship of Michelet's life. Unfortunately, they were often apart. The following year Poinsot decided to pursue a pharmaceutical career, finding apprenticeship and instruction in Melun. Thereafter, Poinsot rarely returned to Paris, until relocating there in September 1817 as a pharmacist's aide. He lived in the same building as the Michelets until April 1820, when he passed his internship and was required to move to Bicêtre. From this period of separation, sixteen letters between Michelet and Poinsot have been preserved, the correspondence and friendship being tragically ended on February 14, 1821, by the premature death of Poinsot from consumption.

Michelet's attachment and identification with Poinsot had been total. "I do not believe that two souls will ever resemble each other more than ours; and we would be, I think, if we could have been placed in the same circumstances, the same man."[19] Michelet clearly remembered their first encounter in Mélot's drab boarding house: "He was a little taller than I, or, at least slender, in a grey-striped cloth coat . . . without pretention . . . . He always laughed, which made me ill at ease; I was always afraid of laughers. But he laughed without malice and the expression on his face was very gentle."[20] In this world of enmity, so full of distrust, Michelet found another, like himself, full of trust and of love. Never having had friends before, Michelet was a little apprehensive at first, but soon opened up and shared his whole world of thoughts and of sentiments, that had too long been pent-up inside. "I talked, talked, talked with more fire than usually belongs to a child of twelve. I did not fear ridicule with him. Timid as I was, this quality attached me endearingly to him."[21] Before Poinsot's departure the next year, they frequently took long walks along the "new boulevards," conversing and laughing together. Michelet was no longer alone. This friendship with Poinsot was among "the most wonderful memories of my life."[22]

Their correspondence of 1820, full of mutual affection, recounted their daily activities and general thoughts. The letters became the medium through which Michelet could express and test his initial ideas on philosophy and history. Often, he took on a lecturing tone, as if to a disciple. "You spoke to me of Condillac and of all the time that you spend reading him. Don't you spend too much on him? . . . In reading too slowly you miss the connection of ideas and, in the works of the great writers, the discovered truths are frequently less useful to the reader than the connection of ideas."[23] Poinsot's untimely death left an irreplacable gap in Michelet's personal life. Wanting to relate and to tell the world of this blissful comradeship, Michelet began a *Life of Poinsot* on September 27, 1821, in which he sketched Poinsot's background before their 1811 meeting. Poinsot's father had sent him away at the age of nine to a boarding school. "It was perhaps by this separation, by this first removal from the paternal home, that begain in him those dispositions to melancholy which rendered him so interesting in his youth, but which perhaps altered his temperament and shortened his life. He always needed to love someone."[24] Although proposing to write a full-length biography, Michelet never again returned to this manuscript.

When the Michelets moved to Dr. Duchemin's sanitarium in October 1815, they quickly became attached to the administrator of the house, forty-five-year-old Mme Fourcy, née Anne Madeleine Christophe. When the house closed three years later, she acquired a boarding house and brought Furcy along with her as manager. Before her death in December 1823, she had become an adviser, if not mother surrogate for Michelet. It was Mme Fourcy who forced him to terminate his first love affair with Thérèse Tarlet. Also, both she and Poinsot were more religiously inclined than Michelet, and it was under their guidance and their care, that he decided to be baptized on June 23, 1916. Performed at the Saint-Médard Church, Michelet received the additional first name of Christophe, while Poinsot was named godfather and Mme Fourcy, godmother.

This religious decision was not totally sudden nor were his two spiritual counselors the only influences. Despite his his irreligious family training, he happened to come across Thomas à Kempis's *Imitation of Jesus Christ* when he was about ten years old. Surrounded by unhappiness, this book struck a internal chord: "These dialogues between God and a sick soul, as mine, moved me deeply; I easily forgot the present . . . and I thought of the future that religion promises us."[25] The book was a temporary relief from his daily miseries, but "these religious stirrings lasted only as long as the distress which had made me want to escape from the present."[26] The memory of this experience, from a book "that had been made for a solitary person like me," found renewed sustenance in his emotional ties with Poinsot and Mme Fourcy.[27] For the moment, the baptism filled a vague religious and moral need. Above all, with these two intimates, Michelet was able to express himself freely and openly. But they both died shortly thereafter, and Michelet increasingly turned to another means of expression—writing.

Not only was the *Mémorial* written between 1820-22, but during these same years Michelet started keeping a *Journal*. In several notebooks he wrote about one hundred pages from May 4, 1820 until July 12, 1823. Then the *Journal* was put aside until 1828, when he began it again and assiduously kept it up until his death. In his first entry, in the full flush of excitement, he predicted that "this *Journal* will have a great advantage, my life will not disappear from me and I will return to it, day by day, with my sentiments, my thoughts, and my actions."[28] But sixteen months months later, after only sporadic insertions, Michelet somberly noted that he had listed only "the principle events of each day" and had "left out completely" the "most useful" and most important information, his "moral experiences."[29]

The *Journal* for the early 1820s remained a somewhat tedious record of daily activities except for two important subjects: his future wife, Pauline, and the ideas of a nascent historian. Soon after Mme Fourcy opened her pension in 1818, she accepted as a lodger, twenty-six-year-old Pauline Rousseau. Pauline had been born illegitimately in Paris six years before Michelet. Her mother, the Baroness de Navailles, née Claude Oudette Gilles Charles, had received her noble name marrying the Baron Henri de Navailles in 1782 just after her sixteenth birthday. The following year she bore him a son, Guillaume, but with her newly acquired social status, she sought to share in the fruits concomitant with that distinction. Rumors abounded about her various amorous affairs, but the first concrete evidence came after she started seeing the star tenor of the opera, Jean-Joseph Rousseau. She became pregnant. With Pauline's birth, the facts became a little cloudy. Pauline never had any papers on her birth, since she was born out-of-wedlock. Michelet often thought that Pauline's father might have been Joseph de Bauffremont, but this was quite unlikely, since he had long passed his seventieth birthday in 1792. To simplify matters for the Baroness, the old Baron died in 1794. Despite another child, who died in infancy, she did not marry Rousseau, who died six years later. The final *coup de théâtre*, the one which obsessed Michelet his whole life, was the Baroness's decision in 1800 to live with her seventeen-year old son. Michelet suspected incest. "Marriage of Monsieur and Madame de Navailles, of the mother and the son: a permanent union, faithful and constantly passionate, lasting thirty-six years, before the public, a union readily admitted and known by all."[30] The Baroness lived until 1832, but communication between her and her daughter and son-in-law was nonexistent.

Always neglected by her mother, Pauline was placed in a series of pensions, and finally in a convent at Meaux in 1814. She remained there until 1817, when, aided by concerned authorities, work for her was found in Paris at Dr. Duchemin's sanitarium. There, she managed to befriend the Michelets and Mme Fourcy before the home closed, paving the way for her immediate acceptance into Mme Fourcy's pension. Soon thereafter Pauline became Michelet's mistress—this was probably his first sexual experience.

Michelet's attitude towards Pauline was never very positive. During their six years together before marriage, Michelet was constantly plagued with doubts about her appearance, personality, and intelligence. In an 1820 letter to Poinsot he asked of himself: "The person whom you are seen with is neither young nor beautiful, but not at all disagreeable. She has her defects but not at all vices. Do you think you deserve someone perfect?"[31] As a highly regarded professor, Michelet retrospectively described these "defects" a bit more succinctly: "She was very fat with little self-respect . . . Myself, I was embarrassed. She scarcely went with my role of a young professor."[32]

Although Michelet sometimes wrote in his *Journal* that he "loved Pauline very much, even physically," these appreciative comments were quite rare.[33] He also had jealous moments but quickly realized that there was "hardly any danger" of Pauline leaving him for another man, since she "knows few people and she is neither beautiful nor pretty."[34] It seems that Michelet, even knowing how he truly felt about Pauline, was the master of his own fate. Even before marriage, he had resigned himself to another unhappy household. "I have chosen someone who resembles me too little in order to hope to taste the good of domestic life. When I see a happy household, I change the direction of my thought; I feel alone, *I will die alone*, as Pascal said."[35] One has to wonder whether he even wanted a "happy household" or wanted to be bothered with a family; the family, at least, was not his major area of life for personal commitment.

Their marriage on May 19, 1824, took place for two central reasons. There was no question of Pauline's love and devotion for Michelet, and because of their many years together Michelet felt that he should do the "honorable" thing, for refusal would reflect "maximum cruelty." Beyond this formal explanation, the direct cause was Pauline's becoming pregnant in December 1823. Their daughter Adèle was born the following August, and their other child Charles four years later. In explaining his approaching marriage to his aunts in Renwez in a letter of March 8,

1824, Michelet capsulized the lack of a real love bond between him and Pauline. The marriage would allow him:

> ... to cut down on his expenses ... she is neither young nor beautiful ... her mother is wealthy ... Mademoiselle Rousseau is 28 years old ... she is not what one could call a Parisian. She's an excellent house cleaner; she is quite capable of managing and directing a large house ... she is more economical than I .... Finally in what appears very important to me in the choice of a wife, her health is excellent. I have observed all of this during the past five years.
>
> Now you are probably wondering why I'm so anxious to get married. First of all, the desire to live more economically ... the maintenance alone of linen is necessary for a man who always has to look his best .... Moreover one must be either a priest or married in order to receive certain places in the University, which require a certain consistency, a certain paternal character.[36]

Aside from reducing Pauline's age and imagining his future mother-in-law's wealth, there was no mention of any human emotion or affection in this letter. Towards the end of this letter Michelet admitted that his impending marriage and family would be based on a "two worlds" concept: "She applies herself to the household as I do to my studies; we will work side by side, and I will have fewer fears of distractions than previously."[37]

This marriage lasted until Pauline's death on July 24, 1839. Initially Michelet felt that marriage would aid his career, reflecting a "certain consistency" in his character, but this particular union became an issue of increasing embarrassment to him, unworthy of "the role of a young professor." Pauline, heavy before marriage, became obese in later years, and may have become an alcoholic. Michelet rarely took Pauline on his many voyages of the 1820s and 1830s. In his letters, he primarily reminded Pauline of the chores she had to do, occasionally slipping in a reference to abstain from her drinking penchants.[38] Her death aroused few pangs of conscience in him, feeling sorry that he had devoted so little attention to her. While he had worked every Sunday, "other families were together enjoying honest amusements."[39] Perhaps unconsciously projecting his own fate, he felt that the most tragic aspect of her death was "her separation from her son."[40] Despite further expressions of guilt, Michelet soon focused, as he had before marriage, on what really mattered to him:

> Half-marriages are risky, full of chances. The most grievous . . . are to love, to attach oneself indissolubly to someone of inferior education, from whom one will always be divorced in spirit. . . .
>
> On the other hand, marriage for long periods is impossible. Was it possible, is it reconcilable with the great work which is the destiny of my life?[41]

Michelet's "destiny" formally commenced when he received a post to teach history on November 13, 1822, at the Collège Sainte-Barbe. Michelet was only able to teach in Paris where the "cohabitation with such a city, has without doubt contributed to the awakening of history in myself."[42] Within the city, he recalled one particularly important childhood experience when he visited the Museum of French Monuments. "It is there . . . that I first received the lively impression of history. I filled these tombs with my imagination. I sensed the dead through the marble, and it was not without some terror that I entered into the lower vaults where Dagobert, Chilpéric, and Frédégonde slept."[43] "Awakened" in Paris, the untraveled Parisian could not be shuffled out into the provinces like the other young professors. Furcy wrote Xavier-Félix Millet that Jules "was named professor of rhetoric at Toulouse," but "he refused, having no intention of leaving Paris. He informed the vice-chancellor of the university of his desire to wait for a position in Paris rather than taking a more lucrative one in the provinces."[44] Fortunately, Michelet was named to a temporary post at his alma mater, the Collège Charlemagne, the year before his appointment to Sainte-Barbe. The future historian of France was first and foremost a Parisian.

His *Journal* revealed that his captivation with history was a more complex phenomenon than the simple visit to the Museum of French Monuments. His passions, largely blocked in his family and in society sought other outlets:

> There is only one way, it is to have a passion. But it is a dangerous way as well. One must choose this passion.

Only four are able to elevate the soul; love of women, love of country, love of men, and lastly, love of God.

The first only elevates by shocks, or rather, it intoxicates. It is the eau-de-vie which appears to give a lot of strength, one thinks himself capable of breaking iron bars, and yet it actually diminishes physical energy. So much for love; when one is no longer intoxicated, one finds himself nearly dead; one begins to drink again and after several bursts of energy, falls into libertinage; the death of the soul.

The love of country does not have these terrible inconveniences. But the noble illusions on which it is based, do they still exist in our country? Think about the fact that the base of governments is no longer virtue, it is security . . . It is now more than ever that patriotism along with the other passions, must lose itself, as streams do in an ocean, in the grand passion of humanity. Do you want to determine your choice? Look for the feelings which have nothing personal, which are disinterested, those especially which do not have an individual for an object, or a class, those which have the great characteristic of generality. The more one abstracts, the more one purifies.

I dare not advise . . . to climb higher than the love of man. In the middle of the distractions of a century which is hardly religious . . . too many barriers separate you; you must cross them little by little. Humanity is the way; it can be felt, it enters us through all the senses.[45]

The "way" out was to release one's passions and one's personality into an area where there was "nothing personal." In this passage, Michelet, whose personal relations were generally so unfruitful, envisioned an ideal implying the negation of individuality. There would be no unhappy encounters if the individual was not the "object." Physical endeavors were unfulfilling, love of God was no longer possible in this irreligious age, and patriotism was both outmoded and too small a unit for commitment. In his attempt to find meaning in life, Michelet turned here to the opposite of individuality; to the largest, most abstract and most inclusive unit of all—humanity. Humanity could swallow up all small units, all contradictions. By casting his lot with "humanity," Michelet could perhaps overcome, in part, past familial and social discord, while renewing the search for personal and societal harmony in the "purified" ocean of humanity.

Often Michelet posed a dichotomy between his own personal existence and that of humanity; a dichotomy which was contained for him in history. "As the season advances, I think less of myself and of my desires, and more of humanity in general."[46] But, more frequently Michelet viewed the study of humanity in history as perhaps the best means of expressing himself and experiencing life. "God has given me in History," Michelet reflected in 1845, "the means of participating in everything."[47] His family life itself made him preeminently qualified to perform this task, for the sufferings "allowed me to acquire more varied knowledge and insights perhaps than other people."[48] From a personal aspect, Michelet was perhaps unwilling to probe into himself in his *Journal* as Rousseau had done in his autobiographies, since the individual was too small a unit. Harmony could come for Michelet only in the interaction between man and society. Having found little love and little unity in his childhood, Michelet hoped that "perhaps in this harmonization of my work, I will find my own harmony."[49]

In the academic world, five months before his marriage, Michelet read in an appendix by J. A. Buchon to Dugald Stewart's newly translated *Histoire abrégée des sciences métaphysiques, morales et politiques depuis la Renaissance des lettres* about a philospher who would forever fascinate him. The philosopher wrote of the harmony of man "in" humanity and the consequent harmony of humanity in the history of the world.[50] Michelet immediately perceived someone speaking directly to him. He found the philosopher's works, read them, and soon began proclaiming, as he did for the rest of his life, that Giambattista Vico was his "only master."

# 3

## *Philosophical Historian*

Michelet's readings and fundamental intellectual concerns during the third decade of his life were recorded in his *Journal des idées*, kept from 1821 until October 1829, and his *Journal de mes lectures*, kept from June 1818 until April 1829. While the former set forth his current ideas and projected scholarly works, the latter reflected these interests by listing the books he had consulted each month. These brief notebooks, each less than thirty pages in published form, show Michelet inquiring into a wide variety of subjects and perusing a myriad of books, ranging from basic classical texts to contemporary works in history and philosophy, and to Shakespeare, Rousseau, and Walter Scott for literary sustenance. At the forefront, though, of Michelet's scholarly priorities during this eleven-year period, were the burgeoning academic fields of history and the philosophy of history. Michelet became acquainted with the primary English and French histories written since the middle of the eighteenth century. While examining these other histories and historians, he also wrote, between 1824 and 1828, three short summaries of modern European history, all intended as basic textbooks for introductory secondary school courses.[1] Despite this solid self-training as a historian, the problems which bothered and engrossed Michelet in the 1820s were in the area of the philosophy of history. The big moments of his life during these years, reading Vico and meeting Cousin, were related directly to his absorption with this field of knowledge. While his *Journal de mes lectures* indicates that he read numerically more histories than philosophies of history, his *Journal des idées* and other 1820s writing evince the preponderant qualitative emphasis he had given to the philosophy of history.

There is danger in singling out Vico as the sole philosophical historian admired and analyzed by Michelet. While Vico's preeminence was avowed eagerly, he still was pondered and commented on, alongside major works of Bossuet, Voltaire, Condorcet, Turgot, Maistre, Kant, Lessing, and Herder. No prominent work in the philosophy of history written since the end of the seventeenth century, on either side of the Rhine, was left unexamined and unread by Michelet. His emphasis was not, for example, on the technical philosophy of Kant nor on the plays of Lessing, but on *The Idea for a Universal History from a Cosmopolitan Point of View* and *The Education of the Human Race*. This feverish exploration of philosophical history was conveyed in a 1824 letter to Cousin. "I recently discovered a curious work of Kant: *Idée de ce que pourrait être l'histoire universelle* . . . Presently, I'm studying Vico, Condorcet, Ferguson, Turgot, and Ancillon . . . and I look forward to knowing Cramer, Walkenaër, Millar, Kant, and Lessing. As for Herder, I've been forced to delay my reading of him."[2]

While Michelet studied philosophies of history, he also started forming his own ideas and planning his own works in these areas. One principal project was to write a *Caractère des peuples trouvé dans leur vocabulaire*. Proposed in 1819, five years before studying Vico's *New Science*, with its "master key" that the first peoples spoke naturally in poetic characters, this undertaking was never completed, but it was mentioned and noted frequently in his *Journal des idées*. The longest passages of this diary in 1823 outlined the need for a "philosophical history of languages." Michelet wanted a composite history of each civilization and of each language, something which Turgot had suggested sixty years earlier. In order to support his ideas, he copied first a sentence from Gibbon, asking for a work that examined "the relationship which exists between the language and the customs of nations"; and then one from Mme de Staël's *De l'Allemagne*, "In studying the spirit and the character of a language, one learns the philosophical history of opinions, customs, etc."[3] A reading of Herder, less than two years later, inspired Michelet to comment in his *Journal des idées*, "My subject of *L'Histoire de la civilisation trouvée dans les langues* was sketched beautifully by Herder."[4]

The interrelation between language and culture was merely one branch in the vast network of possibilities inherent in the philosophy of history. An abundance of other ideas bubbling within Michelet began to be expressed in April 1824, when he met Victor Cousin, the reigning French philosopher. At the Sorbonne, Cousin had acquired impeccable credentials as a leading academic scholar and innovator. He had introduced Hegel and Schelling into the intellectual life of the French university. Since 1816 he had attempted to develop his own philosophy, which he termed "eclecticism" or "spiritualism," and personally saw as a nascent synthesis of the major trends in French, German, and English thought. The expression of a philosophical system in the 1820s was a means itself of opposition to the Restoration regime and its official Catholic doctrine. Cousin's "eclecticism" served that purpose, and fomented the enmity of the government, while it endeared him to French students and writers on the Left Bank. On October 14, 1824, while in Prussia after already having been suspended from teaching by Bourbon supporters, Cousin was arrested by the Prussian government at the request of the French police, who suspected him of revolutionary plotting with his German counterparts. Freed five months later, after the intervention of Hegel, Cousin returned to accolades from his comrades in Paris. However, Cousin's moment of intellectual supremacy and political glory lasted only a few years. By the 1830s he was viewed increasingly as both intellectually stagnant and politically reactionary. But in 1824 Cousin had no recognized equal in his field, and Michelet's meeting with him was of major personal and scholarly significance for this twenty-five-year-old high school teacher.[5]

Michelet was thirsting for a means of studying history and a system which explained the past. His meetings with Cousin enabled him to voice these desires and to speak of the problems which troubled him. Between April and July 1824, he visited Cousin several times and before each discussion prepared a series of questions. These inquiries were broad in scope, reflecting his widening interests in the philosophy of history. Furthermore, these sets of questions indicated that Michelet already had some of his own ideas for a method and an orientation towards the past, before presenting them to Cousin. In one of their first encounters, Michelet wrote in advance:

> To prepare for the study of the philosophy of history, what type of program should one follow in his study of philosophy? The problems of causality and of liberty obviously have to be investigated more deeply . . .

The political sciences. In what order should one study these sciences; by those of law as custom dictates?

History. M. Cousin advises us to study history by fields. But before this, shouldn't whole epochs be studied for a long time (2 or 4 years)? Since all theories are encountered in the study of the history of humanity, shouldn't at least some of the principal ones be touched upon rather than learning history only as a science of facts?[6]

Michelet, thinking that partial inquiries were insufficient, was searching for a method encompassing the large spectrum of history, where streams of philosophy and details of history would be subsumed under general principles and general theory. The next series of questions sketched the essential elements of an ambitious synthetic approach that Michelet visualized:

What does he think of the following steps? 1) Languages, and the study of some authors who have discussed the philosophy of history. 2) Study of history by whole epochs and only as the study of facts (geography-chronology); at the same time, study of the philosophical questions most directly related to history (such as causality, liberty . . . ), study of the theories most directly related to history (such as legislation, political economy, theology). 3) Study of history by fields (religion, constitutional law, style, languages, taste, politics, industry, commerce, sciences, customs, philosophy). 4) Interrelationship of the different areas of history; the study of their reciprocal influence; relations of these interrelations themselves and systematicization of everything . . .

Briefly: 1) Acquisition of instruments. 2) Acquisition of materials. 3) Sorting and classification of materials. 4) Systematicization of the materials. Thereby the edifice, studied at first as it is, is demolished by analysis in order to be further studied in its parts; then according to their reciprocal attractions, the parts resemble each other and the edifice is again raised.[7]

In his quest for a methodology in the philosophy of history, Michelet's proposals incorporated all categories of contemporary historical knowledge. His ideal of one, vast syncretism mirrored, in part, the general system-building temper of the 1820s in men, such as Cousin, Comte, Saint-Simon, Fourier, the Saint-Simonians, and Hegel. This aspiring, young philosophical historian sought a total view of history, where all knowledge coalesced in an "interrelationship" far beyond the narrow confines of political or narrative history.

Upon first meeting Cousin, Michelet wrote that the philosopher's counsel was "excellent for my entire life" and for the "cultivation of my talents."[8] Often, though, Cousin seems to have offered more encouragement than concrete advice. In their session of June 20, 1824, Michelet recorded Cousin's unhelpful and cryptic responses:

> Lamennais, de Bonald—do they not contain something on the general theory of historical criticism? "Nothing."
> Would it not be helpful to confer with de Sismondi and Daunou? "M. de Sismondi is alien to philosophy and Daunou mediocre."
> Descartes and Plato—do they not have something to say on the philosophy of history? "Nothing."[9]

Although inspired by the presence and the ideas of Cousin, Michelet continued his own search for a theory of historical development. Thoughts and expressions from Cousin would seep into Michelet's writings, but there would be an increasing separation in their respective visions of the past.

On August 17, 1825, Michelet delivered a paper, the *Discours sur l'unité de la science*, before the students of the Collège Sainte-Barbe during the annual distribution of prizes. In this essay, written concurrently with his translation of and introduction to Vico, Michelet expounded his theory of knowledge. The views on man and society and the perspectives on history that Michelet expressed on this occasion, would remain with him, in similar form, his whole life. Already, Michelet was committed to understanding and to explaining man's past.

In broad terms Michelet described the unity and harmony of all sciences, both physical and social. "The sciences are one: Languages, Literature, and History, Physics, Mathematics, and Philosophy; these forms of knowledge which appear diverse, are, in reality, interwoven and they form one complete system."[10] The evolution of the sciences was holistic. Despite their variety of forms, they expressed sameness and evenness of development, which Vico had also delineated in his *New Science*. The key element of history which contained, carried, and preserved this unity was humanity. Humanity, the answer that Michelet had detailed in his *Journal* four years earlier and had found again in Vico, was the unit of historical discourse:

> Man is no longer isolated, but a part of an *être collectif* which one calls humanity . . . . The individual appears for an instant, binds himself to the common thought and dies; but the species, which does not die, gathers the eternal fruit of his ephemeral existence. Therefore an immense chain of discoveries and of good deeds unify all the ages; while generations disappear and races perish, the common thought subsists; always the same and always more vast, always under a thousand different forms, this thought contains the identity of the human race, as memory and conscience contain the identity of the individual.[11]

Humanity, the receptacle of man's wisdom, was the unifying agency for each historical epoch. The idea that individual man biologically grows, withers, and dies, while humanity continues to advance, had been formulated fully in Herder's *Ideen*. Man's duty in life, for Michelet, was to unify himself not only with his own historical epoch, but with all past history. Since personal knowledge and worth derived from fulfilling this duty, morality itself became dependent upon the degree of harmony each individual achieved with the history of humanity. As in the current philosophies of history of Saint-Simon and Hegel, the most intelligent, moral, and rational men understood the forces of history and acted within the central thrust of history. Isolated men, removed from the heartbeat of humanity, were without history, without meaning, and probably without morality.

As a mandatory step in the harmonization of each individual with humanity, Michelet proposed the solution of education. Man should study the development of all the sciences, the progress of humanity, and the significant works written by great individuals. In this manner, man would become integrated increasingly with the *être collectif*, which in Michelet's philosophy was a necessity. By immersing oneself in the past and by learning to understand the total process of history, man created the possibilities for passing beyond the accomplishments of previous generations. Even if all of mankind did not harmonize, the educated individuals, those who "embraced a system" and who bound themselves to humanity, would contribute to the advancement of the "common

*31*

thought," and would find their own meaning in life.[12] This understanding of the past along with the new acts, new works, and new discoveries, constituted "the dignity of man and his consolation on earth."[13]

These themes of humanity, harmony, and the unity of the sciences were being analyzed at the same time by Michelet in his study of Vico's *New Science*. This amazingly creative and novel philosophy of history had been written and revised three times by the Neapolitan genius. These editions of 1725, 1730, and 1744 did not cause a ripple in the intellectual tidewaters of the Enlightenment. Copies of the book sent to major eighteenth-century thinkers went unread. Neglected by his own century, it was left to Michelet to bring him into the mainstream of Western European thought. This event was not entirely fortuitous, since, by the 1820s and 1830s, some of Vico's ideas had been expressed in many forms. In decades obsessed with system-building and total structure of philosophical history, Vico's attempted synthesis of Western civilization stood out as the first modern philosophy of history. Michelet, Quinet, Cousin, and later Marx, would all find something in Vico's pregnant interpretations of man and the world he had created. To each of them, Vico had given order and meaning to the enigmatic movement of history, which had become even more complex and confused since the unique experience of the French Revolution.

Five months after reading of Vico's system, Michelet began a translation of the *New Science*, and he immediately received the complete support of Cousin. Discouraged at first, he informed Cousin, "If I find that a translation of Vico is impossible, I will be content with a very detailed extract, and I will combine all my extracts into my treatise on the philosophy of history. The preface will become the work."[14] However, Michelet had fewer difficulties than he expected, and the translation was largely finished by February 1825, although the volume was not published until March 8, 1827. The translation became an immediate success. It was reviewed in all the leading periodicals and specially mentioned by Cousin in his famous Sorbonne course on the philosophy of history in 1828.[15] All through the nineteenth century Michelet's translation was read more frequently than Vico himself. Michelet's romantic rendering popularized and made intelligible the often obscure prose of the *New Science*. The original was repetitive and was constructed loosely, weaving ideas and systems on many levels. Michelet simplified, shortened, and gave more form to Vico's embryonic ideas.

On a personal level, Michelet always acknowledged the crucial importance his discovery of Vico had had for his future historical works. Vico had provided him with the insights into the workings of history that he had been seeking in the early 1820s, insights that he would never disavow. In his letters, diaries, and books he continually paid hommage to his Italian predecessor. His monumental 1869 preface to his *Histoire de France* again reiterated, "Vico was my only master."[16]

Since Vico commanded Michelet's sole intellectual allegiance, it must be asked how he read and what he saw in the *New Science?* Published with the translation was his own essay on the life and philosophy of history of Vico, the *Discours sur le système et la vie de Vico*.[17] Michelet's Vico had explained the unity of all the sciences and had uncovered the order and meaning of world history:

> In this infinite variety of actions and of thoughts, of customs and of languages, which the history of man presents to us, we return frequently to the same traits, the same characteristics. The nations the furthest removed by time and by place follow in their political revolutions, in those of language, a singularly analogous pattern. The object of the new science is to make clear the regular phenomena of apparent accidents and to determine the general laws which govern the former; to trace the course of universal history, eternal, which produces itself in each epoch under the form of particular history; and to describe the ideal circle through which the real world turns. It is at the same time, philosophy and the history of humanity.[18]

The laws of history, manifested in languages, customs, and ideas, had demonstrated the common nature of nations. While the course of nations had moved uniformly in the past, Michelet was not able to adhere to Vico's idea of "analogous patterns" for the future. Despite similarities that could be drawn between the French Revolution and Roman political revolutions, Michelet was too imbued with the general idea of progress permeating early nineteenth-century society to take seriously Vico's dire warning of another *ricorso*. Several years later Michelet suggested that if one had to view "the movement of humanity as an eternal rotation, *corso, ricorso*" one should remember "that if humanity marches in circles, the circles are always expanding."[19] Furthermore, in Michelet's exposition of the Vichian system, he commingled the three absolute states of historical development and of human consciousness. The kernel for Michelet was Vico's description of the natural fitness of things—history, knowledge, sciences, and laws.

"Humanity is its own work," the Vichian sentence most often quoted by Michelet throughout his life, constituted the primary attraction and attribute of the *New Science* in Michelet's eyes.[20] Behind the institutions of societies, sciences of knowledge, and harmonious development of nations, lay man himself, who had created each aspect of his world. The laws and unity of history had not arisen by chance, but had been formulated by the inventive acts of mankind. Although many twentieth-century scholars have focused on the motivational force of fear behind all of man's actions in the Vichian world, Michelet contented himself with glorifying the singular possibility that man created and controlled his world. The productive man, for Michelet, as for Vico, was tied to and expressive of his society. Societal man, not the isolated individual, acted and invented from the very heart of humanity. Each novel expression and each important event occurred in the center of each society.

Four years before reading Vico, Michelet had written, "Look for the feelings which have nothing personal . . . those especially which do not have an individual for an object . . . . Humanity is the way." In Vico, Michelet found a systematic explanation of the historical, where man was humanized in society and where humanity was the unit of history. Four years after his translation, Michelet recalled this orientation towards Vico. Humanity appeared to Vico "as a harmonic system of the civil world. In order to see man . . . Vico placed his faith in man himself, in man humanizing himself in society. It is there that my old Vico is the true prophet of the new order which has begun, and that his book merits the name which he dared to give it: *New Science*."[21]

In the year of Michelet's translation of the *New Science*, there also appeared Edgar Quinet's translation of Herder's *Ideen zur Philosophie der Geschichte der Menscheit*.[22] Quinet, born February 17, 1803 at Bourg en Bresse, was the son of a war commissary who hated Napoleon and of a liberal, Protestant mother. After an unsuccessful attempt at law, he turned to the study of philosophy and of history. Like Michelet, in 1824, he discovered his eighteenth-century spiritual ancestor through Scottish sources; in Quinet's case, from his own brother-in-law. In the midst of his Herder translation in 1825, he met both Cousin and Michelet. Cousin provided the same encouragement that he had been giving to Michelet, while the two young translators began an intimate forty-year friendship. Details on the early years of this relationship are sparse; but by the 1840s, the names Michelet and Quinet were spoken often in the same breath, as these star professors of the Collège de France jointly battled the religious ideas and educational philosophy of the Jesuits.

Quinet's translation was a three-volume abridgment of the *Ideen*. Henri Tronchon has shown, through a comparison of three texts, the French, the original German, and an 1800-1803 English translation by T. O. Churchill, that Quinet followed Churchill's text and not the German Herder.[23] Quinet, who along with Cousin, had been one of the great French proponents of German philosophy in an 1820s Parisian world that rarely had been amenable to either learning the language or reading the abstruse philosophy across the Rhine, had himself, according to Tronchon, not only used the Churchill translation, but probably did not even consult Herder in the original.[24] In this instance, German thought managed to enter France, but indirectly.

Quinet wrote an introduction to his Herder, expressing many of the same basic ideas as Michelet had on the philosophy of history. "The great glory of modern man was to have conceived universal history."[25] This universal, philosophical history had begun with Vico and had advanced during the eighteenth century to Herder. In both philosophies, for Quinet, order and harmony had been given to the grand sweep of history. Quinet's Herder combined general historical law with a clear demonstration of the steady, unyielding progress of humanity. Herder's glorification of the early biological stages of a culture and his attacks against the mixing of indigenous societies were far less important for Quinet than the idea of progress and the ceaseless cultivation of reason. After the appearance of this essay, Michelet enthusiastically wrote Quinet: "Your Introduction already proves that you will be a great writer, but I will wait for more. The Philosophy of History already has had its Copernicus and its Kepler, now it needs its Newton."[26]

While Michelet and Quinet were acquiring reputations as scholars and translators of philosophies of history, Cousin was returning to center stage at the Sorbonne. During the spring of 1828, Cousin gave his first public lectures in eight years. At the height of his fame, Cousin was assured of being read and discussed by all students, scholars, and intellectuals in Paris and beyond. The lectures of Cousin, according to the *Progagateur de la Vérité*, "were printed on all the intersections of the capital, copied by students, reviewed by the master, then printed one by one, and sent to foreign cities, all the way to Moscow . . . The newspapers . . . noted *Le Globe*, analyzed them 'as if they were the speeches of a parliamentary leader.'"[27] On vacation in Germany, later in 1828, Michelet wrote his family, imploring his father to take notes at the Cousin lectures that he was missing.[28]

Cousin entitled his first series of thirteen lectures *Introduction à l'histoire de la philosophie*.[29] After an opening number of definitions, he proceeded to expound a philosophy, that in its barest skeletal form resembled his great hero in Berlin, G.W.F. Hegel. The movement of thought in the history of the world had moved from East to West; for Hegel, the beginnings were China, for Cousin, India, and then, both men went on to Greece, Rome, Christianity, and the modern times. Cousin's own version of the Owl of Minerva revealed that the outstanding element in the history of the West had been the incontestable development of reason. Today everything was "under the domination of reason."[30] Beyond here, though, Hegel's and Cousin's emphases separated. The Cousin lectures showed the steady progress of human reason as a parallel reflection of the history of humanity. Hegel's unit for his philosophy of history had been the "world spirit," which turned and twisted dialectically through civilizations, leaving whole cultures buried and forlorn, until it finally maneuvered its way into Friedrich Wilhelm III's Prussia of the 1820s. Cousin's philosphy, on the contrary, showed a simple linear, external development with neither the dialectical methodology nor the internal soul searching evinced in Hegel's "world spirit." Humanity, Cousin's general unit, like that of his young admirers Michelet and Quinet, was as all-powerful as the "world spirit," but represented institutions and cultural artifacts rather than the progressive, internalization of freedom within the individual. "Humanity embraces everything, profits from everything, advances constantly, and crosses through everything. And when I say humanity, I mean all the powers which represent it in history: industry, the state, religion, art, philosophy. For example, with philosophy, reason advances cease-lessly."[31] Above all, Cousin's "world spirit"—"humanity"—encom-passed modern, cosmopolitan Western civilization, while Hegel's resided in the Germanic world.

Since the nineteenth century, for Cousin, was clearly on the way to a Condorcet form of perfectibility, the task for philosphers was to synthe-size the dominant philosophies of France, Germany, and England. A syncretic work embracing all major cultures, and termed by Cousin "eclecticism," would accelerate the process of progress in society. Cousin's two model philosophers in the last century, by whom he judged modern attempts to extract historical meaning, were Vico and Herder. Despite their brilliance and creativity, though, each had flaws. Vico's *New Science* had too much politics and too little "art and philosophy."[32] The most serious weakness of this work was its inability to explain the unlimited progress of humanity in history, which Cousin considered an a priori truth. Coming at the end of the eighteenth century, after the further development of reason, Herder's *Ideen* was a more complete work than Vico's. Reading Herder as a strict progressionist, Cousin told his students, "The work of Herder is the first great monument presenting the perpetual progress of humanity in all senses and in all directions."[33] The two main problems with Herder's system, unlike Vico's, were that his man was too passive and too bound to nature, and that there were too few laws of history. Nevertheless, Herder's *Ideen* was Cousin's example of the greatest philosophy of history thus far written, which needed only a few more laws and a little more freedom given to mankind, and it would then incarnate a total, ironclad theory of the progress of humanity and of reason through history. This would be the new "eclecticism."

Cousin, Michelet, and Quinet, as reflected in their 1820s writings, treated previous philosophers of history as the most important Western thinkers, and the philosophy of history as a combination of the two most elevated disciplines of knowledge, history and philosophy. In the works of these three men, humanity, signifying the totality of humanity through all ages, was the unit of historical discourse. Their philoso-phies embodied a commitment to moral and scientific progress and, above all, sought to disentangle from the many threads and levels of the past, what Michelet called, "The unity in the history of the human race."[34]

Cousin's impact and influence among young philosophers and historians would recede by the early years of the July Monarchy. As early as
1827, Michelet forecast, despite his personal admiration, an increasing
intellectual distance between himself and Cousin. Ideas and visions were
surging within him, and each time he met Cousin the barriers were
reinforced. "My sentiments for M. Cousin are unchanging, but I fear this
absorbing power that he involuntarily exercises and which makes disciples of all those who approach him. When near him I seek information
more than ideas. I prefer to go more slowly and form my own convictions."[35] In this fertile theoretical period of Michelet's life, his incipient
"convictions" were leading him away from Cousin's general ideas of
"reason" and "eclecticism," while, at the same time, they were leading
him towards a redefinition of the generic unit for French philosophies of
history in the 1820s—humanity. Michelet's 1820 cosmopolitan advice
for the release of one's passions, "humanity is the way," would carry him
only for a decade.

# 4

## Our Only Asylum

Nearly four years after his November 1822 appointment to the Collège Sainte-Barbe, Michelet applied for a professorship at the Ecole Normale. He already had established himself as a promising historian, philosopher, and teacher, with broadening intellectual contacts in the Parisian academic world. In his letter of candidacy to Monseigneur Frayssinous, the rightist minister of public education and former chaplain to Louis XVIII, Michelet recalled the mental and emotional release the university world had served thus far in his personal life. "I belong to the University and to the Academy of Paris more intimately than other people; the first consolations that softened the misfortunes of my family came to me from the University."[1]

Michelet was seeking this position just after the reopening of the school. The Ecole Normale, started in 1795 following an October 30, 1794 (9 Brumaire year III) decree by the Convention authorizing its formation, had the expressed purpose of becoming a training center for France's future educational leaders. Plagued by financial problems, the Ecole Normale lasted less than a year, but was revived by Napoleon in 1808. In September 1822 the institution, having become linked with liberal elements hostile to the Restoration regime, was closed in the wake of the general reaction following the assassination of the Duc de Berry. Reestablished at the end of 1826, it was called the Ecole préparatoire, with the modern name, Ecole Normale Supérieure, dating from the reign of Louis-Philippe.

On February 3, 1827, Michelet was named head lecturer of philosophy and of history at the Ecole Normale. He would remain with this school until his 1838 acceptance of a chair at the Collège de France. In the same letter to Quinet, informing him of his intentions to form his own personal "convictions," Michelet eagerly reported his new teaching assignment. He also disclosed the apolitical character of his ambitions to his heavily politicized friend. "The present state of France is too bitter for you. That's because you only follow the political developments. Do I need to remind you that these developments are subordinated in definition to the progress of enlightenment and are under its control."[2] Politics was secondary to a general philosophical system and to the propagation of that system to other, less enlightened people. "Our philosophical history will have, I hope, a broad and powerful influence on this century, endowing it with this expanding spirit, which contains all areas of knowledge; conceiving and explaining all opinions, all past epochs."[3] His new status at the Ecole Normale would allow him to form his own world view and to impart it to some of France's brightest students.

Philosophy and history, the two disciplines of Michelet's professorship, were, respectively, the subjects of his 1827-28 and 1828-29 courses. In the initial lectures on each, particularly in the second year on history, Michelet attempted to formulate a working definition for the union and synthesis of history and philosophy. Philosophy, according to Michelet, was primarily the study of the individual and his mental equipment. Alone, philosophy was an inadequate explanation of human knowledge, failing to account for the human species as a whole and the concrete acts of men in time and space. Therefore, the other, complementary half of study necessary for a complete understanding of mankind, was history.[4] History contained the facts of collective human behavior and of social movements. While philosophy was preoccupied with the individual, history introduced the ingredient of societal man. Philosophers of history studied man in society, who had created the institutions and the morality of the present world. This societal man "who exists in time and space" was synonymous with humanity. "I define, therefore, history as the development of humanity, a development which ceaselessly advances."[5] In essence, through these definitions, Michelet's synthesis of philosophy and of history, the philosophy of history, was a study of social man, leaving the pure, timeless study of individual man for technical philosophers.

Michelet was not totally averse to metaphysics, having focused his 1827-28 course on the individual theories of psychology, physiology, memory, knowledge, association of ideas, imagination, and method. In August 1829, when the new minister of public education, de Montbel, decided to separate the chairs of philosophy and of history at the Ecole Normale, Michelet "opted for philosophy."[6] This decision, however, probably did not mean metaphysics, but most likely signified the philosophy of history, since this had been Michelet's main intellectual interest for the past five years. Moreover, the historical manuals, which he had written in the 1820s, were, to a great extent, factual histories of names and dates within a rigid political framework. The philosophy of history evinced in his Sainte-Barbe lecture, his introduction to Vico, his 1828-29 course, and his diaries, was noticeably absent in these summary histories. Within this context, his "opting" was, in large part, for the synthetic, theoretical, and all-encompassing philosophy of history rather than mere, factual history.

Michelet's personal decision, however, was unacceptable to the educational authorities, who proceeded to assign him to the professorship of history, alone. This administrative act apparently resolved for Michelet the profession which he would practice for the rest of his life. But this important moment in his career did not end his interest in the philosophy of history. His major work of this period strictly on the philosophy of history, the *Introduction à l'histoire universelle*, was written in 1830-31, while his famous historical works were characterized by a synthetic conception of the movement of French history. The questions that he had asked Cousin in 1824, those which he had posed, along with his proposed solutions, in his *Discours sur le système et la vie de Vico* and his *Discours sur l'unité de la science*, would be asked again in reformulated form, answered again, and then synthesized anew in his mature works.

Michelet was a thirty-one-year-old professional historian when, during three exhilarating days of July 1830, the Bourbons were overthrown and French society, apparently, was transformed. Personally, Michelet later attached crucial value to the July Revolution as the key political, social, and moral event affecting his life's work. It seems, though, that Michelet was not at all prepared for nor actively involved during the Three Glorious Days; in fact, he continued, according to the dates on his lectures, to give his course at the Ecole Normale.[7] His 1827 letter to

Quinet, asserting the secondary position of politics in his philosophy, was probably a fair assessment of his thinking on the eve of the July Revolution.[8] As late as April 28, 1830, on a trip through Dauphine, Michelet viewed the monarchy as one integral element in his quest for a unitary system. "Royalism, that is, the unity of the country materialized in a man, is still more necessary than is often believed."[9] But, beyond the political changes of the July Days, Michelet sensed, as did so many other intellectuals, a profound renovation of the French spirit, a renewal that had evidently been lacking in the restrictive atmosphere of French Restoration society. Two weeks after the installation of Louis-Philippe, Michelet enthusiastically informed Quinet of the new élan in Paris and the new opportunities available for scholars. "You must come immediately, my friend, new things are materializing. New positions are being grabbed quickly. You'll find one easily if you arrive soon. Your friends are in power. Guizot to the ministry of the interior and to that of public education, Villemain, Vatismenil or Cousin."[10]

Michelet, though playing no active role in the Revolution nor in the new government, wrote of the historical importance of the events. In his *Introduction à l'histoire universelle*, largely written at the end of 1830 and published the following April, he interpreted the July Revolution as a unique moment in the history of the world. It was the "first revolution without heroes, without names even; there was no individual on whom the glory could be concentrated. Society did everything . . . no one prepared it, no one led it; no one figure eclipsed the others. After the victory, one looked for a hero; and one found only a people."[11] This Revolution was the concretization of Michelet's philosophy that societal man made history. As in Delacroix's majestic painting, liberty, so long repressed, emerged as the symbol and rallying point during the Three Glorious Days. Individuals had suspended their own interests and had attached themselves to the higher strata of society and of humanity. The combined efforts led to the rebirth of liberty in France. In his 1869 preface to the *Histoire de France* Michelet recalled: "My first pages after July, written on the burning stones, were a glance at the world, the universal History, as a combat of liberty, and its inevitable victory over the fatal world; all was an eternal July."[12]

According to Michelet's 1869 recollections, the July Revolution also sparked the emergence of his full vision of France and inspired him to write her history. "This laborious work of around forty years was conceived in the moment of illumination of July. During those memorable days, a great light appeared, and I perceived France."[13] Although Michelet may have overdramatized this "moment" of creativity, the July Revolution did mark a turning point in his fundamental assumptions and goals. But his decision to write a history of France was not totally sudden. As early as 1826, in his *Journal des idées,* he had proposed various titles for his own histories of France, primarily for the sixteenth century. His historical manuals of the 1820s had dwelt mostly on French history since the reign of Louis XIV. Furthermore, his 1828-29 course had sketched the history of France, had reviewed the related historiography, and had concluded with the powerful judgment: "We still don't really have a history of France."[14] Nevertheless, Michelet had suggested, in addition to histories of France, many other forms and topics of histories before 1830. It is only after July 1830 that one notices in Michelet's writings an increased propensity to write solely the history of France.

As Michelet moved towards writing a history of France, so, too, did his unit of historical discourse narrow from humanity to France. His broad, cosmopolitan use of the word humanity in the 1820s had become decidedly more ambiguous by the time of his 1828-29 history course. In these lectures, Michelet readily acknowledged that humanity had made history in the past, but in the present era, "France is the true center of Europe."[15] Modern humanity and modern France were often used interchangeably in his concluding sessions, but this ambiguity practically disappeared after 1830. In Michelet's 1831 *Introduction à l'histoire universelle*, the progress of humanity became virtually synonymous with the course of modern French history. As Hegel, in his *Philosophy of History*, had attributed to Germany the status of being at the forefront of history, so now did Michelet ascribe that honor to France. The movement of Western civilization had traveled from large, loosely defined centers of cultures and institutions to the tight, restrictive geographical boundaries of a nation.

The *Introduction à l'histoire universelle*, although generally modeled after his 1829-29 course, added his new complete portrait of France, as he traced the flow of world history from its origins in India to contemporary French society. Michelet's characterization of India as the cradle of civilization had become currently common in philosophies of history by 1831. The India craze had received its first modern thrust in Western society through the seminal 1784 translation of Sanskrit texts by William Jones. Back across the Channel, Anguetil-Duperron published his second volume of *Recherches sur l'Inde* in 1787, giving the first authentic version of the four Upanishads. In the early nineteenth century, a whole generation of German poets and philosophers, already identifying strongly with their Greek ancestry, turned also to India as the original, timeless utopia of mankind. These Germans, primarily Schelling and Creuzer, were read deeply and carefully by Quinet and Cousin, who in turn recommended their works to Michelet. Cousin's 1828 course had portrayed India in much the same manner that Michelet did three years later.

The domain of liberty had enlarged progressively from India, to Persia, Greece, Rome, and into the modern world. Since the Middle Ages, Italy, Germany, and England had all made valuable contributions to the advancement of humanity. Now France, superior in culture and civilization, possessed and controlled the future fate of mankind. "France acts and reasons, decrees, and combats; she moves the world; she makes history and relates history."[16] The conclusion to the *Introduction à l'histoire universelle* heralded: "Our country leads the modern world . . . into the mysterious paths of the future."[17]

Even before the initial 1833 volumes of his *Histoire de France*, Michelet had formed his "own convictions" and had broken decisively with Cousin. While Cousin in 1828 had focused on previous philosophies and historical institutions as evidence of the abstract rise of reason in history, Michelet, in 1831, revealed the growing liberty of humanity through the concrete manifestations of man's creations: the arts, customs, and major events. Poetry, literature, and the July Revolution were as much the criteria for a philosophy of history for Michelet, as reflective, technical works of philosophy. Cousin had taught his students that the great nineteenth-century philosophy of history would be a synthesis of all major European forms of thought. Three years later, Michelet redefined the scope of this project to the present torchbearer of humanity, France. There was, however, still some residue from his 1820s cosmopolitan philosophy in the *Introduction à l'histoire universelle*. In this work Michelet announced future plans to write not only a history of France, but also histories of Italy and of the German Reformation. These latter two histories were never completed. By 1833, with the appearance of the first two volumes of the *Histoire de France*, humanity, as a philosophical preconception of Michelet's, and as his central unit of historical discourse, solely resided in and represented his mother country.

On a higher plane, Cousin's philosophy of history, as well as Vico's, Herder's, and Hegel's, was ultimately a theodicy. Michelet, although briefly adhering to the theodicy formula in his *Introduction à l'histoire universelle*, was like contemporary French system-makers, such as Saint-Simon, Fourier, and the Saint-Simonians, who were searching for a new, total explanation of man and society. These solutions often broke with the existing theodicy tradition, because it was presumed that the old Christian explanation of history had perished in the debris of the French Revolution. These men were erecting new worlds on top of Christianity, much as the early Christians had done to the Roman world. In an August 7, 1831 entry in his *Journal*, Michelet passionately set forth the scope and ramifications of France as a unit of historical discourse, which was more than the fount and matrix of modern humanity. Near the seaport of Le Havre at the time, Michelet described, both for his writings and his personal life, the religious and moral significance now embodied in his beloved nation:

> . . . I suffer from an empty pit within. . . . I felt the fiber of individuality tearing itself to pieces. The general, the universal, the eternal, that is the country of man.
>
> It is to you that I turn for aid, my noble country; You must take the place of God, whom we miss; you must fill within us the incommensurable abyss left by an extinguished Christianity. You must become the equivalent of the infinite. We all feel our individuality perishing. Let the feelings of social well-being, of human universality, and of the universality of the world be born again! Then perhaps we can move once more towards God![18]

At least temporarily, the *patrie* was replacing God as the giver of moral and spiritual comfort and as the source capable of uniting mankind. The center of this newly deified symbol for man to worship, Michelet added, was the city:

## Jules Michelet

Yes, the infinite has become sterile, since God left it and went into exile: sterile, deserted, devastated, we roll about there like a pebble on a beach. . . . Individuality perishes with the barbarous life, universality perishes with religion. Ah! but this shipwreck should be welcomed by the city; the city is our only asylum. And it should be able to transfigure itself into heaven! It is time that I part; the sight of this sterile infinite saddens me to the point of tears.[19]

# 5

## *These Catacombs of Manuscripts*

Before the venerated faculty of the renowned Sorbonne, Michelet fervently intoned, on January 9, 1834, the credo of a historian, living in a totally historicized world. He gave this *Discours d'ouverture prononcé à la Faculté des Lettres* while temporarily assisting Guizot, now a minister in Louis-Philippe's government, with his professorial duties.[1] Michelet opened this address in a solemn, respectful tone:

> It is a serious matter to speak of history in a place so profoundly historical. These walls which evoke so many memories, this audience assembled from all parts of France, overwhelms me and unsettles my speech; in this unique moment, in this narrow space, history appears to me immense and varied, in all the complexity of times and places. Since the thirteenth century, since the reign of St. Louis, the name of the Sorbonne recalls the great school of France, or should we say rather, that of the world; the most famous people of the Middle Ages sat on these benches.[2]

Following this reverent introduction, Michelet evoked the names of great Frenchmen—Malebranche, Arnaud, Pascal, Fénélon, Molière, Voltaire, and Turgot—all of whom had studied, taught, or lived near the Sorbonne. Turgot, eighty-four years earlier in his Sorbonne lectures, had formulated "the true base of a philosophy of history," and Guizot had carried on this tradition.[3] In this moment of praise for one of his colleagues, Michelet wondered when Guizot would return to the Sorbonne and again show the elevation of history "to the dignity of law?"[4]

Michelet quickly indicated his own acceptance of the importance ascribed to the discipline of history by embracing a full-blown concep-

47

tion of modern man's domination by history. This belief, expressed in flowing romantic language, was accompanied by the assumption that France itself was a collective, emotional being:

> Men and houses, we are all stamped by past epochs. We have in us, as young men, I do not know how many ideas, and ancient sentiments, of which we are not even aware. These traces from ancient times are confused, indistinct, often intruders in our soul. We find ourselves knowing what we have not learned; we remember what we have not seen; we feel the voiceless prolongation of emotions from those whom we have not known. One is astonished at the seriousness of these young faces. Our fathers ask us why in this age of power, we march pensively and hunched over. The reason is that history is in us, the centuries weigh heavily, we carry the world.[5]

All past ideas, thoughts, and emotions had entered into the bloodstream of the new generation of Frenchmen. There was no escaping history, since consciously or unconsciously, it formed each aspect of Michelet's individual. All men were completely historical beings. "All the centuries have worked for us."[6] Modern man was the end product of the steady progress of French civilization. Each epoch had contributed to this advancement of culture and society. The fourteenth and fifteenth centuries solidified the survival of France; the sixteenth century "gave us" religious liberty.[7]

Michelet acknowledged that many in his audience might question the modern principles of progress; both scientific and moral. But Michelet, himself, felt none of these uncertainties. "Whatever may be our doubts, our uneasiness, in these periods of transition, we believe firmly in progress, science, and liberty."[8] This trinity of modern morality, Michelet concluded, could best be comprehended and furthered if we continually grasped the repository of all elements of the present, namely, the past. "It is history that we have to grasp . . .Let's address ourselves to all past centuries; spell them out, interpret the prophecies of the past; and then perhaps we can distinguish there the morning ray of the future."[9]

Adhering to his own advice, Michelet ardently committed himself to an examination of the history that "is in us." He personally saw as his most significant opportunity for extracting all possible meaning from French history, his appointment to the Archives Nationales on October 21, 1830. On that date, Guizot announced Michelet's assignment to, what was then called, the Archives du Royaume. Michelet entered the hôtel de Soubise on November 2, 1830, as head archivist of the historical section, a post he would retain for nearly twenty-two years.

Michelet always attributed extraordinary value, as he had done only with the July Revolution of the same year, to his position of archivist. Surrounded by the parched remains of France, he sought to learn every detail of her history. Until 1852, he worked at the Archives almost every day, studying documents, beginning inventory systems, administering the activities of the historical section, aiding other scholars, and locating precious materials for his histories. Archival research in the 1830s helped immensely for numerous sections of his *Histoire de France*. At the end of his second volume of the *Histoire de France*, written in 1833, Michelet claimed that his job at the Archives "has made it the author's duty to investigate the history of our antiquities," since this was "the place which inspired them."[10]

In 1833, while discussing his first days at the Archives, Michelet recalled his astonishment upon entering the rooms of manuscripts, and his phenomenal vision of the documents and their possibilities. These worn, dusty pieces of paper contained the very heart of French history, as Michelet imaginatively recounted, in Ezekiel-like imagery, their future worth for him:

> As for me, when I first entered these catacombs of manuscripts, this wonderful necropolis of national monuments, I would willingly have exclaimed, like the German on entering the monastery of St. Vannes— "Here is the place I have chosen and where I will remain forever."
>
> However, I was not slow to discern in the midst of the apparent silence of the galleries, a movement and a murmur which were not those of death. These papers and parchments, so long deserted, desired no better than to be restored to the light of day. These papers are not just papers, but lives of men, of provinces, and of nations . . .
>
> Softly, my dear friends, let us proceed in order, if you please. All of you have your claim on history. The individual is good, that is, as individual; the general, as general. Feudalism is in the right, the monarchy more so,

and, still more, the Empire. I am yours, Godfrey—yours, Richelieu—yours, Bonaparte! . . .

And, as I breathed on their dust, I saw them rise up. They rose from the sepulcher, one the hand, the other the head, as in the Last Judgment of Michelangelo or in the Dance of Death. This frenzied dance, which they performed around me, I have tried to reproduce in this work.[11]

Into the valley of death Michelet went to make live again the holy remains of France. He poured his whole being into this enterprise, exclaiming first in his 1833 *Histoire de France*, and frequently thereafter, "This book is my life."[12] This personal stimulation within the Archives, Michelet reiterated in slightly different fashion in his 1869 preface to his *Histoire de France*:

In these solitary galleries of the Archives where I wandered for twenty years in profound silence, some murmurs came to my ears. The distant sufferings of so many souls, smothered in past epochs, moaned in a soft voice. The austere reality complained against art and said to him [Michelet] often some bitter things: "What amuses you? Are you a Walter Scott in order to tell at great length the picturesque detail, the coarse tables of Philip the Good, the vain wish of Faisan? Do you know that our martyrs for the past four hundred years wait for you? Do you know that the courageous of Courtray, of Rosebecque, do not yet have a monument that history owes to them?" The hired chroniclers, the chaplain Froissart, the gossipy Monstrelet do not suffice them. It is in firm faith, the hope in justice, that they have given their life. They should have the right to say: "History! reckon with us. Your creditors summon you. We have accepted death for a line from you."[13]

Michelet was able to give "a line" to each of France's martyrs in his histories. He often mentioned his indebtedness to the Archives for providing him with the raw material for his re-creation of French history. In his 1868 preface to the *Histoire de la Révolution française*, he emphasized again, that this work "was born in the heart of the Archives."[14] These constant reminders to his readers of the importance of the archives was far from a passing fancy. In addition to his qualitative attacks on other historians' visions of France and of the French Revolution, Michelet always hammered home the inferior amount of quantitative research other historians had done in relation to him. Writing to his son Charles on December 28, 1851, Michelet grudgingly admitted that there were "many good things in Mignet, Thiers, and Lamartine," but added, that their works were limited in scope, because "they did no research in the archives and only followed *Mémoires*, which are often strongly suspect."[15] Louis Blanc's version of the French Revolution was rejected out-of-hand by Michelet on the basis of his research alone.

> Can one write the history of revolutionary Paris in London? It can be done only in Paris. In London, it is true, there is a jolly collection of French documents: printed materials, brochures, and periodicals . . . But a collection of an amateur, of detached curiosities, that do not at all replace the official deposits where all follows, where one finds the order and the facts, and then their connections; where frequently an event is represented twenty, thirty, forty times, in its different versions; and then it can be studied, judged, and verified. These possibilities are afforded by the three great bodies of revolutionary archives of Paris.[16]

In historical polemics, Michelet continually kept at the fore of the controversy the superior value, by definition, of his histories, created from "the heart of the Archives."

Alongside the personal research at the Archives, Michelet also administered the historical section for twenty-two years. The documents on Michelet the administrator and director, housed at the Archives Nationales and in the Fonds Baudoüin-Demesnil at the Bibliothèque historique de la ville de Paris, are rather sparse.[17] They consist primarily of monthly reports made to the heads of the Archives, Daunou and Letronne, occasional suggestions for a new method of inventory within the historical section, reports on specific archival material, and analyses of provincial archives. Pierre Claude François Daunou had been an active legislator and educational reformer during the Directory. He became the first president of the Conseil des Cinq-Cents and president of the Institut. Admired by Napoleon, he rose progressively through the archival hierarchy, becoming head of the Archives in 1804. Relieved of his functions during the Restoration, he lectured at the Collège de France, only to return to the Archives after the July Revolution, remaining there until his death on June 20, 1840. Jean-Baptiste Letronne, who preceded Michelet as professor of history and morals at the Collège de France, headed the Archives after Daunou, until his death in 1849.

Michelet had not been trained as an archivist and therefore was forced to learn his trade quickly after entering the Archives. Rather than merely assigning the inventory of unedited boxes to the other employees, as was frequently the procedure, he decided to participate actively in the long, often tedious process of ordering and cataloguing the immense amount of material. Vast quantities of manuscripts had been discovered and sent to the Archives during and after the French Revolution. Official papers gathering dust in private, aristocratic castles, monarchical estates, and governmental buildings, suddenly came to the attention of archivists and historians in the decades after 1789. In a very real sense, Michelet's research on the history of France and the Revolution was original work with documents accessible for the first time. According to Michelet, among the approximately 150,000 boxes of papers and parchments at the Archives, the chief collection was the *Trésor des Chartes*. They contained "a series of the acts of the government from the thirteenth century, . . . the diplomatic acts of the Middle Ages, and among others, those which brought about the union of the provinces. . . . These constituted the ancient arsenal from which our kings drew forth weapons to break the strongholds of feudalism."[18] Michelet was absorbed, throughout the 1830s, with this assemblage of official documents, reports, and laws.

His monthly reports to Daunou and Letronne were generally about one and one-half pages in length, which included one or two sentences on the specific work of each employee in the historical section. Occasionally the reports were expanded into lengthier statements, revelatory of Michelet's sense of the historical possibilities inherent in the manuscripts and of a methodological approach to a new system of classification. Michelet was not solely a methodical archivist, listing new papers and collections, but more fundamentally, a sensitive historian always looking for the intellectual, political, and cultural meaning contained within this maze of 150,000 unedited boxes. Less than a week after his initiation into his new job, he wrote Daunou of a simple, straightforward method of classification. This inventory system, Michelet suggested, thinking in large units, should center around "a reign or an entire century."[19] With his historical imagination actively engaged,

Michelet told Daunou the following month that, by using the materials of the *Trésor des Chartes*, he envisaged the future portrait of "a complete history of the customs of the time."[20]

In the final sentences of his monthly reports, those capsulizing his own work, Michelet periodically mentioned that he had aided the research of other historians. Reports of 1833, 1838, and 1840 noted that he had responded to research requests from such men as Amédée and Augustin Thierry, Mignet, and Montalembert.[21] In a letter of January 9, 1833, he informed Sismondi that his position at the Archives would allow him "to do something for you in your research."[22]

As chief national, historical archivist, Michelet considered it his duty not only to procure and study documents in Paris, but in all of France as well. From 1830 to 1844 he visited all of the provinces of the country, seeking to educate himself totally on France. In this quest of "becoming France," or as Michelet often phrased it, "marrying France," he visited and made detailed reports from many of the provincial archives.[23] In 1835, under the authorization of Minister of Public Education Guizot, he examined all of the provincial archives in southwestern France. The principal stops were at Poitiers, Toulouse, Montauban, Cahors, Limoges, Bourges, and Orléans. After his return to Paris, he drafted a *Rapport au ministre de l'Instruction publique sur les bibliothèques et archives des départements du sud-ouest de la France*.[24] In response to specific questions posed by Guizot, Michelet presented in this report, city by city, the number of books, manuscripts, the method of classification, and the most important documents available in each archive.[25] An 1837 trip to Belgium and Holland carried Michelet first through several archives in northern France, which he reported to Daunou.[26] In the central archives of Belgium and Holland, Michelet studied their systems of classification and also searched for materials to use in his *Histoire de France*. The following year he investigated the archives at Besançon as well as several Italian and Swiss archives.[27]

This personal effort at collecting all of France's history transferred itself into concrete proposals by Michelet at the Archives. In 1833, and for the next two decades, Michelet called for the centralization of all the archives of France into the central depository in Paris. Michelet continually exhorted all of the provincial archives to send their valuable material to Paris. Although his pleas were met with resistance, he felt that his idea of one archive for all of France would eventually come to fruition. "Although the provinces refuse to entrust us with their archives, as do several of the ministers, they will be forced to get rid some day of the accumulating mass. That day will be ours, for we are death. All gravitates to us. . . . We need only wait . . . in patience since we die not."[28] At the Archives Nationales proper, the philosophical thrust of all of Michelet's reports for twenty-two years was towards a centralized, unified classification. All of France's history, for Michelet, could be placed in files, then arranged, hierarchized, and harmonized under one shelter, the hôtel de Soubise.[29] "Let but one great effort at classification serve as the thread through this chaos."[30]

As Michelet's vision upon first entering the Archives related directly to his inspiration of France's history, so, too, did his desire for a unified inventory relate to his view of the movement of French history. In his 1833 essay on his vision of and work at the Archives, Michelet consciously correlated these themes of the archival inspiration in "these catacombs of manuscripts"; a history of France from "this frenzied dance, which they performed around me"; one, centralized archive after "one great effort at classification"; and the progressive unity of France. Before the nineteenth century, each province had had an archive, but now the time had come to have only one, representing all of France undivided. The organization of the Archives should mirror the image of France he hoped to portray in his *Histoire de France*:

> The France of the present day, in its oneness and identity, may very well forget that old, heterogeneous France. . . . The Gascon may not choose to recognize Gascony, nor the Provençal, Provence; to which I answer that there is no longer a Provence or a Gascony, but a France. This France I now present is with all the differences of its ancient and original diversities into provinces. The latter volumes of my history will show her in her unity.[31]

# 6

## *Paris Is The World*

In a letter appearing in the *Courrier français* on July 13, 1820, Augustin Thierry expressed his belief that "we do not yet possess a history of France."[1] For this former disciple of Saint-Simon, the current books and articles on France were incomplete. "The history of France written by our modern writers is not the true history of the country; this history is still buried in the dust of contemporary chronicles."[2] Thierry called for a return to the original sources, as Michelet himself would come to do, in order to write a comprehensive history of France. While humbly noting that he was incapable of fulfilling such an undertaking, Thierry proposed that someone was needed with a broad "basis of feeling and judgment . . . and a lively enough sensibility to enable him to attach himself to the destiny of a whole nation, as that of one man, and to follow it through the centuries as one follows a friend in a perilous voyage."[3]

Thierry's desire for a truly national historian sensitized to each period of French history and attuned to the varying fortunes of the country, as if each internal change were part of his own life, presaged Michelet's monumental seventeen-volume *Histoire de France*. This work of love and devotion took thirty-four years to complete. The first six volumes, which covered the history of France until the end of the Middle Ages, appeared between 1833 and 1844. The seventh volume, the Renaissance, did not appear until 1855, although Michelet had lectured on this subject at the Collège de France in 1840. During this break in his chronological history of France, Michelet wrote—from 1846 to 1853—his historical classic, *Histoire de la Révolution française*. Removed from his positions of professor and chief historical archivist during the Second Empire,

Michelet was forced to write the last eleven volumes without the full benefit of the manuscripts and documents which he so highly valued. But, despite the fewer number of details in the last volumes, Michelet was still able to compose, unlike any other French historian of his century, complex psychological portraits of individuals, of societies, and of the national mentality for each period of history. He himself traveled all over France, having seen every French province by as early as 1844. His life and his work converged in his long attachment to "a friend in a perilous voyage." Michelet captured the essence of this unique bond between himself and the *Histoire de France*, when he exclaimed: "This book is my life."[4]

Michelet had begun his *Histoire de France* after an already vast outpouring of histories in this area during the 1820s. Historical writing had become a major expression of intellectual thought in the decades after the Revolution and the Empire. These mammoth works often espoused major philosophical systems not always in harmony with the conservative Catholic viewpoints of the Restoration government. In 1834 Augustin Thierry noted this increased importance of history as a comprehensive field of knowledge:

> I had the good fortune to see what I most desired, historical works becoming popular, and the best writers devoting themselves to them by preference. The number and importance of the publications which appeared successively from 1824 to the end of 1830, so many extensive works, each of which presented in a new light, and reestablished in some way either an ancient or modern historical period—such an abundance of efforts and talents gave rise to the opinion, now well accepted, that history would be the stamp of the nineteenth century and would give its name as philosophy had done for the eighteenth century.[5]

In this six-year span, Thierry published his *Lettres sur l'histoire de France* and *Histoire de la conquête de l'Angleterre*; his brother Amédée wrote his three-volume *Histoire des Gaulois*; Prosper de Barante wrote his twelve-volume *Histoire des Ducs de Burgogne*; Henri Martin began his seventeen-volume *Histoire de France*; J. C. L. Simonde de Sismondi wrote many of his thirty-one volumes of *Histoire des Français*; and François Guizot wrote his *Essais sur l'histoire de France* and published his courses on the history of modern civilization and the history of France, given at the Sorbonne in 1828-29 and 1829-30, respectively. These men were writing and theorizing on the origins of France, the course of her history, and the important ingredients of the past which had formed modern France. Men of varying political orientations were attempting to reconstruct the unbroken and unifying elements in French history in order to explain both the French Revolution and the movement of contemporary history. Voltaire's debunking of the Middle Ages less than a century earlier was, for the moment, unacceptable to these historians who were searching for the origins of institutions and, in often biological imagery, the foundations of modern French society. Common to these historians were the traditionalist preconceptions, in men such as Joseph de Maistre and the Vicomte de Bonald, that the Middle Ages were a high point of civilization. From this perspective, in contrast with Voltaire's flippancy towards the past, the only meaningful institutions and societies had been manifested in time and history. If an institution, government, or society had not existed for a long period of history, then it had very little validity. Often these historians were diametrically opposed to the overall philosophies of Maistre and Bonald, but their general ideas on the value of history and of the Middle Ages were strikingly similar. In this glorification of the Middle Ages as a formative epoch in the history of France, Michelet was no exception.

In their works, Augustin Thierry, Barante, Guizot, and Sismondi all mentioned the importance of research and of the use of original documents.[6] They felt that this was the first time historians had relied extensively upon primary sources. Guizot established a research group, the "Commission des monuments historiques," and published a lengthy series of documents, the *Mémoires rélatifs à l'histoire de France*. Much like Michelet, these historians thought the dried parchments would reveal the meaning and significance of French history. But, as with later generations of historians, their individual forms and methods of writing history resulted in different selections and uses of documents and diversified interpretations of French history.

For the Thierry brothers, Amédée and Augustin, the central element around which all French history revolved was race. They used the word race in broad cultural, social, and political terms to denote the two groupings of French people, the indigenous Gauls and the Germanic

Franks. Amédée, in his *Histoire des Gaulois*, and Augustin, in his second letter, "Sur la fausse couleur donnée aux premiers temps de l'histoire de France, et la fausseté de la méthode suivie par les historiens," analyzed numerous subgroupings of races within these two main races.[7] However, despite the varieties of minor races, the Thierry brothers ascribed basic political, religious, and social characteristics to the generic units of Gauls and Franks. By describing the origins and union of the Gauls, Amédée felt he was also portraying, at the same time, the inherent character and personality of the Gauls for "1700 years."[8] Henri Martin agreed that Amédée had laid the "cornerstone of a history of France" and, following his lead, attempted in his *Histoire de France* to evince the continued importance of the Gauls throughout the history of France.[9] Augustin, also having decided that his brother had written the definitive work on the Gauls, focused much of his research on the Germanic origins of the Franks.[10] Although admitting the complex mixture of peoples comprising the Franks, Augustin adhered to a general thesis in his various essays of the "two hostile camps on the soil of France"—the Franks and the Gauls; throughout the Middle Ages the incompatibility of two nations inhabiting one country explained all of the conflicts and crises in French history.[11]

Unlike the two Thierrys and Martin, Sismondi, a Genevan Protestant, discounted the importance of race in French history. In great detail he chronologically narrated the development of laws and the formation and actions of governments. Legal modifications and governmental edicts were the twin pillars of history. Guizot, in his 1829-30 Sorbonne courses on the history of French civilization, attempted to expand Sismondi's ideas on laws and governments. After recommending to his students Sismondi's *Histoire des Français* as the best history of France, he proceeded to inform them that it was unfortunately incomplete.[12] Sismondi's exposition of the institutions and the political development of France was too sketchy and too untheoretical for Guizot. Guizot's France became a nation with a fully developed government in the sixteenth century. In his philosophical and often historically abstract lectures, Guizot described the essential elements of the political system, religious structure, and legal doctrines which eventually evolved into a full-blown institutional framework of a nation. These areas of history contained "the germs of everything which is necessary to form a nation and a government."[13] While the establishment of key institutions was intrinsically the history of France, the main social manifestation, paralleling the continual formation of the nation, was the appearance of the middle class.

Augustin Thierry's reliance upon race as a causal explanation for conflicts and events was attacked by Guizot.[14] Laws had replaced races as a dominant principle of history between the ninth and eleventh centuries.[15] The varieties of legislation in regions of France could more accurately be explained, as Michelet would come to assert, by social and geographical factors rather than race alone.

Michelet was well-acquainted with the historical works of the two Thierrys, Sismondi, and Guizot. His *Journal de mes lectures* shows that he had read each of their works immediately after publication.[16] He had attended or received the notes from each of Guizot's lectures of 1828-29 and 1829-30. It was natural, therefore, that when he wrote his original preface to his *Histoire de France* in 1833, that each of these major historical writers would be mentioned. As a new historian of his country, Michelet paid homage to the creative and innovative works of his contemporaries. The Thierry brothers were lauded for their realization of the importance of race in French history, and Michelet added that he had kept in mind throughout the writing of his first two volumes, "their wonderful histories."[17] Michelet's most flattering comments were saved for Guizot, the foremost historian of the Restoration and then liberal political leader in the July Monarchy, who had personally arranged Michelet's appointment to the Archives Nationales. Michelet thought that Guizot, in his Sorbonne courses, had gone beyond "the history of facts and had seen the history of ideas. No analysis of social and intellectual factors had existed before his *Cours*."[18]

This original preface praising his fellow historians was dropped after 1837 from all further editions of the *Histoire de France*. Throughout the remainder of his life, Michelet increasingly qualified his admiration for these histories and increasingly minimized any possible influence these men may have had on his own histories. By 1841 Michelet no longer singled out Augustin Thierry for his novel ideas on race, but rather criticized him for his narrow theory of history. "It is not only necessary to have a theory of race . . . but also a geography."[19] In his unpublished 1868 preface to his entire *Histoire de France*, Michelet emphatically denied any influence of Guizot on his own writings.[20]

Michelet summarized his cumulative attitudes toward these other works in his final 1869 preface. He noted, as Augustin Thierry had thirty years earlier, that there had been an "outpouring" of histories between 1920 and 1830, but added, as a critique, that they were all written from "diverse and particular points of view."[21] Thinking of Thierry and Guizot, Michelet offered as examples of limited historical perspectives, "sole preoccupation with race or with institutions."[22] These particularistic outlooks "always have something a little artificial, which claim to clarify and yet give false perspectives about the whole of history and conceal its superior harmony."[23] Sismondi, as with Thierry and Guizot, could "rarely rise to a full conception of history."[24] Michelet, in 1869, thought that only he had "penetrated into the infinite detail of various developments" of French history.[25] No one before him had "embraced history in the living unity of its natural and geographical elements which had constituted it. Primarily, I saw her as a soul and as a person."[26] He had labeled his novel and unique form of history writing as early as 1846. "Thierry called it a *narration* and M. Guizot an *analysis*. I have named it *resurrection* and that name will remain."[27] Unlike all of the other historians who had written on one aspect of France, whether it was race, institutions, government, religion, or laws, Michelet felt that he had been the first to unite and integrate all of French history, to synthesize the multiple organs of a country as if it were a person. His *Histoire de France* was "the resurrection of the fullness of life" of "this body."[28]

Despite Michelet's 1869 critique of the history of races as incomplete history, the initial volume and one-half of his *Histoire de France* was primarily a racial interpretation of the first one thousand years of French history. Quoting and footnoting the Thierry brothers frequently, Michelet went into lengthy discussions on the origins of the Gauls or Celtic peoples and the various subsidiary races which had composed them. Although occasionally differing in interpretation on specific matters, Michelet's focus scarcely diverged from Amédée Thierry's textbook history of the Gauls. On the Franks and their influence, Michelet relied on both Augustin Thierry and Guizot. He sided, on this issue, with Thierry's interpretation that the Franks had little lasting impact on the character of most Frenchmen as opposed to Guizot's glorification of the German spirit of independence, brought in by the Franks and inherited by the French.[29]

Nearly midway through his first volume Michelet realized that his history of "France" had not begun yet, as he commented on the true impact of races alone:

> Let us not give too much importance to the primitive element of the Celtic genius, or to the additions from without. The Celts have contributed to the result, there can be no doubt; so have Rome, Greece, and the Germans. But who has united, fused, converted these elements? Who has transmuted, transformed, and made a single body of them? Who has eliminated out of them our France? France herself, by that internal travail and mysterious production, compounded of necessity and of liberty, which it is the province of history to explain. Such has been the accumulation of races in our Gaul—race upon race, people upon people, Gauls, Cymry, Bolg,—from one quarter; Iberians from other quarters again; Greeks and Romans; the catalogue is closed by the Germans. This said, have we said—France? Rather, all remains to be said. France has formed herself out of these elements, while any other union might have been the result. Oil and sugar consist of the same chemical elements. But the elements given all is not given; there remains the mystery of a special and peculiar nature to be accounted for. And how much more this fact has to be insisted upon, when the question is of a living and active union, such as a nation; a union, susceptible of internal development and self-modification! Now, this development and these successive modifications, through which our country is undergoing constant change, are the subject matter of French history.[30]

The formation and composition of France was a far more complex process than the development and interrelationship of the specific races. Michelet discovered the unaccounted for mysteries of France's "special and peculiar nature" through a geographical description of his beloved country.

In the pages immediately preceding volume 2, book 3, the famous *Tableau de la France*, Michelet summarized his impressions of the physical and psychological conditions of France around the year 1000. Various races had populated as well as governed France. The Romans and Charlemagne had tried to impose order and establish unity, but in each case their attainments had been evanescent. According to Michelet, France was extremely chaotic and divided in the year 1000, and he located the prima facie evidence for these conditions in the geographical make-up of the country. Rivers, mountains, and valleys separated societies and regions, while men were prisoners of their specific geographical areas. "The basins of the Seine and Loire, those of the Meuse, the Saône, and the Rhone" were not united, because, during this period of history, "rivers and mountains enter their protests against unity. Division triumphs; each point of space asserts its independence. The valley becomes a kingdom; the mountain, a kingdom."[31] Since these geographical factors were so all powerful, Michelet decided to stop at this moment in his chronological history of France, to ascertain the static attributes of each province:

> Let us try to disentangle this vast subject by marking in a precise manner the original character of the provinces where these dynasties have come to land. Each of them obeys visibly in its historical development diverse influences of the soil and of the climate... Mere geography becomes history.[32]

Michelet's declaration of a geographical basis for history broke sharply with the historical methods of the Thierry brothers, Sismondi, and Guizot. The *Tableau de la France* signaled this parting of the ways. His 1869 assessment, that "without a geographical basis, the people, the makers of history, seem to be walking on air, as in those Chinese pictures where the ground is wanting," was completely lacking in the historical theories of his contemporaries.[33] Eighteenth-century theorists on climate and geography—Montesquieu, Turgot, and Herder—were more in harmony with Michelet's general inclinations and intuitions. Turgot had sketched a *Plans d'ouvrages: sur la géographie politique*, but he was thinking in terms of nations, not a myriad of subdivisions within a country.[34] Michelet's work and ideas were reminiscent of Herder's poetic descriptions of characters and peoples, molded by a particular climate and an inherent genetic power. This genetic power, so mysteriously evoked in the *Ideen*, and then only applied to nations or religions, frequently became in the *Tableau de la France* the concrete manifestations of racial or provincial groupings. In both Herder and Michelet, unlike Montesquieu, history and geography welded together to give full characterizations of a people conforming to time, place, and their general personalities.

Michelet had discussed the importance of geography as history in his 1828-29 Ecole Normale course and had written most of the *Tableau de la France* for his June and July 1832 course. The "moral geography," as he termed it in 1868, of the *Tableau de la France* was philosophical and literary.[35] In this theoretical and artistic section of the *Histoire de France* one of the more creative and imaginative historical works of the nineteenth century, Michelet was passionately illuminating the "soul" of France.

In the *Tableau de la France*, Michelet's idea of his historical method—a unified history of all the internal elements of a people—first presented itself. The *Tableau de la France* was a reflective, geographical panorama of France around the year 1000 when she "displayed herself for the first time in her geographic form."[36] This geographical completeness enabled Michelet to describe, in infinite detail, the forms of a heterogeneous France. Political and physical divisions corresponded at this juncture in the history of France. "The true starting point of our history is a political division of France, founded on its natural and physical division. At first, history is altogether geography. It is impossible to describe the feudal period . . . without first tracing the peculiarities of the provinces."[37] In rapturous poetical passages, Michelet began his geographical interpretation of "the peculiarities of the provinces":

Let us ascend one of the highest summits of the Vosges, or, if you choose, let us seat ourselves on the Jura—our back to the Alps. We will notice . . . an undulating line, extending from the wood-crowned hills of Luxembourg and of Ardennes to the balloon-shaped hills of the Vosges, and then along the viny slopes of Burgundy to the volcanic crags of the Cevennes, and to the vast wall of the Pyrenees. This line marks the watershed. On its western side descent to the ocean, the Seine, the Loire, and the Garonne; on the other, the Meuse flows to the north, the Saône and Rhone to the south. In the distance are two continental islands, as it were—Brittany, low and rugged, of quartz and granite only, a huge shoal

63

of the current of the strait; and Auvergne, green and coarse, a vast extinct fire, with its forty volcanoes.[38]

These images of topographical conditions suggested the imprinting and shaping of each region by the forces of nature. As Michelet neared Brittany, he noticed that the increased density of the forests, "the solitude of La Trappe, where the monks lead a difficult life, the expressive names of the towns Fougères and Rennes, and the grey waters of the Mayenne and Villaine, all announce the wildness of the country."[39] Geography, climate, and the Celtic origins of the people forged the Breton character of "untameable resistance and of blind, intrepid opposition."[40]

Michelet traveled through each French province, relating, in the same eloquent manner, the geographical, climatological, and racial composition of each region. The main racial elements were the Celts or Gauls, the Iberians, and the Germanic tribes. But Michelet's idea of race was very general, and his use of the word race most often embraced all of these factors—racial, geographical, and climatological—at the same time. Even people from the provinces, such as Brittany or Burgundy, were referred to as races.[41] The great variety or provinces arose not only from racial characteristics, but also from manifold nuances of craggy peaks, twisting tributaries, wide-open valleys, and the corresponding modifications in weather conditions. Nature imposed variety on the Celts or Gauls as they moved into different areas of the country. No two provinces were the same. Often, in Michelet's poetical vision, a regional character was formed in order to protect the inhabitants against natural influences. The people in the mountains of Dauphine, for example, had "to love one another," because "nature apparently loves them very little"; their lives were only made tolerable by their "good hearts and good sense . . . , exposed as they are on bleak mountain ridges that face the north, or living in the depths of those gloomy shafts down which sweeps the accursed Alpine wind."[42]

Michelet's marvelous characterizations of regional customs and sensibilities were, in his viewpoint, a general depiction of heterogeneous France during the Middle Ages. These were not the people of modern France. Despite his astonishing ability to create these vivid portraits of a diversified France, Michelet did not intend this book to be construed as a contemporary characterization of Frenchmen. These were the static conditions of an embryonic country, which would one day mature.

Important theoretical statements in the *Tableau de la France* gave form and meaning to the complementary, literary descriptions. Michelet declared, in the paragraph prior to the *Tableau de la France,* that each of the provinces "obeys visibly in its historical development diverse influences of the soil and of the climate . . . local *fatalités* are all-powerful."[43] These "all-powerful" *fatalités*, according to Michelet, were geographical and climatological conditions along with racial qualities. He had first indicated the philosophical importance he attached to the concept of *fatalité* in his opening sentence of the *Introduction à l'histoire universelle.* The world had begun with a struggle "of man against nature, of the spirit against matter, of liberty against fate. History is nothing other than the tale of this interminable struggle."[44] *Fatalité* was the great enemy of liberty and progress. Frequently, in the *Introduction à l'histoire universelle*, Michelet referred to the "fatal power of nature," namely, race, climate, and geography. The combined effects of these factors did not engender a healthy variety of individuals, but rather had deleterious consequences on man's psychological state. "These powerful local influences, identifying man with the earth, attaching him at least in heart and spirit to his mountain, to his native valley, keep him in a state of isolation, of dispersion, of mutual hostility."[45] Isolation, localism, nature, hostility, and *fatalité* all went together in Michelet's vision of specific regions.

Although Michelet is noted as the celebrator of the heterogeneity of France, because of his *Tableau de la France*, he was not in favor of heterogeneity but unity. He had characterized ancient France so that he could now proceed to theorize on the beneficial change and transformation of the country since the year 1000. The problem was how to destroy those forces of individuation which had opposed unity some eight centuries earlier. Since the *fatalités* of races signified for Michelet the negative characteristics of a region determined by race, geography, and climate, he naturally had to consider, while solving this key problem, the major racial theories discussed in Paris during the early 1830s.

The two main theorists on racial change for Michelet were Dr. William Frédéric Edwards and Augustin Thierry. Edwards had published his principal work. *Des caractères philosophiques des races humaines considérées dans leurs rapports avec l'histoire: Lettre à M. Amédée Thierry*, in 1829.[46] In an entry of March 12, 1829, in his *Journal des idées*, Michelet noted that "on the question of races," he had "to consult . . . Dr. Edwards."[47] Two months later he met Edwards for the first time.[48] The two men began a close friendship and Edwards became Michelet's personal physician. Some of the doctor's treatments and advice for Michelet's problems of frequent headaches and nervous strain from overwork, are preserved at the Bibliothèque historique de la ville de Paris.[49]

In his book, Edwards investigated the races of France through first-hand observation. He had traveled around the country in order to acquire knowledge of the present-day characteristics of the races. Through this technique, he hoped to establish the changes races had undergone over the centuries. Scientific evidence for ancient traits depended upon works such as the *Histoire des Gaulois*, but Edwards felt that conclusions could be drawn for racial change by comparing textbook knowledge on races and his own hypotheses. His "fundamental conclusion" from his data was "that peoples belonging to a variety of races" could mix with their neighbors, but would still "conserve . . . elements of the primitive types."[50] Personal observation had demonstrated to him that the main characteristics of each people remained the same through the centuries "in most of the population, despite the influence of climate, the mixture of races, foreign invasions, and the progress of civilization."[51]

Michelet used the phrase "persistence of the races" to connote Edwards's theory as well as Thierry's ideas on the continuity of the Franks and the Gauls in French history. In his *Introduction à l'histoire universelle* and *Histoire de France*, Michelet took issue with their interpretations. He suggested that Dr. Edwards, who "expressed for the first time, I believe, the widespread principle of the persistence of the races," should take more account of "the mixing of the races."[52] Michelet attacked Thierry and Edwards, in a lengthy footnote in his *Histoire de France*, for their ideas on the "persistence of the races," and he contrasted their misinterpretations with another 1829 work, Rev. Thomas Price's *An Essay on the Physiognomy and Physiology of the Present Inhabitants of Britain, with Reference to their Origin as Goths and Celts*.[53] In contrast to Edwards and Thierry, Price argued for the mutability of the races, and, although

Michelet did not agree with the details of Price's study, he concurred with his theory.[54]

In the *Introduction à l'histoire universelle* Michelet introduced his own theory, similar to Price's conception, that there had been a fusion of the races through history. Unlike Herder's fear of racial and cultural contamination, Michelet posited this interbreeding as essential to progress and unity. "The crossing of the races, the mixture of opposing civilizations, is the most powerful auxiliary of liberty. The diverse *fatalités* which they carry into this mixture, are cancelled out and neutralized."[55]

Only in France did Michelet foresee the fusion of the races. He also thought, as he expanded his conception of the fusion of the races in the *Tableau de la France*, that this fusion already had occurred in his native Paris. The barriers of race, geography, and climate had been erased there, in part, because Paris was the center of the country. This center was not located geographically, for that "would be Bourges and the Bourbonnois . . . No, the center was located more by political considerations than natural, more human than material."[56] Viewed in this manner, there was no question of the centrality of Paris. "The history of the center of the center, of Paris, of the Ile-de-France, is the history of the whole monarchy."[57] Among all of the provincial personalities, which he had characterized in the *Tableau de la France*, not one of them had created the true France. Paris, alone, "had both received and given the national character; it is not a country, but the epitome of the country."[58]

The fusion of the races in Paris was entirely beneficial to the character of the citizenry. Lack of the *fatalités* of race, geography, and climate had made Paris cosmopolitan and universal. The "wiping out of every local and provincial feeling" in Paris was not at all "negative," but helped account for the "Parisian mind," which was "the most complex and the highest form of French genius."[59]

Paris was "the sensorium" of France.[60] The capital had incorporated, as part of her nature, the highest qualities from each area of the country. "The center knows itself and knows all the other parts."[61] As one left Paris towards any of the borders, individuals became "less French."[62] The Parisian character, the loftiest expression of the "French character," was distinguished by a "social spirit."[63] This "social spirit" was the direct opposite of provincial and local natures. While teaching at the Ecole Normale, Michelet was able to observe through his students, his specific ideas on the individual character of provincial peoples and the social character of Parisians:

> I've always found an interesting spectacle in these generations of students, constantly renewed, who appear before my eyes each year during my courses, and then leave me and flow away, but each one in the process giving me some interesting memory. Especially at the Ecole Normale this sight is quite striking. The students who came to us from all the provinces and who represented so innocently their native types, offered in their assemblage a composite of France. Through them I began to better understand the diverse nationalities which compose my country. While I related to these young students the history of the past, their features, their gestures, the forms of their language, represented to me, unbeknownst to them, another history, which was profound and true in many respects. In some of them I recognized the ingenious races of the Midi, that Roman or Iberian blood of Provence and of Languedoc, by which France is related to Italy and Spain, and which one day ought to unite under its influence all the peoples of the Latin language. Others represented to me the stubborn Celtic race, the resistant element of the ancient world, those iron heads with their lively poetry and their insular nationality on the continent. Elsewhere I found the conquering and quarrelsome people of Normandy, the most heroic during heroic times, the most industrious of the industrial age . . . .On the other hand, the blue eyes and blond heads made me hopefully think of French Germany, thrown as a bridge between two races and two civilizations. Finally the absence of indigenous characteristics, the indecisive features, the spontaneous ability, the universal capacity, indicated to me Paris, the head and thought of France.[64]

Without "indigenous characteristics" Parisians had no racial characteristics and no identifying traits derived from geography and climate. The very essence of the "social spirit" of Parisians was their lack of individually distinguishable markings. Michelet could examine in detail all of the other Frenchmen by means of their provincial determinisms, but Parisians were identifiable only by their "indecisive features."

There was no individualism amongst Parisians but only a "social spirit." Michelet's view that provinces could be intricately depicted while Paris could not be analyzed into individual parts, since it was an object of wholeness and of unity, contrasted sharply with other contemporary portrayals, such as Balzac's, of Paris. At the same time that

Michclet was praising the absence of traits and *fatalités* in Paris, Balzac was dissecting every nuance of social and psychological differentiation in the nation's capital. While Balzac described the greed, distrust, and selfishness of Parisians, Michelet saw only their "social spirit"—a wholly positive characteristic resulting from the "wiping out" of "provincial feelings."

In his *Journal* Michelet derived the sociable nature of Paris from a more personal angle:

> This city has been everything to me. I was born here. I have lived here, I will pass all my days here . . . All my emotions, all my traditions are tied to it, as are my past and my future . . . My Paris is not a particular monument or epoch. I loved this city before noticing any object of art. The most beautiful thing in her is neither Notre-Dame nor any other structure, but "herself." The beauty of the buildings is even secondary in this city. Walk along the quais and the boulevards and you will sense without looking for detail, that you are in the midst of the capital of human sociability.[65]

Because of this personal attachment, it was appropriate that Michelet's manuscripts should have been deposited not at the Archives Nationales nor at the Bibliothèque Nationale but at the Bibliothèque historique de la ville de Paris.

Paris was the center of France and contained the best of all things French. For Michelet no other country could reproduce such a situation, because they all lacked a center. Paris, between the Seine and Marne, was a city of "beautiful harmony"; "the most lovely of all cities, ancient and modern. Rome and London present nothing like it; they are cast on one side of their rivers alone."[66] Deprived of a center, other countries could not negate their local *fatalités* in order to achieve unity and harmony. Italy could never progress, because it was weighed down by the *fatalités* of "local cultures and customs."[67]

Only Paris was naturally harmonized. She was "the 'mediator of France' . . . where men think and ideas are formed."[68] "Modern Paris is beautiful in both immensity and uniformity, as a Babel and a desert. There is fantastic variety, incorporating all of the architectural styles, representing the epitome of the world."[69] Paris formed ideas, culture, and civilization not only for France but for the whole world. "The Seine flows and carries the thought of France to the Ocean, to England, to America."[70] Since Michelet, in 1831, had placed all of his faith in the "city" as "our only asylum," his Parisian origins allowed him to partake of and belong to the highest culture Western civilization had to offer. Michelet's ideas on Paris were not just part of his youth or his early writings in the 1830s, but lifelong preconceptions. In his *Histoire de la Révolution française* he neared the end of this momentous event only to reflect: "The all? Is it only France? Don't believe it. Paris is the world."[71]

# 7
## History Effaces Geography

Throughout the first six volumes of his *Histoire de France* Michelet described the slow but inexorable unification of France. Unity of the country politically and union of his fellow Frenchmen in feeling were Michelet's fondest desires. By the eleventh century, France had formed herself into the perfect hexagonal geography, but, except for Paris, there was no national harmony. With succeeding generations and monarchical regimes during the Middle Ages, feudal and provincial diversities began to be superseded by political, emotive, and social centralization. This centralization was always praised by Michelet as further evidence of the ineluctable progress and unity of the country. He recorded each step in the disappearance of the local *fatalités* and customs of a heterogeneous France and the concurrent emergence of homogeneous, harmonious France.

The increased centralization of the country in the Middle Ages was described in the other national histories of the 1820s and 1830s. Sismondi, however, reacted negatively to each new encroachment by the central monarchy at the expense of feudal values and traditions. For Guizot the development of France was similar to that of the dominant nations of Europe. In his lectures he subordinated French civilization to the progressive, uniform evolution of European civilization.[1] Désiré Nisard, the nineteenth-century French classicist, perceived this distinction: "Guizot is dominated by the march of civilization; Michelet by the unity of France."[2] Augustin Thierry, instead of searching for the unity of France during the Middle Ages, placed his allegiance in the fortunes of the nascent third estate. "We are the sons of the third estate," he exclaimed in his "Sur l'antipathie de race qui divise la nation française," and their history was the true history of France.[3] Henri Martin portrayed "the progressive development of national unity" in his *Histoire de France*, but by "unity," he only meant the political unity of France.[4]

Michelet's unity was, at the same time, political, social, and psychological. After characterizing the particularities of each region of France, he conveyed the emotive overtones behind a centralized, unified France in the most famous passage of the *Tableau de la France*, the last sentence of which was often quoted by de Gaulle.

> . . . we must not take France piece by piece, but embrace her in her entirety. It is precisely because centralization is powerful and because general life strong and energetic, that local life is weak. This is what constitutes the beauty of our country. France does not have the calculating head of England, ever perfecting new schemes of trade and money-making; but then she doesn't have the desert of the Scottish Highlands, nor that cancer, Ireland. She does not have like Germany and Italy, twenty central points of science and of art. She has but one of them; and but one center of social life. England is an empire; Germany, a country, a race; France is a person.[5]

In order to make France this one unified being, the local *fatalités* of language, climate, geography, and race had to be transcended.

One mechanism of transcendence, the fusion of the races, with the consequent annihilation of all *fatalités*, had occurred within Paris, but this process was insufficient and too slow for the provinces. There were, however, additional mechanisms in Michelet's histories which fostered national unity. In his *Histoire de France* certain attributes of human nature were set forth as the prime dynamic elements underlying the inevitable process of French unification. In his first volume Michelet discussed the transformation of the Celtic peoples in France and ascribed a "lively sympathy" to their character:

> This tendency to equality, this leveling desposition, which kept men aloof from each other in matters of law, needed the balance of a close and lively sympathy which would attach man to man who, though isolated and independent due to their equality before the law, would be joined to his

fellow man by voluntary bonds; and this is what at last took place in France, and accounts for its greatness.[6]

This positing of a "lively sympathy" which fomented "voluntary bonds" among Frenchmen was a baseless assumption by Michelet. No historical reason or analysis was given for the emergence of this trait.

Michelet enlarged and expanded his idea of the "lively sympathy" of French people into a key philosophical and psychological precept in his *Tableau de la France*. The "condensation of France into oneness and annihilation of provincial feeling" was steadily accomplished "by quick and lively sympathy of the Gallic character; its social instinct did the rest."[7] The natural "lively sympathy" which accelerated the unity of the country, was a general, social phenomenon. This "lively sympathy" stood in contrast to Michelet's far different psychology of individual man.

In Michelet's psychology of human nature, man was an egotist who acted out of self-interest. Rare, indeed, were the individuals who were motivated by unselfish motive. "Individual man is a materialist, and spontaneously attaches himself to local and private interests."[8] The quality of sympathy and social instinct, which only Frenchmen possessed, overcame the daily problems and frustrations of individuals and attached them to the country. "Lively sympathy" transformed obsession with "local and private interests" into the "voluntary bonds" amongst Frenchmen. This sympathy was not between men in a individual relationship, since they acted out of self-interest, buy only occurred within the larger, abstract unit of France.

> . . . each race is powerfully influenced by its own land. Little by little, the internal strength of man will disengage and uproot him from this narrow spot. He will leave it, reject it, trample it under foot, and require, instead of his native village, town, or province, a great country by which he may himself become a sharer in the destinies of the world. The idea of such a country, an abstract idea which depends little on the senses, will lead him, by a new effort, to the idea of a universal country, of the city of Providence.[9]

Michelet was presenting his own version of a common dialectical device in philosophies of history. In Vico and Hegel, man also acted out of selfish, private motives, but his actions were conversely turned into public benefits. Hegel had termed his mechanism the "cunning of reason." In both philosophies, God had foreordained the reason and logic of history regardless of personal behavior. Since Michelet's history was not a theodicy, his interpretation of human motivation and the movement of history was more akin to the French sensationalist and English utilitarian theories propounded during the previous century. His language of egotism, self-interest, and unselfishness was typical of the vocabulary in the writings of Adam Smith, Saint-Simon, and the Saint-Simonians. In fact, Adam Smith, whom Michelet had read in July 1824, had used the terminology of sympathy and social instinct as natural qualities in his *Theory of Moral Sentiments* and of egotism and self-interest in his *Wealth of Nations*.[10] His concept of an "invisible hand" was similar to Michelet's idea of a natural, undefined sympathy leading to progress and unity despite the selfish acts of mankind. Michelet's complement to the "cunning of reason" and "invisible hand" had become a "cunning of sympathy."

The Saint-Simonians, one of whose lectures Michelet had attended in 1831, spoke of the declining egotism and antagonism in the world as association and love enlarged. But they thought the whole world would eventually be one of association, whereas Michelet had only inculcated Frenchmen with the sympathy needed to transcend personal interests and behavior. Perhaps, though, behind Michelet's continual castigation of individuality and his concomitant belief in spontaneous, social love bereft of private egos, stood the theorist of the general will—Jean-Jacques Rousseau.

Michelet's definition of human nature along national lines was reminiscent of Hegel's approach. In Michelet's case, his views on France contrasted strikingly with the character and personality of the people across the Channel. As with many Frenchmen, Michelet saw England as the traditional enemy of France. England became the recipient of Michelet's greatest attacks on any people or society. Not until after the Prussian war did he severely upbraid the character and personality of another country. Until that time, Michelet, at each opportunity in his works and letters, impugned the English character and assailed the historical actions of English governments.

In his *Histoire de France* Michelet pointed out the continual hostility of England towards France during the Middle Ages. The eleventh, twelfth, fourteenth, and fifteenth centuries witnessed virulent political and military conflicts between these two powers. The battles with Normandy in the twelfth century, though, were little in comparison with the gigantic struggles of the fifteenth century, personified in the heroic opposition of Joan of Arc to the "empire" on French soil. The clashes with England were so constant and so powerful, that Michelet discerned the French nation itself forming and uniting as a result of these interminable confrontations. "The struggle with England has done France immense service. It has confirmed and stamped her nationality. By banding against the common enemy, the provinces have become one people."[11] France was "indebted to her enemy for the recognition of herself as a nation."[12] In his January 9, 1834 opening discourse at the Sorbonne, Michelet reiterated, with further imagery, this theme. "France is grateful to the English. England taught her to know herself. England is the merciless guide in this painful initiation. It is the demon who tempts her and tests her, who shoves her, pricks her in the back through these circles of Dante's hell, which some call the fourteenth century."[13]

What kind of people had chosen to confront France throughout the Middle Ages? In his *Introducation à l'histoire universelle*, Michelet deprecated England's "egoist and materialist politics."[14] Despite competing principles in the country, such as "industrialism and feudalism," all Englishmen were "in agreement on one point, the acquisition and the enjoyment of wealth."[15] The materialistic English, who lacked a perfect internal geographical configuration, as in France, were also egotistical people, ensconced in individualistic "pride."[16] In contrast with the French capacity to overcome "private interests," the English character contained no mechanism to remedy their complete "unsociability."[17] The selfish and "inflexible pride of England has placed an eternal obstacle to the fusion of the races as a solution to these conditions."[18]

The aggressive, warlike England of the past had bred a selfish people. From August 5 to September 5, 1834, Michelet visited England to gain first-hand impressions of the country which he had berated continually in his writings. His diary for this month, without any exceptions, was totally scornful of the English society and English way of life. Many of his caustic entries were typical of observations made by foreign commentators against the effects of industrialization. Unlike the beauty of Paris, the evil symptoms of a new society pervaded Michelet's senses upon arriving in London. "Nowhere, as here, did misery seem to affect me so, in this road filled with beautiful horses and carriages, . . . mendacity, begging, baseness, and moral degradation."[19] Living conditions were miserable and suffering was widespread in every city. On the outskirts of Manchester "the little weavers perish from hunger."[20]

Beyond the condemnation of industrialism, Michelet incessantly criticized the contemporary English personality. Much like in his *Histoire de France*, Michelet described the country as one "of insolence and inequality."[21] England was the epitome of "pride and exclusion," where mutual bonds of affection did not exist.[22] In England even the "household servants remained strangers" to their "masters."[23]

On several fundamental matters, Michelet's England was the direct opposite of France. Their disproportionate geography, with "no great image of centralization like the Louvre," totally hindered any form of unification.[24] Moreover, the pride and selfishness of the people "had placed an eternal obstacle to the fusion of the races." In France, also, men generally acted out of private, egotistical interests. However, most importantly, Michelet did not discover in the English mentality that Gallic sympathy which had allowed for the transcendence of petty concerns in France. Without sympathy and sociability there was no higher mechanism to unify or harmonize the country. Deprived of a means of attaching themselves to larger units—of forming "one great house" as the French—the English people could only retreat further into exclusive patterns and seclude themselves from one another.[25] Michelet footnoted in his *Histoire de la Révolution française* an interesting consequence from this world of egotism and individuality. Unable to find an internal solution to inequality, the English, the "empire," in Michelet's view, had transferred their problems onto external territories:

England would have died, had she not found, from century to century, an exterior diversion for her interior evil—aristocratic injustice, in the spoilation of Spain; in the eighteenth, the spoilation of France and the conquest of India; in the nineteenth, a new colonial extension, and an immense manufacturing development.[26]

England was condemned to divisiveness by Michelet. Within France, on the contrary, harmony progressed through history. This was not

76

merely a natural process catalyzed by the fusion of the races and by the "lively sympathy" of Frenchmen. Although this sympathy was a necessary ingredient, there was, for Michelet, another dynamic element which continually activated "lively sympathy" and accelerated the inevitable unification. Actions of great individuals also helped engender the French nation. "France has made France and the fatal element of race appears to me secondary. France is the daughter of liberty. In human progress, the essential part is the lively force which one calls man. *Man is his own Prometheus.*"[27] Man, whom Michelet had glorified in Vico's *New Science*, created and controlled his world. The free, overt deeds of men further removed the society from the harmful effects of local *fatalités*. This was the central point on which Michelet had criticized Thierry's racial theories. "Alongside the development of races, there is another . . . the free activites of men . . . . We remain attached to the earth by races, but we have in us a power of locomotion by which we can imprint the movement of histroy. That is what M. Thierry has neglected."[28]

In his *Introduction à l'histoire universelle* Michelet had posed "liberty and fate" as the primary conflict in the past, while history had been exposed and catalogued in the *Tableau de la France*. "Liberty . . .only submits to reason, to law, which knows no peace between itself and fate. Hardened forever in combat, it constitutes the dignity of man . . . . And it will harden no doubt, as long as the human will stiffens itself against the influences of race and climate."[30] Nature was the adversary and the free acts of mankind removed segments of French society from the restrictions caused by race, climate, and geography. This was *not* a concept of individual liberty, whereby men could do anything they wished, but a very specific form in which actions led to the cancellation of regional specificity and particularity, and to the increase of sociability and harmony. In this manner, individual efforts led directly to a free France unencumbered by regional *fatalités*. "France wants liberty in equality . . . and it ought to be attained by the mixing of peoples . . . by the neutralization of the opposing *fatalités* of race and climate."[31] Alongside Gallic sympathy, the liberty of man facilitated the harmonization of French society.

Within this context, the only positive actions by individuals in the *Histoire de France* were those which Michelet considered as enhancing unification. His philosophy of history revolved around the twin themes of unification and centralization; no action, institution, or event which did not further these goals was beneficial to the history of France. Only the specific role Michelet ascribed to liberty and natural sympathy reflected the steady evolution of heterogeneous France to "oneness." Sismondi commented on Michelet's orientation by contrasting their styles in a letter of April 5, 1840. He told Michelet that his *Histoire de France*:

> ... was so different from mine that it requires an effort on my part to recall the same events which we relate in such diverse manners. . . . I see that you would like to realize your goal, very French, by wanting to arouse enthusiasm for France. Desirous of power, you look at conquests, united assemblages, aggrandizement, as a good, as a sufficient aim for the efforts of Frenchmen. I am not French. I don't have to look for impartiality, it comes to me naturally; belonging to a small people, unselfish in all struggles that I relate, I only see the advantage of humanity, of justice, of respect for the rights of all; and I belong yet to the Middle Ages by my preference for resistance rather than force, for local powers opposed to centralization, and for individual existences.[32]

In his *Histoire de France* Michelet intertwined historical personages with progressive centralization of France. The two institutions around which France had attempted to unite during the Middle Ages were the Church and the monarchy. For Michelet the Carolingian empire had been a false unity. Charlemagne, as a representative of a foreign power, had been unable to truly bring together the heterogeneous parts of the country.[33] From the dissolution of this empire until the thirteenth century, the Church had been the central political, religious, and institutional focus for France. But the Church both "utterly failed" to unite itself, and did not induce "real unity, that of minds and of wills," anywhere in the country.[34]

Although Michelet's desire for a union "of minds and of wills" à la Rousseau, had not occurred under religious suzerainty, the Church had nurtured and supported the institution which would replace it as the unifying element of France—the monarchy. In dialectical fashion, the Church initially had used the "docile " Capets to thwart the growing power of the aggressive Normans, but, in the process, the Church had strengthened the Capets so much and "raised them so high that they were enabled to lower the Church itself."[35]

The ensuing battle between the Church and the monarchy reached its culmination during the reign of St. Louis, with the monarchy emerging as the clear and dominant victor under Philip the Fair. St. Louis symbolized in himself the brief union of Church and monarchy, but he also further dismantled ecclesiastical power. His actions against the Church were popular and successful, because "royalty had assumed in the eyes of the people religious authority, and the idea of sanctity was attached to it."[36]

In the fifth volume of Sismondi's *Histoire des Français*, he described the political transformation from a confederation of feudal powers to an absolute regime under St. Louis. However, the most significant result for Sismondi in this movement was the tragic loss of personal liberties.[37] Michelet also was aware of the extinction of feudal rights, but his judgments did not focus on the loss of personal liberties, but rather on the positive aspects of increasing centralization and unification. Although St. Louis, in Michelet's opinion, wanted to preserve feudal privileges, he acted for the "good of justice" and for the good of France by disregarding his own values and sacrificing "feudal rights which he would have desired."[38]

Under Philip the Fair the monarchy had become the only institution representing France and able to unite the people. Again, Michelet's concerns were not with the character of Philip the Fair in his individual actions, but with the whole of his accomplishments. He had bolstered the French monarchy, and this alone made him worthy of respect and admiration. "Whether or not Philip the Fair was a wicked man or a bad king, there is no mistaking his reign as the grand era of civil order in France, the foundation of the modern monarchy."[39]

In the twelfth, thirteenth, and fourteenth centuries, guided by the power and authority of the monarchy, France gradually became a nation. "She lost something of the religious and chivalrous character which had confounded her with the rest of Christendom during the whole Middle Ages and saw herself for the first time in her national and prosaic aspect."[40] Under the unifying force of the monarchy the "national era of France" commenced.[41] Until the fourteenth century France had been "less France than Christian"; she had been dominated "by other states, by feudalism, and the Church," but the day was coming "little by little, where she will have a feeling of herself."[42]

The monarchy had given form to France, but the "feeling of herself" was supplied not by a king, but by a little peasant girl, the only authentic individual and hero in the first six volumes of the *Histoire de France*, Joan of Arc. Michelet's singling out of Joan as the supreme embodiment of France and French ideals was a common assertion in the other, contemporary histories of France. In both Guizot and Martin, for example, Joan represented the moral union of the French nation, the French mind, and French patriotism.[43] Michelet's version of Joan has undergone an exhaustive examination by the twentieth-century positivistic literary historian Gustave Rudler.[44] He shows the historical inaccuracies on each page, concluding: "One must admit that this work is not brilliant. The analysis . . . is very weak. I think I've furnished the proof for this."[45] From another perspective, though, this section of Joan of Arc in the fifth volume of the *Histoire de France* was one of the most brilliant of Michelet's achievements. In this work of pure inspiration, Michelet poetically evoked the moral, religious, and political unification of France in one person. For over four volumes of writings and fifteen hundred years of history, he had pointed to the unification and harmonization of France. Now he was reliving and "resurrecting" the history of the first individual who represented, in every way, Michelet's idea of a Frenchman. She was France.

Joan was the first person who touched an emotional chord in every Frenchman. Gallic sympathy overcame private interests when Joan acted and spoke. "Little by little, the whole of France became interested in the fate of one town."[46] The other individuals in the *Histoire de France* who contributed to centralization and harmony did so despite their selfishness or egotism. Joan, alone, was a genuine hero for Michelet, because her character and the ideals of France were one and the same. Even in her battle against the English, all of the other French counselors gave divisive and unharmonious advice. Only Joan did not give "opinions dictated by self-interest."[47] In the highest sense, lack of self-interest, for Michelet, was synonymous with France.

Joan became the eternal symbol of the national sense of all the French people. She had given Frenchmen a momentary "feel of herself," and Michelet hoped that one day all of his countrymen would follow her example and bind themselves together in love and harmony with France. After finishing the composition of this book, Michelet personally felt that his perception of the past had changed, and that he had been able, through "concentration and reflection," to "fathom all the apparent diversities" of French history, and to "give them in my historical writing the unity they had in reality."[48]

The greatest centralizing monarch of the fifteenth century was Louis XI. He consciously destroyed the feudal power and feudal traditions of the provinces. By subduing "Picardy, Burgundy, Provence, and Roussillon, Maine and Anjou," Louis XI "laid the foundation of perpetual peace for the provinces of the center."[49] For Sismondi, Louis XI's repression of feudalism was evidence of a complete tyrant. In his novel *Quentin Durward*, Walter Scott chided Louis XI for destroying feudal values and traditions in his dynastic struggles with the Duke of Burgundy. Scott's romantic style of writing and dramatization of history were similar in method and tone to Michelet's. Since Scott was his favorite novelist, Michelet read virtually all of his works.[50] But, despite the concordance of their styles, their judgments on human nature and its relation to history were diametrically opposed. Scott's Louis XI was a selfish, tyrannical creature, because of heartless onslaughts against the last bastions of feudalism. Louis XI's character, Scott caustically wrote, was "inconsistent with the principles of chivalry," since "the principle of devoting toil, talents and time, to the accomplishment of objects, from which no personal advantage could, in the nature of things, be obtained," was foreign to his nature.[51]

Personal greed and lust for power had extinguished priceless feudal values in *Quentin Durward*. Michelet's interpretation, on the other hand, was from a different perspective. He could concur with Scott and Sismondi that Louis XI was selfish and tyrannical. His psychology of human nature had admitted that individuals were vain and egotistical. However, at the same time, Michelet's definition of man allowed complex views within the framework of man and society. There were certain negative aspects to Louis XI, but he was also part of a larger society. And the relationship between man and society overshadowed personal attributes. In society, Louis XI had facilitated the centralization of France, and this, above all, made him an outstanding man and monarch. Unlike Scott and Sismondi, Michelet did not bemoan the fate of chivalry and honor codes, but rejoiced in the further unification of France.

## Jules Michelet

In the conclusion of his *Tableau de la France* Michelet reflected upon the course of French history and the current state of France. From the Roman empire through the rule of Christianity, Charlemagne, Louis XIV, French Revolution leaders, and Napoleon, provincial *fatalités* had either been eradicated or overcome. This was the aim of centralization, because "the nation whose centralization is the most perfect, is likewise that which, by its example, and by the energy of its action, has done the most to forward the centralization of the world."[52] The centralizing actions of individuals had helped in the inexorable process of the "condensation of France into oneness and annihilation of provincial feeling." Even if some *fatalités* had remained, Michelet wanted to show how his vision of total harmony under the aegis of France transcended all differences. He wanted all Frenchmen overcome by emotion of *patrie*:

Strange! These provinces, differing in climate, customs, and language, have comprehended and loved one another, until they feel themselves one. The Gascon has been uneasy about Flanders, the Burgundian has rejoiced or suffered from what has taken place in the Pyrenees; the Breton, seated on the shores of the ocean, has felt the blows struck on the Rhine.

In this manner has been formed the general, the universal spirit of the country; the local has disappeared daily; the influence of soil, climate, and race has given way before social and political action. Local *fatalités* have been overcome, and man has escaped from the tyranny of material circumstances. The Frenchman of the North has enjoyed the South, and gathered life from her sun. The southerner has gained something of the tenacity, seriousness, and reflectiveness of the North. Society and liberty have subdued nature and history has effaced geography. In this marvelous transformation, spirit has triumphed over matter, the general over the particular, and the ideal over the real. Individual man is a a materialist and spontaneously attaches himself to local and private interests. Human society is a spiritualist; it tends unceasingly to free itself from the miseries of local existence in order to attain the lofty and abstract unity of *la patrie*.[53]

In Hegelian cadence Michelet intoned the inevitable goals of France— the progressive centralization, the fusion of the races, the continual flowering of Gallic sympathy, the transcendence of private interests by social love and affection, and the effacing of geographical *fatalités* through time and history—all of them coalescing in *la patrie*. In his *Journal* Michelet included another dimension of *la patrie* which he had hoped to find in his study of her history and eventual union with her:

> Why do I love France? So young and so reasonable . . . She is lively, she is merry; sometimes she makes fun of you. Leave and see if you can get along without her. You will return very quickly. . . . I love [the provinces] and thank them for rendering to me the adored mother, such as she was to another age, when, younger, she was less herself. They are for me the degrees, the stations towards the supreme maternal beauty.[54]

Michelet, in the *Introduction à l'histoire universelle*, thought he discerned in the July Revolution the culmination of French history. "Society was everything," and all men loved each other and France.[55] He gradually realized near the completion of his history of the Middle Ages that this was not the case. By 1842 personal tragedy had overcome him. At the same time he noticed an increasing conflict between his theories on the harmonization of France and present-day realities. No longer did nature, geography, climate, and race appear to be the complete list of *fatalités*. Man-made *fatalités*, secondary in the *Histoire de France*, now became the pressing areas of his concern. The new barriers he perceived hindering the harmonization and unification of France encompassed social class conflicts, religious ideas, educational philosophies, and political ideals. He would have to combat, solve, and eradicate these new *fatalités* before France could finally mirror "oneness."

# 8

## *The New Clergy*

In 1843 Michelet entered new areas of intellectual activity. For the next eleven years, along with his history writing, he became involved in the current political, social, religious, and educational problems of his society. The nexus of his contemporary concerns and analyses was education. Since 1838 he had been professor of history and morals at the Collège de France, and increasingly had seen in his position the authority to assume the functions of prime educator of France. Already an accomplished historian, he now took just as seriously the other half of his title, proclaiming: "I am professor of history and morals."[1] In *Des jésuites* and *Du prêtre, de la femme, de la famille*, Michelet asserted the sole right of the university to educate the youth of France, and in *Le Peuple* and his published course of 1847-48, Michelet proposed educational remedies to the social class conflicts searing the skin of France. These works, not his histories, were widely read in the 1840s. During his lifetime, Michelet's reputation and the general conception of his ideas were derived from the extensive dissemination of these popular pamphlets.

His heightened interest in the present, which occurred at the same time as a deep personal crisis in his life, involved a new interpretation and attitude towards the past. Although his commitment to France was not questioned, Michelet attacked throughout the 1840s both Catholicism and the Middle Ages, which he had just recreated in his *Histoire de France*. His *Journal* records this startling historical reorientation. In August 1840 he contrasted the passivity of Christianity during the Middle Ages with the creativity of the Renaissance. "Two ways of enduring life: to accept it, to approve it, as the Christians, or to remake it, as the artists. Christian resignation was not part of the Renaissance as men, no longer accepting the world, began to remake it."[2] By August 13, 1841, Michelet's feelings of modernity and of the need to engage in contemporary struggles was associated with his distaste for the Middle Ages. "All has perished for me: antiquity, the Middle Ages; I now sense myself deeply modern. The contemplation of monuments, dreamy speculation, no longer make any sense. Today, action, action!"[3] At Le Havre in 1831 Michelet had forecast the temporary replacement of Christianity by the *patrie*, but his severe condemnation of the Middle Ages and its chief symbol, the Catholic Church, only burst forth in the 1840s. "In the Middle Ages everything coexisted, but coexisted harmoniously in a religious form; in the modern age all coexists in a religious form, no less religious, and very specific; *la patrie*."[4]

Great individuals such as Joan of Arc were never criticized, but, by 1843, the whole tenor of the Middle Ages had changed in Michelet's writings. For the rest of his life he commonly referred to the Middle Ages as "barbaric," "warlike," "somber," "a world of hate," "frightful," "intolerable," and "a world of illusion."[5] His historical magnum opus, *Histoire de la Révolution française*, showed how the ideas and spirit of the French Révolution had passed infinitely beyond Christianity. In a diary notation of 1843 Michelet bade farewell, with some finality, to his ideals of the past: "My dreams of the Middle Ages . . . are ended . . . . Goodby Church, goodby my mother and my daughter . . . All that I have loved and known, I have left for the infinite unknown, for the obscure regions, where I sense without having known it yet, the new God of the future."[6]

The period of trying to free himself from previous historical conceptions coincided with Michelet's desperate attempt to overcome the most sorrowful year of his life, 1842. The soul-searching and internal turbulence was first precipitated by the death of his wife Pauline on July 24, 1839. His *Journal* for the following month is filled with a passionate examination of their relationship and their meaning to each other. He did not try to gloss over the defects of their marriage and the deficiencies of the deceased in order to imagine a rapport which never existed. Instead, Michelet's reflections conveyed the loss of a good wife, whose spirit and intelligence were unfortunately not on a level with his own. The remorse and guilt which Michelet may have felt was explained away

*85*

by a comparison of their educational differences. He warned that the most harmful type of marriage was with someone of an inferior education. Michelet had failed with Pauline, in part, because he had been unable to educate her. "This death weighs heavily on me; perhaps if I could have changed this poor soul, if I could have seriously devoted myself to doing so."[7] But, unable to accept the blame for her shortcomings, Michelet proceeded to recall that probably no one could have changed Pauline after her miserable childhood. Already emotionally and intellectually removed from her husband, she tried to keep up her appearance, but "in the last years, she sagged, she abandoned herself."[8]

In November 1839 Michelet met and began a friendship with one of his auditors at the Collège de France, Alfred Dumesnil. Dumesnil was an eighteen-year-old son of a Rouen banker, who had gained access to Michelet with a letter of introduction from a former Michelet student at the Ecole Normale. This young provincial bourgeois became totally captivated by the personality and courses of Michelet. In 1840 he wrote to his childhood friend Eugène Noël:

> How I regret not being able to describe to you what Michelet does when he expresses his ideas and retraces the past; how he is animated, incisive, sometimes enthusiastic, often sensitive, always deeply spiritual.
>
> He is sometimes a narrator expressing himself simply and concisely, sometimes an economist, sometimes an artist, sometimes a poet, and always a philosopher, a moralist, a lover of what is good in the past in order to educate posterity.[9]

The following year Eugène came to hear Michelet, and together with Alfred, they became intimate friends and disciples of the famous historian. Hundreds of letters were exchanged between the three of them during the next decade, and in this correspondence Michelet expressed his feelings more openly than with anyone else. For Michelet, these friends represented the youth of France, and he often discussed his new ideas with them before conveying them to his audience at the Collège de France. Alfred, a frequent Michelet houseguest for several years, eventually became his son-in-law by marrying Adèle on August 3, 1843. But this close contact with Alfred was initially most important for Michelet, because of his May 24, 1840 meeting with Alfred's mother, Mme Dumesnil. She shortly became the first woman Michelet ever loved.

One year younger than Michelet, Mme Dumesnil, née Fantelin, married at seventeen a wealthy Rouen banker and property-holder nineteen years her senior, in order to ease desperate family financial circumstances. Concern and devotion for her only son brought her to Paris in 1840 to inquire after his health and education. From her very first visit to Michelet's home, she sought the historian's advice on these matters. Mme Dumesnil and Michelet began to see each other regularly, and, after she returned to Rouen, an active correspondence ensued. In January 1841 Michelet visited her family, and the following month she traveled again to Paris.

A tender, emotional bond with Mme Dumesnil totally rejuvenated Michelet, who now had been a widower for nearly two years. At the end of April 1841 he wrote her enthusiastically on the progress of his work and added at the end: "Why do I speak to you this way Madame? Because you have won my confidence and you have inspired me more than anyone else."[10] This resurgence of spirit helped catalyze, the following month, Michelet's original conception of the Renaissance as a distinct epoch in Western civilization, arising in organic form after the Middle Ages.[11] He wrote to Alfred on May 15: "I have never yet raised up such a great mass, never reconciled so many seemingly discordant elements in a living unity. All these elements were in me for a long time, but only as knowledge; today they have become my sentiments, my own thoughts."[12] Michelet felt that his own heightened spirits had coalesced with his novel vision of the past. "I had remained immobile for several months in the presence of my disorganized material; unity and life suddenly began to vivify this chaos of dead things."[13] This emotional euphoria and historical discovery of May 1841 were great moments "of exaltation."[14]

Just when Michelet felt revitalized, though, the most difficult year of his life began, culminating with the death of Mme Dumesnil from cancer on May 31, 1842. In order to be cared for, she moved into Michelet's home on rue des Postes in June 1841 and spent much of her last year there, including her last days. Their vacations were spent together—in August a trip to Fontainebleau with their children and in September a week's stay at the Dumesnil country home at Vascoeuil.

There were moments of happiness in the fall of 1841, but by February 1842 the doctors and surgeons informed Michelet that there was no longer any hope. Mme Dumesnil decided to have a confessor, which greatly grieved Michelet, who had broken with Catholic practices.

> Yesterday, Monday, Mme Cartier, in the absence of the priest Guerry, proposed the priest Beauvrais; thirty-six years old, more spirutual than intellectual. I was doubly afflicted: it all escaped me.... After the surgeons, she had wanted a foreign magnetizer, then the confessor. In such a crisis the soul moves away from those who love but cannot help. It asks for help from unknown persons, from foreigners. That, for me, is an unexpected form of death, to feel the confidence and affection of the soul die. It is death for my entire self.[15]

Her death emotionally and mentally incapacitated Michelet for several months. Except for seven lectures in April and May, Michelet did not teach during 1842 at the Collège de France.[16] He had been excused for reasons of health both during her illness and after her death. "In the midst of this death, slow and without horror, I tried to look for new reasons to live."[17] But the harsh reality of losing the first woman he had loved overcame him completely. "All is finished . . . .One year . . . that one year contains so many things, events, emotions! One year to cross three worlds: cruel drama of a cruel unity."[18] Having been "born alone," Michelet, once again, had to "live as if I were alone."[19] Her passing had extinguished his rejuvenated spirit and had brought him within the clutches of emotional death. "It is I who died. I sense it and will continue to sense it. Where am I in this empty and widowed house? I look for myself but I am no longer there."[20]

Michelet tried to recover by traveling to Germany for six weeks with his children and Alfred, but his letters upon returning show that he remained deeply depressed. "My heart is sick," he wrote to Alfred on August 10, 1842.[21] He mournfully sensed in a letter of September 1 that, "I am death, nothing more . . . if I have life in me it has sought refuge in a corner of my heart so obscure that I do not know where it is."[22] This same, sorrowful state was confided to Alfred three days later, but Michelet also managed to add a few words of hope. "Personally, my body and mind are in terrible shape. Truthfully, I foresee nothing in this world. The more I try, the less I desire. The world is closed for me . . . . To live, to last. This hope remains with me yet."[23] The desire, though, to escape from the pain and the shock did not immediately materialize. Although Michelet had finally recovered his "capacity to work," he still seemed "to be descending a rapid slope where nothing will keep me up."[24] In mid-September Alfred informed Eugène, after visiting Michelet, that his father-in-law's suffering had seriously affected his emotional and mental frame of mind:

> I found M. Michelet extremely pale and sometimes visibly altered; he suffers in both his chest and heart. But what is far more serious is that morally he appears very sick, worse than I expected. Three days ago he said he had never been lower in his life. His children are uneasy and concerned with his state. There is a danger that in this depression his health will not hold up. He tries to work but the trouble he has producing discourages him. Nearly every night he reads old chronicles, unable to sleep.[25]

Michelet remained considerably distraught over his irretrievable loss. His words were not those of guilt followed by an analysis of two different spirits, as with Pauline, but they were of profound and timeless loneliness. "I no longer hope nor desire to live, my body and mind are worse each day. Dizziness and nausea warn me ceaselessly that my stomach and head are no better than my chest. . . . The sentiment of the harmony of the world diminishes in me each day."[26]

By December 1842, however, at the same time that Michelet was completing his intellectual break with the past, he seems to have recovered from the worst moments of his crisis. "I am doing well, my friend, as least, I have rebegun my life, my work . . . . On the whole this suspension of work has been good for me. I am better oriented than before."[27] On December 7 Michelet told Alfred, "One must return," and he informed him of a bundle of new ideas surging within him.[28] His letters to his son-in-law no longer spoke of his personal distress, as they had done incessantly only two months earlier, but again discussed his ideas and projects. "I have retaken all my works since 1833, in art, law, and religion. All of this will converge easily into my new movement."[29] He thought of writing a history of "modern society," and hoped that "in this harmonization of my work, I will find my own harmony."[30]

## Jules Michelet

Thomas Couture's famous portrait of Michelet, now hanging in the Musée Carnavalet, was painted mostly during the sad days of May and September 1842. Michelet, immaculately dressed in formal attire, is sitting slightly forward in his chair. His head is turned towards the right, confronting the viewer directly. There is the sharp nose, square chin, and the long, slender left hand resting comfortably on his knee. Scattered on his desk and the floor are books and papers arranged haphazardly, perhaps indicative of Michelet's rapid method of examining materials and sources. The majestic pose, the sharp features, and the imposing collection of thick works is disturbed, however, by the right hand and lips. The fist is closed and the fingers tensed, while the lips are pursed, revealing the storm and passion within. The eyes are deeply set, covered by strained eyelids. On top, the long, wavy white hair flows smoothly but the sides are disheveled and turbulent. Beneath the attempt to portray a calm, dignified professor, the overall nervous energy comes through as the dominant element of Michelet's temperament. Was it not perhaps this energy, captured so successfully by Couture and internalized during his slow breaking away from the Middle Ages and Catholicism and his depressive crisis of 1842, that burst forth in 1843 as a deep commitment to the future and a strong attack against the Jesuits?

Michelet's confrontation with the Jesuits, his first polemic as a historian, became one of the focal points of a widespread French debate between the Catholics and the universities over education. The general issue was commonly referred to as the "freedom of teaching." Since the Napoleonic period, universities had been given nearly complete control over secondary education in France. By controlling the curriculum and intellectual orientation of high school students, universities directly influenced each new generation of administrators, civil servants, and professionals. Under the July Monarchy, Catholics increasingly fought to open secondary schools legally free of strict university control. Their campaign was accelerated after an elementary school reform, the Guizot Law, passed in 1833. An 1836 law, also under Guizot's direction, containing provisions for "freedom of teaching" in secondary schools, passed in the Chamber of Deputies only to die with the resignation of the government.

For many intellectuals in Paris, among them Michelet, the active attempt by the Church to increase her role in society was an act of divisiveness. These men dreamt of national unity, and the Church's intrusion into the realization of that quest injected internal hatred and disunity into the path of progress. Moreover, the "Jesuit problem" entered the complicated controversy by the early 1840s. The Jesuits had returned to Paris in 1833, opening one "monastery" after another. At the same time, their influence, with the decline of Gallican authority against the state and the expanding popularity of ultramontane doctrines among priests, rapidly spread within the French church. In 1841 the Church decided to open up a highly charged campaign against the university "monopoly" of secondary education by initiating attacks on unsympathetic professors through the Catholic press, books, sermons, and speeches. In their counterattack, the resurgence of the Jesuits, the old nemesis of enlightened French intellectuals, became the primary target of university defenders. The government, led in this issue by Minister of Public Education Villemain, was also against the further proliferation of Jesuit "monasteries" in Paris, and was resentful of their desire to gain a foothold in the French educational system.

The principal organ of the Catholic press was *L'Univers*, directed by Louis Veuillot. *L'Univers* had started publication in 1833 under Abbé Migne, who considered this paper to be in the spirit of *L'Avenir*. However, Veuillot took over control of the newspaper in 1842 and immediately began a vitriolic assault upon the universities, which incidentally helped raise the number of subscribers from 1,800 to 7,000 within five years.[31] On March 31, 1842, *L'Univers* accused eighteen professors at the Collège de France and the Sorbonne, among them Michelet and Quinet, of subversive teaching.

This attempt to undermine the reputation of university professors as a means of convincing parliamentarians to reform the educational system, was also carried on by a Jesuit circle in Lyon. Their major work, *Monopole Universitaire*, was published in April 1843, and it became the most widely publicized attack on professors. For these Jesuits, university control of secondary schools meant nothing less than "suicide, parricide, homicide, infanticide, dueling, rape, incest, adultery."[32] Michelet was singled out as an "impure blasphemer," whose courses were a lesson in "impiety."[33]

Jesuit and Catholic smears on the center and pinnacle of French learning, the Collège de France, aroused the indignation of Michelet and

Quinet, who, along with their colleague Mickiewicz, soon came to symbolize the Collège de France itself and its tradition of liberty and freedom of thought. In the press, regardless of political and religious orientation, these three men were always named together as professors with the same ideas and outlooks. They attracted the largest number of auditors in the history of the Collège de France, with Michelet being the most popular. Room 7 where Michelet taught upwards of one thousand students was later remodeled to prevent large gatherings of political agitators. Journalists in 1848 commonly referred to Michelet, Mickiewicz, and Quinet as catalysts for the revolutionary temper which culminated in the February 1848 overthrow of the July Monarchy. Michelet himself was to believe this interpretation.[34] In 1884, republican leaders of the Third Republic placed a plaque in the northwest corner of the Collège de France memorializing the legendary fame of these three professors.[35]

Adam Mickiewicz, born the same year as Michelet in Russian-occupied Poland, became, by the 1830s, the leading Polish nationalist poet, calling on the Poles to rise up and cast off the wicked hegemony of Russia. After imprisonment in Poland and a literary life in Moscow cultural circles, Mickiewicz became an exile espousing the cause of Polish freedom. His 1832 *Books of the Polish Nation and of the Polish Pilgrims* was intended to give spiritual and political guidance to the large number of émigrés in the West. This work was translated in 1833 by Montalembert, since Mickiewicz's philosophy was based on Christian principles. His last major work, *Pan Tadeusz*, published the following year, became the national Polish epic poem.

The career of Mickiewicz at the Collège de France was stormy and brief, lasting from December 22, 1840 until May 28, 1844. In July 1840, with the aid of Villemain, a new chair of Slavic languages and literature was created to which Mickiewicz was named. His dynamic style of lecturing created a revolutionary fervor among his auditors, who began to associate the coming upheaval not only with the freedom of Poland but also with a religious and political renovation of France.

A major transformation of Mickiewicz's ideas began after a July 30, 1841 meeting with Andrzej Towianski, a Lithuanian mystic. Towianski quickly became Mickiewicz's spiritual master by first promising and then curing the poet's mentally disturbed wife. Towianski, and later

Mickiewicz in his courses, forecast that seven emissaries would be sent by God to finish Christ's work. The first messiah, Napoleon, failed because of too little spiritual emphasis, but the second emissary, Towianski, would spread the word of the "new revelation." Polish émigrés, furious at losing their political and literary leader to the warped mind of Towianski, accused the mystic of being a Russian spy, while the French government, fearful of his Napoleonic ideas, expelled Towianski on July 20, 1842, for "agitating" Polish émigrés.[36]

Despite attacks from official religious circles, Mickiewicz continued teaching two more years on Towianski's vision. His final courses, entitled "The Official Church and Messianism" and "The Church and the Messiah," showed the hidden hand of God in Slavic history. Mickiewicz taught that faith alone, much to the chagrin of Polish émigrés, would free Poland. Once everyone was reborn spiritually, Poland would become independent and together with France would lead the world into a new millenium. The spiritual awakening would unite all followers of Towianski with Napoleon's soul. Napoleon "understood the divine nature of Christ and explained it better than any theologian."[37] This advocacy of a Napoleonic cult upset not only the government authorities, who accused Mickiewicz of the "most reprehensible attacks against the social order, government, and Catholic religion," but also infuriated Michelet, who eternally despised the Emperor and his myth-makers.[38] After his lecture on May 28, 1844, the government dismissed him under the guise of a leave of absence. Mickiewicz had given his last lecture at the Collège de France. In this final session, preaching beneath a portrait of Napoleon, Mickiewicz called for signs of adherence to the "new revelation." At the end of the sermon, one follower, Maria Rutkowska, ecstatically threw herself at the poet's feet.[39]

Michelet and Quinet were not as mystically inclined as Mickiewicz, although Quinet did admire Napoleon. However, their joint attacks against the Jesuits generated a far larger response and outrage from the Catholic Church. Quinet had been appointed to the Collège de France in July 1841 to occupy the newly created chair of Southern European languages and literature. Simultaneously, and apparently without previous consultation, the two men began lecturing on Jesuitism during the spring of 1843. They published their lectures together on July 15, 1843, and *Des jésuites* became an instant best seller. It sold "five thousand copies in ten days," and went through five editions, averaging two thousand copies each, before the end of the year.[40] By the time of the seventh edition in early 1845, over two hundred articles and books had appeared either praising or condemning the ideas of Michelet and Quinet.

The impassioned lectures of Michelet read like many modern pamphlets exposing an internal conspiracy instigated by foreigners. The Jesuits were outsiders infecting the very soul of France with their "police" system:

> Let God give us ten times the political, military, and other tyrannies that we have suffered rather than have such a police stain our France! . . . There is one good thing about tyranny, it often awakens national feeling; it [tyranny] is then broken or it breaks itself. But if this national feeling is extinguished, gangrene sets in your flesh and bones, and then how can one get rid of it?[41]

Although Michelet estimated that approximately one thousand Jesuits were in France, he felt that during the previous decade they had increasingly infiltrated the Church and converted to their ideas a great portion of the forty thousand priests in France. While they spied on the whole society, their own workings were unknown to the public. "One hardly knows what is done in these seminaries, hedged in as they are against interference from the authorities, except by the nothingness of their results. Their textbooks . . . considered by the rest of the world as rubbish, are forced down our unfortunate young priests."[42]

Jesuits, for Michelet, were omnipresent. They converted unsuspecting people, they deceived them, and they "kidnapped" children by teaching them their doctrine. "While we sleep, they surprised, like wolves, defenseless peoples, priests, women, and nunneries."[43] Essentially, Jesuitism for France would mean "the death of liberty" and triumph of "the counterrevolution."[44] While the Lyon circle calumnied Michelet and other professors, the Jesuits ordered "young saints" to attack relentlessly higher education, and to disrupt the free lectures given at the Collège de France.[45]

Michelet contrasted organic, spiritual forms of life with the sterile "machinism" of the Jesuits.[46] This machinism, a word Quinet also used to signify the Jesuits, involved annihilating the will and freedom of their subjects. Through their demands of total obedience, people under the guidance of Jesuits became "like a stick, like a corpse."[47] There was no common feeling of brotherhood or unity amongst the Jesuits, because their hierarchical structure necessitated telling their devotees what to do and think. Once ensnared in their gigantic net, members proceeded "blindly from one stage to the next."[48] Their spy system, both on the general society and on their own followers, had engendered a world of total distrust. "They are suspicious of each other for fear of mutual betrayals."[49]

The Jesuit conspiracy was trying to destroy Michelet's most cherished ideal—France. These invaders from Rome proposed educational theories contrary to human nature. In addition to the required mechanical obedience and the concomitant mutual distrust, they had falsified the history of France. Michelet examined, before his auditors, the official Jesuit history of France. This textbook, which unsuspecting children were forced to memorize, "slandered and blasphemed France."[50] Time after time, Michelet alleged, the authors had sided with England rather than France in their interpretation of historical events.

Quinet, likewise, pictured the issue as a confrontation between the Jesuits and France. Although his lectures were reasoned, historical analyses of Loyola's ideas, devoid of Michelet's conspiratorial theories, he ultimately concluded: "Two incompatible principles are in combat, one of which must destroy the other. Jesuitism must destroy the spirit of France or France must destroy the spirit of Jesuitism."[51]

In this general confrontation over educational control, Michelet could not have foreigners instructing young French children. To foster national unity the universities had to direct education, unassisted by the Jesuits. These anti-French spies were the "enemies of France."[52] Moreover, Michelet, the educator, told the audience that he had been obligated to discuss these topics before the public. As "professor of morals and history," it ."was not only his right but his duty " to have analyzed this vitally important subject.[53]

On May 16, 1843, during the outrage over his lectures, Michelet wrote the *Journal des débats*: "I don't speak out often. Most of my life has flowed in silence. I have written forcefully lately, and during that time I have never disputed, never responded."[54] But Michelet could not contain the storm unleashed upon the publication in July of his and Quinet's lectures. For months every major newspaper carried debates, accusations, and commentaries on their writings. The articles were, at the same time, political, religious, and educational. In general, the liberal press, such as *Le National, Le Constitutionnel, Courrier français, Le Siècle, Journal des débats,* and *Revue des Deux Mondes,* defended Michelet and Quinet. When one of these liberal publications published an article hostile to the two professors, as *Revue des Deux Mondes* did on October 15, 1843, it caused a big sensation, since their readers were generally not of that opinion.[55] Meanwhile the rightist and Catholic press called for the dismissal of Michelet and Quinet from the Collège de France. *L'Univers* was the most acrimonious, but even the more moderate *Le Correspondant,* under the influence of Montalembert, criticized *Des jésuites* in measured, reasoned tones. Michelet followed the whole debate very closely, well aware of the power of the press. Thinking of Jesuit publications, Michelet wrote in his diary, "What are my six or eight thousand copies against such newspapers as theirs, which print thirty thousand?"[56]

In September 1843 the Jesuits of Lyon published their rebuttal under the title *L'Université jugée par elle-même.* They accused Michelet of being "anti-Catholic, pantheist, impious, immoral, full of ignorance, of bad faith, and self-contradictory."[57] Repeating what they had "demonstrated" in *Monopole Universitaire,* they concluded that "the University and MM. Michelet and Quinet in particular insult in their lectures all belief and all religions; attack the bases of all moral, religious, and social beliefs; and impose by their monopoly of teaching, impieties, and blasphemies."[58] Impervious to these bitter epithets, Michelet remained fully committed to his cause. He wrote Quinet on June 5, 1843: "Our enemies retake the offensive. They have the men and we have the youth, the Schools."[59] Alfred cautioned him that the controversy was becoming too dangerous. Michelet, aware of the moral, religious, educational, and political importance of this issue for his own philosophy and ideal of France, responded: "It stops dangers greater than you could possibly imagine."[60]

Michelet continued his diatribe against the Jesuits and their attempts to usurp the educational system in France in *Du prêtre, de la femme, de la famille.* Published on January 15, 1845, this extension of his Jesuit lectures had the same overwhelming public success; it sold "fourteen thousand copies in eight months," went through nine English editions within a year, and was even translated into Arabic.[61]

In addition to repeating his same interpretation of the false and harmful educational indoctrination used by the Jesuits, Michelet also expanded his denunciations by assailing priests and Catholicism in general. Furthermore, he uncovered the historical roots of Jesuit evil. This historical presentation had been strikingly absent from his *Des jésuites*. Since the principal confrontation was over education, it had now become incumbent upon Michelet to examine the method of French education during the seventeenth and eighteenth centuries, because it had been set up by the Jesuits. In this analysis, Michelet perceived the origins of most of his previous themes such as annihilation of will, obedience, distrust of human nature, and lack of freedom and liberty. According to Michelet, the mechanistic, passive educational system of the Jesuits had inhibited moral and intellectual progress within France. While the Jesuits perfected their machine for "narrowing the heads of men and flattening their minds," great geniuses such as Descartes and Voltaire arose, because they were able to escape from this system designed to stifle invention and creativity.[62] With the Jesuits expelled from French educational control since the 1760s Michelet wanted no new recrudescence of Jesuit educators. Modern priests and Catholicism in France were succumbing to the devious ideas of the Jesuits. Michelet hoped that by presenting both the historical effects of Jesuit education and the contemporary conspiratorial efforts, those reading his book would help him combat this threat of tyranny.

During the 1843 controversy the Government, not wanting any interference from the Church, had been sympathetic to the ideas of Michelet and Quinet. Michelet, who taught Princess Clémentine, daughter of Louis-Philippe, had been invited to dine with the Duc de Montpensier on May 29, 1843, during the height of the Catholic protest. Moreover, Villemain, a former professor of Michelet's, had been firmly committed to the liberal, university cause in his powerful position of minister of public education. But on December 20, 1844, he was replaced by the more conservative Salvandy. The new minister thought the lectures of Michelet and Quinet were far too extreme and wanted to end them, while the government had come increasingly under attack by the liberal and radical elements in Paris and could no longer openly side with their causes.

Immediately after the publication of *Du prêtre* the minister of the interior, the minister of justice, and the prosecuting attorney for Paris began discussing legal sanctions against Michelet. The two ministers asked the chief prosecuting attorney to rule on the legal merits of the book. Noting the government pressure "to disapprove of the work," the prosecuting attorney, after careful scrutiny, decided that "other means" would have to be found. He reasoned that, despite the outrageous tone and accusations of Michelet, French laws did not cover "attacks against religion."[63] Therefore, any attempted legal action by the government risked the possibility of backfiring and making Michelet a martyr. If the government intervened, "everyone would regard this intervention as direct policy of the government," and if the jury acquitted Michelet, his group would "have achieved a glowing triumph which could only, to their profit, escalate political passions as well as irreligious attitudes."[64]

Government involvement increased in March 1845 because of a widely circulated letter of protest against the courses of Michelet and Quinet, entitled "Eighty-nine residents of Marseilles addressed to the Chamber of Peers." For these "typical" Catholic residents of Marseilles, the courses of these professors, "paid for by the State," did not respect the Catholic religion.[65] They wanted sanctions imposed by the House of Lords against Michelet and Quinet. This action would demonstrate that the parliamentarians "defend and maintain the liberty of religion and protect, in conformity with the Constitution, the religion of the majority of Frenchmen."[66]

The Chamber of Peers debated this issue on April 14, 1845, with the transcript appearing the following day in *Le Moniteur universel*. The Chamber of Peers, agreeing with the opinion of the chairman Tascher, recommended an end to the university campaign against established religion. The pernicious works of these professors, according to Tascher, degraded religion. In *Du prêtre*, for example, Michelet characterized "the holy immutability of Catholic dogma as likened to death."[67] Tascher questioned, as had the Marseilles residents, the wisdom of allowing professors at the Collège de France to be exempt from all control. Noninterference by the government had allowed the expression of moral values contrary to those of the state. While not in favor of Catholic control of education, Tascher wanted stricter governmental supervision of the course material in order to prevent possible outbreaks of political, religious, or social hostility against the government.

Michelet escaped, for the time being, from official government action, but Quinet resigned in the fall of 1845 after inordinate pressure from Salvandy. Quinet wanted the word "institutions" included in the title of his chair so that he could continue lecturing on religion. Salvandy refused, and Quinet, unwilling to compromise by teaching only a literature course which limited his educational freedom, left the Collège de France. In the next few years Michelet's problems with the government would increase, while religious authorities would continue to regard him as a great enemy. On the same day as the debate in the Chamber of Peers, his *Du prêtre* was placed on the Index.

The response from intellectuals to Michelet's new works varied. Tocqueville was hostile, because he believed in the reconciliation of the Church with modern democracy. Enfantin, the former high priest of the Saint-Simonians, wrote Michelet on February 28, 1845, and criticized him for his blanket condemnation of priests.[68] Enfantin felt that the functions of priests were not harmful, but rather quite valuable in any society. Priests were a source of "consolation and of hope" for women and the family. Moral priests, like Enfantin himself, could be aided by the priests of the Gallican Church in "regenerating and recreating the human priesthood with a new formula from the will of God, showing humanity its destiny of peace, association, and fraternity."[69] Unlike Enfantin, George Sand felt that Michelet only wanted to change the attitudes of the priests, not outlaw them. She wrote to Michelet on April 1, 1845: "I am a utopian, you are a reformer, it is not the same spirit. I find that you expend too much energy and genius in attacking a trivial subject. You want to reform the Church and change the priests; myself, I want neither the priests nor the Church."[70]

Both Enfantin and Sand were expressing their own viewpoints, but failed to comprehend fully Michelet's perception of the issues. The subject was not "trivial." As a variant on the Saint-Simonian theme of artists and moralists leading the society, Michelet wanted the educators and universities, primarily the Collège de France, to guide society. Michelet could not accept Enfantin's repeated call for a "human priesthood," because the central area of controversy was between France and outsiders. The Jesuits were not part of the organic whole of *la patrie*. Michelet wanted to retain the priesthood, as Sand had told him, but not priests within the Church. He had broken completely with the Church and wanted new priests outside of the old religion. The new clergy of priests, Michelet felt, were the educators of Frenchmen, who should now lead the struggle against all hindrances to French unity and harmony. Michelet sensed this role in his comments to his auditors on "his duty and right" as professor of morals and history. Other professors, though, as he noted in his diary on January 25, 1844, had not yet understood their new function as moral directors of French society: "The University is not without reproach; it has not yet sensed that it must be the ministry of the future."[71]

# 9
## *The People*

Combatting the outside intervention of the Jesuits was a serious affair for Michelet. But as historian of France's unity he had to arrest, by 1845, a potentially more lethal drug already injected into the inner soul of France. External agents could be exiled, but the critical internal problem of social class conflicts had to be analyzed, diagnosed, and remedied before Frenchmen could live harmoniously. To rid France of the social contagion of class hatreds became Michelet's urgent educational challenge in *Le Peuple*. This work, the most revelatory of Michelet's social class preconceptions, was written in the fall of 1845 and published on January 28, 1846. He had become concerned about class problems during a trip to Lyon in March and April 1839, where ex-Saint-Simonians such as Arlès-Dufour and Jean Reynaud showed him the miserable conditions of workers.[1] Now, he hoped, with the appearance of *Le Peuple*, that his educational solutions to these problems would be studied and implemented, thereby healing the wounds of the country. Michelet was exuberant over the success of the book, telling his aunts of sales of "1000 copies in Paris in one day alone."[2] Already, in a letter of February 23, 1846, Michelet sensed the educational impact of his ideas on others: "Let me tell you what I have told no one else: this is much more than a success of petty vanity, it is a success of the heart. I have received from some vain and selfish men a good response, a moment of emotion which could be the beginning of a real improvement in their attitudes."[3]

The term "the people" had had a long history in France of various and ever-changing meanings. By the 1840s the phrase had taken on another new definition and new form by coming to signify the disparate groups, including workers, peasants, and the urban poor, who were not part of the bourgeoisie. Lamennais had popularized this use of the term in the 1830s. His *Paroles d'un croyant*, a blistering tirade, in Old Testament imagery, against oppressors of the poor, was dedicated "to the people."[4] His sympathy for the poor and his belief in a unique love bond between "the people" and God were elaborated upon further in his 1837 *Le livre du peuple*. "The people" became common currency in radical political circles as early as 1840. In the *Revue indépendante*, controlled by Pierre Leroux and George Sand, "the people" were glowingly idealized as the saviors of France. "We wait for it [future revelation] from everyone; we sense it in the French masses; one word which we believe in, is our Messiah, it is the People, and that idea is embodied not in one man but in thousands of men."[5] Conversely, mention of "the people" to the bourgeoisie in the 1840s struck them with terror. To them, as Louis Chevalier has shown, "the people" comprised the laboring and dangerous classes of Paris, whose daily criminal acts were slowly undermining the political and social fabric of the city.[6]

Michelet did not fear "the people," as did the bourgeoisie, but glorified them, as did the social reformers. In his stirring introduction, dedicated to Edgar Quinet, he began: "This book is more than a book; it is myself, and that is why it belongs to you."[7] He was eminently qualified to write of "the people" because he had come from them. "I have made this book out of myself, out of my life, and out of my heart. It is the product of my experience rather than of my studies."[8] Others, such as Eugène Sue in his *Les mystères de Paris*, had shown the seamy side of lower class life where cities were "nothing but a place where police tracked down habitual criminals and escaped convicts."[9] Michelet, though, because of his origins, felt that he could explain "the people" to the public more deeply and more accurately:

And I, who have sprung from them, who have lived and toiled and suffered with them, who more than any other has earned the right to say that I know them—I am coming forward now against all these views to establish the personality of the people.

I have not taken this personality from the surface, in its picturesque or dramatic aspects. I have not seen it from the outside, but experienced it from within.[10]

As evidence that he had "sprung from them" and understood them, Michelet recounted the story of his childhood. He and his family, in this introduction, were portrayed as typical examples of "the people." This 1846 version of his youth focused on societal injustices harming the fortunes of the family. The passages revealing the inner tensions of the household, the most significant sections of the *Mémorial*, were totally absent in this revised autobiography. Both families were "originally peasants" who faced continual economic hardships.[11] "Poverty," and not "awkwardness," as in the *Mémorial*, was the reason for the rancor and biting laughter of his classmates.[12]

Near the end of his introduction Michelet exclaimed: "I am still one of the people."[13] However, by his own analysis in *Le Peuple*, Michelet was destined to become part of another class. He parents were not simply "peasant" in origin; his mother came from peasant property-holders and his father was a literate artisan. The different classes Michelet inherited from his parents and his own new status created an apparent crisis in his social and class identity. His class uncertainty may have triggered his ideal solutions for both the problems of France and those of himself. Michelet's social world in *Le Peuple* presented the horns of these dilemmas.

For Michelet, France in 1846 was a country in chaos because of class hatreds and class conflict. Protruding from the pages of *Le Peuple* was the conscious recognition of class strife, which was threatening to destroy the very fabric of French society. His chapter titles themselves connoted the "bondage" of each class to another. Unlike many of the leftist writers in Paris who wrote mostly on the urban poor and the working class created by the recent industrialization, Michelet began his socio-economic analysis with the peasant. He attempted to reverse the devastating, satirical portrait of peasants in Balzac's *Les Paysans* which had been serialized after December 1844 in *La Presse*. Michelet mocked Balzac in the opening pages of *Le Peuple*: "A genre painter, admirable for his genius for details, delights in depicting a loathsome village alehouse, a tavern for rogues and thieves. And beneath this hideous sketch he has the nerve to write the word which is the name of the greater part of the inhabitants of France."[14]

The peasantry was the backbone of France. "The land of France belongs to the fifteen or twenty million peasants who farm it."[15] This most numerous class cultivated and developed the land, thereby providing the food for the other classes. For Michelet, these peasants possessed the attributes of hard and persistent work, sobriety, frugality, and austere morals. But the contemporary peasant, like every other class, was neither happy nor satisfied. His living conditions were miserable. "Look at his food and compare it with that of the urban worker; the latter eats better every day than the peasant on Sunday."[16] The helpless peasant was continually taken advantage of by bankers, moneylenders, and lawyers, who pried his land and money away from him. The result was that "the peasant isolates himself and becomes more and more bitter. His heart is too constricted to be opened to any feeling of goodwill. He hates the rich, he hates his neighbor, he hates the world."[17] The government, meanwhile, collected the majority of France's taxes from the peasantry, but concentrated on industrial instead of agricultural development. The downtrodden peasant, unable to exist on his meager income, dreamt of a better life in the city. Rather than being contented with his own position in life, the peasant had come to envy the worker as a better, happier, and more economically satisfied man. "The worker, even with the little he earns for a living, is the object of the peasant's envy."[18]

Although the country was "poor," the city, according to Michelet, was probably "more wretched.[19] The lowest social strata in the captivating yet hate-ridden city was the working class. The workers had one major superiority over other social classes, namely, a natural disposition to aid others, particularly the members of their own families. In addition to aiding his family, the worker was the best of companions. Their inexpensive machine-made products clothed the poor, but this labor was accomplished at a great personal price. This "progress and obvious advance of the masses" had, nevertheless, created a "miserable, stunted group of machine-men who live but half a life."[20] The worker was enslaved by the machine and had given up "the free possession of his soul."[21] The debased factory worker, overcome by boredom and monotony, had lost "every intellectual interest"; his is a work which requires neither strength nor skill and never asks for thought! Nothing, nothing, and always nothing! No moral force could withstand that!"[22] The only relief workers had from this mental and physical enslavement was drinking. Michelet's assumption that all workers were prone to become alcoholics was a common assertion in the 1840s. In Michelet's view, this dependence on liquor further destroyed any instinctual aptitudes or any intellectual inclinations workers may have possessed.

Michelet sympathized with the miserable lives led by workers, who were broken in will by submission to the machine. However, he always characterized workers harshly, never identified with their political and social causes, and never admitted to their being more than a tiny minority of "the people." His ideal leaned more to the peasant and to the social class just above the workers, that of the artisans. The artisan, the class of his father, was not enslaved by machines, and was, consequently, more independent. This completely free man, for Michelet, was morally superior to men from other socio-economic classes. While this appeared to be one of the most attractive classes, problems had arisen because of the bourgeois aspirations of many formerly contented artisans. Much like the other classes, most artisans thought that there were greater earthly rewards on the next social level. Michelet, himself, in his autobiographical portrait, revealed a decided ambivalence towards artisans, when friends of the family suggested that he might become a printer like his father:

> If my parents had followed reason, made me an artisan and saved themselves, would I then have been lost? No, I see among artisans men of such merit, men who are quite the equals of men of letters in intelligence and are their superiors in character. But what difficulties I would have encountered! What a struggle against the lack of every opportunity; against the *fatalité* of the times.[23]

Michelet's next class, comprised of small manufacturers, had the good qualities of being active and energetic and engaging in a patriotic struggle against foreign industry. But the manufacturer was always on the brink of ruin, instigated by greedy bourgeois, who loaned him money or supplied him with goods. In frustration, he vented his anger on his workers, goading them to be more productive. "A man in this state of mind is not very tender-hearted. It would be a miracle if he were kind and gentle to his employees and his workers."[24] The manufacturer, therefore, was being exploited by a class above him while fomenting enmity against himself from a class below him. Michelet, however, felt that the manufacturer's hatred of workers was unnecessary:

> Frequently, the manufacturer and his family hate the worker because they think they are hated by him. I must say, contrary to common opinion, that they are often mistaken about this. In the great factories the worker hates the foreman, whose tyranny he feels directly, while that of the master is more remote and thus less odious to him.[25]

Despite the manufacturer's problems, the men of the next class, the shopkeepers, were in even more desperate straits. They continually pressured the manufacturer to supply them with goods quickly and cheaply. At the same time the shopkeeper was besieged with the complaints of his customers who were constantly pestering him for bargains, and who were rarely satisfied with their purchases. "The shopkeeper must outwit these people or fail. He is always waging a two-front war; a war of cheating and cunning against the unreasonable customer, and a war of vexations and outrageous demands against the manufacturer."[26]

Michelet thought that the shopkeeper was the most deceitful of men—one who valued money more than personal honor or integrity. He was always lying and cheating. "I do not hesitate to affirm that for a man of honor the position of the most dependent worker is one of freedom compared with this. A serf in body, he is free in soul. For to enslave your soul and sacrifice your integrity ... is the lowest form of serfdom."[27]

Above the shopkeeper was the public servant, who was underpaid, neglected, and shifted from task to task and city to city at the whim of some superior. Many of them could not marry because their "salaries cannot support a family."[28] These civil servants were in bondage to their superiors, because they had to be careful that their political and religious ideas did not affront the administration. Michelet also included among public servants the primary school teachers. Their pitifully low salaries did not befit their new function acquired during the French Revolution. "The country that pays the least to those that instruct the people—and let us blush to confess it—is France ... .On the contrary, the true

France, that of the Revolution, declared that teaching was a holy office and that the schoolmaster was equal to the priest."[29]

The next class, the bourgeoisie, was one of the most important, yet one that Michelet did not define precisely. It was "not easy to define the limits of this class, to say where it begins or where it ends."[30] Generally the members of this class were owners of property, involved in a large industrial enterprise, or engaged in some form of commercial activity. Michelet emphasized again and again that there were many poor bourgeois. This economic indefinability of the bourgeoisie demonstrated for Michelet the incorrectness of socialist interpretations such as Louis Blanc's, who attempted to divide France along lines of rich and poor.[31] The previous classes which Michelet had discussed comprised "the people," but the indeterminate structure of the bourgeoisie prevented their being opposed to "the people." "Thus thank God, the bourgeoisie cannot, strictly speaking, be opposed to the people, as some believe, which would be no less than creating two nations."[32]

The bourgeoisie were an essential part of French society. Michelet vehemently criticized socialist doctrines that called for an end to private property or private enterprise. His main enemy on the question of property was Proudhon, whose *Qu'est-ce que la propriété?* and *Avertissement aux propriétaires* he often tried to refute. For Michelet unlimited access to property was a fundamental principle in France; this access had marked the freeing of the peasantry. "France is the last country in the world in which private property will be abolished. If, as someone of that school said, 'Property is nothing but theft,' then we have twenty-five million thieves here who are not about to give up their loot."[33]

Unfortunately, most of the rich bourgeois had lost contact with the other segments of society. He knew the rest of France "only through the police reports" or through "his servants who rob him and laugh at him."[34] These wealthy people had closed themselves off physically from the poor by living in their own private ghettos, and psychically by following a philosophy which emphasized that they should always fear and distrust the poor. This physical and psychical separation had made these materially secure people lose their souls in Michelet's eyes, for they could not enjoy any happiness by living in total terror of the lower classes. This serious situation was only degenerating further as each new day brought new fears and new distrust. "So they shut themselves up more and more. They barricade and solidly wall up their doors and minds—no more daylight, not the slightest crack to let in a ray of light."[35]

Ascending the social scale, morality had gradually decreased:

> We have seen this man of today grow smaller with every step that seemed to lift him up. As a peasant, he had morality, sobriety, and thrift. As a workman, he was a good companion and a great help to his family. As a manufacturer, he was active, energetic, and filled with an industrial patriotism which struggled against foreign industry. But he has left all as he has risen, and nothing has taken its place. His house is full, his coffer is full, and his soul is empty.[36]

The imagery in Michelet's description of the social world changed from the warmth of the lower classes to the cold, sterile chill of the rich bourgeois:

> How cold it is if I go higher! It is like the cold of the Alps. I reach the region of snows. Moral vegetation gradually disappears, and the flower of nationality grows pale. It is like a world seized in a single night by a sudden frost of selfishness and fear. If I ascend one step higher, even fear ceases. There is the pure egotism of the calculator who has no fatherland, where people are no longer people but only numbers. There is a true glacier, abandoned by nature. Let me come down. The cold is too great for me there, and I cannot breathe.[37]

Michelet did not mention the aristocracy as a class. Might it be because they posed no threat to Michelet or because most Parisian aristocrats were not politically active during the regime of Louis-Philippe? Might Michelet's lack of concern reflect the changing ingredients of status, where wealth became as important as birth in post-Bourbon France?

Michelet's was a France in which each class was in bondage to another, hence a France full of hate and envy. His idea of "the people" was not merely all of the social levels beneath the bourgeoisie but also included what he saw as a shared ideal among these classes. But these classes could only truly mirror this cloudy concept termed "the people" if they shed their antagonisms towards their fellow Frenchmen.

The stringent demands Michelet placed upon "the people"—to become loving and fraternal as the real means of reflecting their true character—could only be accomplished by interaction with the educators of France. Although not formally presented like the social classes, Michelet characterized in passages throughout *Le Peuple* another group of classes, namely, the professional classes. Professionals such as bankers, lawyers, and moneylenders, Michelet mentioned only to attack, because they had taken advantage of all segments of society. The profession that Michelet was obsessed with, the one which he considered himself to belong to, was the educational class. The assumption of the existence of such a class, referred to variously by Michelet in *Le Peuple* and his *Journal* as *gens de lettres*, *hommes de lettres*, or *les esprits cultivés*, had been common since the eighteenth century when *gens de lettres* appeared on the title page of *L'Encyclopédie* and Voltaire proselytized for a lettered class.

In addition to the social classes living in disharmony, the educational class and "the people" were divided. Michelet set up a dichotomy whereby "the people" were men of action and instinct, while the men of the educational class were reflective by nature and engaged in passive study. "The man of the people is above all a man of instinct and action."[38] The friction between these two types of men was present in both Michelet's attempt to formulate his own social identity and in his attempt to solve France's problems engendered by class hatred. Although Michelet stated in the introduction to *Le Peuple* that he was "still one of the people," he now clearly identified with the educational class vis-à-vis "the people." "We, the cultivated minds . . . what difficulties we have in recognizing any good qualities in the people."[39] Likewise, the men of reflection, men such as Michelet himself, were not understood by "the people." "They laugh at the learned man for leading the life of a cripple. In their opinion he is a loafer. They have no idea of the powers of reflection, meditation."[40]

The misunderstanding between the educational class—"we"—and "the people"—"they"—was the greatest evil confronting France:

> They [the people] misunderstand the powers of study and persevering reflection by which discoveries are made. We [the cultivated minds] misunderstand the instinct, the inspiration, and the energy which make heroes.

You can be sure that this is the greatest evil in the world. We hate one another, we despise one another; that is to say, we do not know one another.[41]

Michelet was not sure which type of man was better. Occasionally he stated that men of instinct were equal to or even superior to men of reflection. More often, however, he seemed to be on the side of his own educational class, who alone could improve France's condition. "Next to the conversation of men of genius and of the most eminent scholars, that of the people is certainly the most instructive. If you cannot talk with Béranger, Lamennais, or Lamartine [as he did], go into the fields and chat with a peasant."[42] This separation between the educational class and the men of instinct and action, "the people," had to be bridged before the class hatred in France could begin to be assuaged. "The separation of men and classes is due principally to the absurd opposition between instinct and reflection that has been established in our time."[43]

What kinds of solutions were there to end the class strife in France? Michelet, the educator, felt that he alone could solve this problem. "It is like standing at the foot of a gigantic monument which I must move all alone."[44] His two natural advantages of having come from "the people" and of being able to analyze the situation historically had prepared him for this exalted task.[45] Other men of letters, not having as great an understanding of the problems involved, could not propose proper solutions. Many writers neglected the high moral standards of the lower classes, and only described the minor criminal elements in their midst. "Close examination clearly shows, however, that these artists, famous dramatists before everything else, have depicted under the name of the people a limited class whose life, full of accidents, violence, and felonies, offered them ... successful horror stories."[46] Writers also misunderstood the issues and the problems, because many of them believed that "the people" were primarily factory workers. "It is a numerous class, but a small minority nonetheless. Those who take it for their model have no right to use the caption, 'This is a portrait of the people.'"[47]

One solution Michelet thought to be an unmitigated disaster was to change classes. He derisively called men who became part of another class, members of the bastard class. "Everyone is changing his social rank today; they all rise, or think they rise."[48] All that had resulted from these phony desires was a tasteless hodgepodge of a "bastard class." In contrast to those who wanted to rise in class, Michelet desired "strong men . . . who will not want to rise, men born of the people who will wish to remain of the people."[49] These "strong men" should also marry within their own class, because "changes of ranks" not only prevented "all inner improvement," but they also produced "vulgar, pretentious, and barren" mixtures.[50] Although Michelet wanted class harmony and mutual understanding of differences he did *not* believe that social mobility nurtured these aims. One striking message of Michelet seemed to be—stay in the class in which you were born.

Michelet's remedy for the envy, hate, and misunderstanding prevalent in the country was education. He diagnosed the problems confronting France, as Lamennais and the Saint-Simonians had, as primarily moral. "The partial remedies that may be applied are no doubt good, but the basic remedy is a general one. We must cure the soul."[51] Moral reform, what Lamennais had called "love and charity," would cure class hatreds.[52] The instilling of love would probably not affect the old, corrupted bourgeois, but at least their children and "the people" could learn to love one another.[53]

Education as a panacea for social amelioration involved a major change in Michelet's psychology of human nature. In his *Histoire de France* he had assumed that most men acted out of self-interest, but he had not discussed the origins of their behavior. Now, in the 40s, after a decisive break with the Middle Ages, Michelet was able to modify his idea of man's internal psyche. One whole chapter in *Le Peuple* entitled "Is the natural instinct of the child perverse?" confronted directly the concept of original sin postulated by the "horrible" Middle Ages. Michelet steadfastly denied this harmful interpretation of human nature. Instead, he felt that love was the true innate principle of mankind. The hate and envy proliferating throughout France could be mitigated by appealing to the original, natural instincts of Frenchmen. "Man . . . must be taught envy, for he does not know it by himself."[54] This revised theory of human nature made hatred and egotism much like social disharmony and the Jesuits; they were artificial and, therefore, solvable *fatalités*.

Michelet's call for a moral and psychological revolution could be easily achieved if educators inculcated love and understanding in the schools and in their writings. The poor and the rich should be taught in the same classrooms. There, the rich would talk to the poor, and they would find gentility and warmth in these impecunious people. Likewise, Michelet felt, the poor would see that they need not envy the rich, since the poor were morally superior.

> If only the two children, the poor one and the rich one, had been sitting on the benches of the same school, if only they commonly considered themselves connected by friendship though separated by careers, they would do more good between them than all the politicians and all the moral lessons in the world. They would preserve in their unselfish, innocent friendship the sacred bond of the City. The rich man would know life and inequality, and would shudder at it. All his efforts would be to share with his poor friend. The poor man would show greatness of heart, and console him for being rich.[55]

Children of all classes (in contrast to the present situation) must go to school together and learn to love one another as fellow human beings. The educators themselves must preach this love and brotherhood so that each man would realize his own positive qualities that made him the equal of any man. In this way, classes would no longer envy nor fear each other.

This apparent simplicity of solution contrasted sharply with Lamennais's apocalyptic tone in *Paroles d'un croyant*. "There will be a great battle and the angel of justice and the angel of love will fight with those who have armed themselves to reestablish among men the kingdom of justice and the kingdom of love."[56] Secondly, while liberal and radical thinkers such as Proudhon, and even the religious Lamennais, spoke of various political and economic reforms to go along with a moral regeneration, Michelet felt that his moral and educational reforms would suffice. Michelet fervently believed in this solution, because, unlike Lamennais, Leroux, and the Saint-Simonians who preached universal love, his moral reform was totally nationalistic. Lamennais, in his *Le livre du peuple*, had warned against "exclusive patriotism" and the "fatal consequences" from this "selfishness of nations"; "It isolates, it divides the inhabitants of different countries and incites them to mutual harm instead of mutual aid; it is the father of that bloody and horrible monster called war."[57] But Michelet did not want, as Lamennais did, the union of "the people" with God, but rather with France.

In contrast to Lamennais's admonition against the "selfishness of nations," Michelet discerned in nations a unifying moral force. "Nationalities are so far from disappearing that I see them every day developing morally, and becoming persons instead of collections of men as they once were."[58] As the educators had become the new moral clergy, so too had *la patrie* completely replaced Christianity as the new religion. "France is a religion," Michelet proclaimed, and his highest educational aims were to unify classes through a common love of France.[59] There was "no education without faith," and that education would come after everyone put their "faith in France":[60]

> To put our faith in France again and to hope for her future, we must go back into her past and fathom her natural genius. And if you do so seriously and sincerely, you will see that this consequence inevitably follows. From the past you will deduce the future; the mission of France will rise before you and appear in full light. You will believe, and you will love to believe. Faith is nothing more.[61]

Love for France was needed in order to prevent internal divisions and possible civil war:

> One people! One country! One France! Never, Never, I beg you, must we become two nations! Without unity we perish. How is it that you fail to see this?
> Frenchmen of every condition, of every class, and of every party remember one thing! You have on earth only one sure friend—France![62]

Consequently, Michelet dreamt of a "great national school" where children of all classes would come together to "learn France"; children would go to this school "for a year or two" before their specialized educations began, and they would "sit together and learn nothing but France."[63]

By learning "nothing but France," this larger unit of *la patrie* would swallow up the particulars of class conflicts. The poor child would learn "that if the rich man is rich, it is not his fault: he was born that way, and his riches often make him poor in basic values—poor in will power and moral strength."[64] In this atmosphere France would appear as she was truly capable of being—a harmonic expression of multiplicity in unity.

"There our country would appear young and delightful in all her variety and all her harmony—a wealth of characters, faces, and races, a rainbow with a hundred colors. Every rank, every fortune, and every dress . . . all together on the same benches."[65]

In his quest for loving harmony, Michelet broadened the meaning of "the people" onto a level above being merely the poor or several social classes. In its highest sense "the people" reflected fully the moral qualities embodied in *la patrie*. A future flowering of "the people" would become synonymous with the soul of France. Everyone would learn that his "mother is France" and would unite with her in love and friendship.[66] Union with this loving mother might also end Michelet's need to assuage the pain of his own unfulfilled relationship with his mother.

Within this context of mother France, the very idea of social classes was divisive for Michelet, since these groups separated France into parts. He wanted one whole organic entity which could not be defined through socio-economic categories. Therefore "the people" could not ultimately signify several social classes, but had to connote all of France. The term "the people" was Michelet's unitary answer to the various other scholarly attempts to separate France into classes. Everyone could eventually unite with "the people" since they reflected *la patrie*. Michelet had thus driven this unique conception of one moral class and no social classes to a plane where everyone could belong and, hopefully, where even class conflicts would finally wither away.

This emotive nationalism, ingrained and spread by educators, was a long-range ideal for Michelet. For the moment only men of genius could reflect the most elevated possibilities of "the people" and speak for *la patrie*:

> The people, in the highest sense of the concept, are seldom found among the people. When I observe them here or there, they are not the people, but a certain class or some partial manifestation of the people, altered and ephemeral. The people exist in truth and in their highest power only in the man of genius; in him resides their great soul.[67]

The man of genius combined "the instinct of the simple and the reflection of the wise," and, for the present, he alone transcended all classes and categories.[68]

This man of genius who combined the best characteristics of Frenchmen and represented "the people" in "the highest sense of the concept" was not only Michelet's ideal, but perhaps also his attempt to alleviate the anxiety of his own class identity. In Michelet's social world it was difficult to change classes, and those that did were usually referred to as members of the bastard class. Yet Michelet's mother was from complex, peasant origins; his father was an artisan; and now he was a member of the educational class. Within his world view, his social identity had changed, but he considered his origins essential to his overall identity. He thought *Le Peuple* both personally and publicly ended the estrangement between the men of letters and "the people." Nevertheless, Michelet consciously recognized that he had changed classes and that the instincts and spontaneity of his ancestry were beginning to leave him. "Even they who have traversed, like me, different classes, and who, through all sorts of trials, have preserved the fruitful instinct of the people, have no less lost by the way, in inward struggles, a great part of their strength. It is late—I feel it; the evening is coming on."[69] Although wishing to recapture the active, instinctual side of his heritage, Michelet, even after the February revolution which he so applauded, could not bring himself to accept a post with the new regime. His role was passive. Faced with the conflict between instinct and reflection and the conflict between his parents' classes and his own, he tried to find his social definition in an ideal solution of *la patrie* or "the people" where everyone could be a part of France, where everyone would be part of this larger class—the numerous social classes, all of his ancestors, and himself.

# 10

## *Education And Expulsion*

In Flaubert's *L'Education sentimentale* the lawyer Deslauriers, who lost each of his cases in court and who trained law students for the exams which they failed, asked Frédéric Moreau to help finance his new plan: a mass subscription newspaper which would spread his ideas.[1] The importance ascribed to the power of the press to control events and to influence opinions, satirized here by Flaubert, was one of the great novelties of the 1840s. As Michelet rhetorically asked in *Le Peuple*: "What is the Press in the modern times, but the holy ark?"[2] Newspapers had been around for centuries, but they only discovered, partly due to technological inventions in printing, their mass appeal in Paris during the July Monarchy. Subscriptions to newspapers had risen in Paris from 70,000 in 1836 to some 200,000 on the eve of the February revolution. One of the liberal dailies, *La Presse*, was begun in 1836 by the enterprising publisher Emile de Girardin, who increased the space for advertising and cut subscription rates in half, thereby accounting for an astonishing circulation of 70,000 by 1847. This wide diffusion of newspapers does not even begin to assess the number of readers since many men were accustomed to reading the papers available in most of the local cafés. In the months after February 1848 over one hundred men, many like Deslauriers, started newspapers on the Left Bank, hoping to inculcate their social and political ideas into their readers. For inherent in this great belief in the power of the press was the concomitant belief in the power of the word. The spoken or, especially, the printed word, men assumed, could easily mold the ideas and sentiments of Frenchmen.

Michelet had two means for spreading his ideas—books such as *Le Peuple* and his popular courses at the Collège de France. Throughout the period 1847 to 1854 Michelet felt that his mission was to educate his fellow countrymen in order to unify France. In these years after the writing of *Le Peuple*, Michelet expanded and formulated more fully his ideas for an educational solution to class conflicts—expanding and reiterating these thoughts even after his 1852 expulsions from the Collège de France and the Archives Nationales. While revealing through the spoken work his analysis of a divided France and his vision of a harmonious France, Michelet also decided in December 1847, as premier historian and *moraliste* at the Collège de France, to begin publishing each lecture. In this manner, each course would hopefully reach the hearts and minds of more people.

Michelet's confidence on the effect of his words was apparently confirmed both by the enormous crowds which tried to hear each lecture and by the continual government surveillance of the lectures and the auditors. Contemporary estimates ranged from eight hundred to twelve hundred people cramming the largest room in the Collège de France. Hundreds would arrive hours early in order to prepare for the "experience" of coming into contact with the magnetic personality of Michelet. Sentences from the master reverberated through the hushed audience; one word alone, according to Quinet's wife, was capable of "sending electric shocks" through the hypnotized listeners.[3] Eugène Noël, writing to his parents, gave his own impressions of these lectures:

> You cannot imagine the thunder of applause which welcomed the professor. With calm reestablished, an astonishing silence permeated the crowd and allowed M. Michelet to speak. He said that he was going to speak on a subject on which everyone would be in agreement, namely, *la patrie*, of which there was only one opinion in France; and then applause burst out everywhere once again. And then you know what he did? He smiled to his ecstatic audience . . . M. Michelet smiled like everyone else; then in the midst of this joy, he uttered some words so noble, so patriotic, so true, and so unexpected that the applause, the cries of approval, exploded with a greater force than I have ever heard. . . . When the lecture ended, everyone remained in the courtyard and on rue Saint-Jacques for a half-hour in the rain, hoping that M. Michelet would pass by so that they could salute him.[4]

The public enthusiasm for Michelet's course increasingly displeased the government. For some time Minister of Public Education Salvandy had wanted to quiet Michelet because of his attacks on religion. By December 1847 general appeals in Paris for a political and social upheaval had heightened the fears of Louis-Philippe and his cabinet. Michelet's lectures, in the heart of the Left Bank, attracted many of the "undesirable" young radicals and revolutionaries. Numerous policemen, including many plainclothesmen, regularly attended Michelet's sessions, and they remained with the auditors who gathered in the courtyard after each lecture. The sudden outbreak of unruly demonstrations generated by Michelet's speeches was an ever-present danger and threat in the minds of the authorities.

Michelet, aware of his lowered standing with the government since the departure of Villemain and cognizant of the anti-monarchical sentiments of his auditors, began his winter 1847-48 course in a precarious position. Press censorship was being strictly enforced in the capital, and he knew that his course could be closed at any moment. But he decided to give no quarter and to lecture on the topics which he had already prepared.

Michelet proposed in his first lecture of December 16, 1847, to speak of the future unity of France. He recalled for his audience the 1833 *Tableau de la France* and his mistaken assumption that France was then nearly one:

> Let us not deceive ourselves, what prevents us often from having unity is that we think we have it . . . Should I not accuse myself for having made hymns and odes to the unity of France? I wrote in 1833 on the harmony of the provinces, I thought I had heard a lyre and I listened to the great harmony of it. But all of this is only a beginning; we are at the dawn of things, never lose that from view.[5]

His fallacy had been that moral and spiritual unity resulted automatically from administrative centralization. While this centralization was essential, he now saw that other methods, primarily education, were necessary to bring about moral unity. The spirit of Michelet's vision was clearly the same as in 1833, but, in 1847, he only foresaw the fruition of his dream in the future. Apparently, the press would be the medium for this message:

Gentlemen, what will be the means of realizing this moral union? You have all responded that it is the communication of thought, it is in the press.

Is not the press in effect the universal intermediary? What a sight, when from the post office, one watches newspapers leave by the thousands, these representatives of diverse opinions, who will carry until the distant frontiers the tradition of the parties, the voice of polemic, harmonizing nevertheless in a certain unity of language and of ideas! This spectacle is great in the morning when the presses stop, when the engines cease to smoke, when the paper leaves rapidly, when the pages are scattered all over France. Who does not believe that the national soul is going to circulate now by all the means of this great mechanism?[6]

Michelet, however, the great believer in the power of the word, had sensed by 1847 that despite all of the positive attributes inherent in the press, it had failed in its most important function. The press, used by Michelet in the broadest sense of the term, "had not reached the people."[7] Only a minority of Frenchmen had ever reaped the benefits of a divine press. "The daily newspapers fulfill a sacred mission, but the essential nature of this mission is an abstract and subtle discussion which invincibly closes it from the people."[8]

France, Michelet continued in his next two lectures, was divided into the literate and the illiterate:

The people! Are we not all the people? . . . I mean by this word the thirty million men, I ought to say thirty-two, who are unacquainted with your books, with your newspapers, with your theaters and even with the laws which they obey. . . . Gentlemen, there are thirty million men who have nearly nothing in common with you; that is the point of departure.[9]

In *Le Peuple* Michelet had characterized "the people" socio-economically, as the poor divided from the wealthy classes, and educationally, as the instinctive separated from the reflective. From these late 1847 lectures through his last major social writings in 1854 Michelet spoke almost exclusively of "the people" in terms of literate versus illiterate. The major problem separating classes was neither economic, social nor political but educational. "The people" were the thirty million individuals in France who did not read. This clear demarcation of literacy between "the people" and the rest of France showed even more distinctly the chasm between Michelet himself and these thirty million people with whom he tried to identify. For with this modified definition of "the people" Michelet, within his own terminology, did not "spring" from "the people." His father, who had died the previous year, was a printer, a profession of the educated elite of the artisan class.

The problem now posed to his auditors was finding a means of communication with the illiterate majority of France. His suggestions, which would be continually broadened over the next few years, were along the lines of an aural and visual culture for "the people." He did *not* propose to make the illiterate literate, but instead envisioned a form of communication between the educated and "the people" which did not require significant use of the printed word. For example, one means of spiritual contact between the two groups of France should be a national theater group traveling all through the country. "In the future the theater should unquestionably be the most powerful means of education, of bringing men together: it is the best hope perhaps of a national renovation. I am thinking of an immensely popular theater . . . circulating even into the tiniest villages."[10] Another way "to unite the two divided peoples" was through personal, "oral communication."[11] Educated people should not merely write books or articles in the newspapers, but should go out and speak as equals to those who do not read.

Michelet wanted his students, the youth of France, to become the mediators between the educated and "the people." Since 1842 Michelet had been expressing his faith in the youth because they were unshackled by the dying religion of the past. In *Le Peuple* Michelet described the young bourgeois as uncorrupted, unlike their parents, by the class hatred of their time.[12] Michelet spoke of the new role he had devised for the youth in a letter to Eugène Noël on December 9, 1847: "I am going to start, I believe, a useful course on the state of spirits: 'On social discord and union.' There I will speak of the role of the *young man*. I will give him the world, place the future in his hand."[13] The young were Michelet's personal agents for communicating his ideas and closing the gap between the educated and uneducated. As Michelet had been the mediator between his father and mother, and then between the social classes, and then between men of instinct and men of reflection (all three unsuccessfully), now the young should be the new mediators of France:

As the child is mediator in his family, the young man ought to be mediator in the city. In domestic quarrels when the father is on one side of the table and the mother on the other, it is the child who takes the hand of one and places it in the other . . . Likewise in the city. This is why you will see, or rather what you will do, for you are the ones who will act.[14]

Michelet, in his constant ambivalence towards "the people," was not primarily trying to change the attitudes of the educated nor even of the wealthy, but rather continually attempting to communicate with and to change "the people." Béranger, the great national poet and composer of songs for "the people," had a strikingly different approach to the lower classes than his friend Michelet. Without the unconsciously patronizing outlook of Michelet, Béranger felt it was not the duty of educators to arouse the instincts and passions of "the people." When Michelet besieged Béranger with his ideas on eliminating the barriers between men, Béranger understood the contradictory relationship of Michelet with "the people," and he responded: "Let them do it themselves; who are you to arrogate to yourself the aristocratic privilege of wanting to enlighten the people? Let them do it, they will find their illumination and they will succeed; they will see themselves in the clearness which could not possibly be seen by you."[15]

Before Michelet arrived at the Collège de France to give his third lecture a student mocked a recent speech by Louis-Philippe. The crowd laughed and then sang republican songs until Michelet entered the hall. But the undercover police reported this as a serious incident inimical to the interests of the July Monarchy, and therefore gave the government a pretext to suspend the course indefinitely. Michelet was advised of this decision on January 2, 1848, and the following day he protested the action in a letter to Letronne, the director of the Collège de France:

From Mickiewicz to Quinet, and from Quinet to me, it is a coup d'état in three blows. Mickiewicz had ignited a flame over Europe, founding the marriage of peoples, . . . of France and the Slavs. Quinet had given the overall unity of literary, political, and religious questions, coming together in the soul. Myself, I had, in this chair of morals and of history, begun a moral work between all . . . on the subject of the times: social and moral unity; pacifying as much as was in me, the war of the classes, which weighs heavily on us, removing the barriers, more apparent than real, which separate and make hostile these classes whose interests are fundamentally the same.[16]

On January 7, 1848, about two thousand students protested in the Latin Quarter against Michelet's suspension.[17] He expressed, in a letter to his aunts, his satisfaction over the public support accorded him, but emphasized that the recent series of events had not motivated him to become personally involved in attacks against the government. "I am a writer, and I will remain such, wanting nothing more."[18] However, Michelet's voice was not stifled. He decided after the decree of January 2 to continue publishing, week by week, his remaining lectures of the term.

In the next seven lectures, undelivered but published, Michelet reiterated his same themes. Béranger's sharp rebuke did not affect Michelet, who continued to see in himself the person most qualified to interpret and to solve the problems of "the people":

> What should the man of the people say in the presence of the scholar? "Here is a man who by a special education, by the acquisition of knowledge available only through reading and study, represents the lives of fifty men; a considerable part of the human experience has accumulated within him. One word from him would convey to me this knowledge . . . This man is necessary for me."[19]

If Michelet's educational remedies were followed, he felt that a moral fraternity would supersede the temporary barriers between classes. An education about France did not require literacy, only love.

Apparently this nationalism of the heart, which Michelet had tried to inculcate again and again over the past two years, finally began with the February revolution. The overthrow of the monarchy catapulted many of Michelet's literary friends into national political prominence. On the first day of the revolt, February 22, Michelet wrote his friend Lamartine, who would soon become head of the Provisional Government:

> Blood flows as you can see, the government no longer dares call up the national guard . . . It is rumored that two thousand men are encircled in the Marais and that we are going to have another massacre . . .

If the Chamber still has a drop of French blood in its heart it must immediately make a strong statement that the control of Paris be given to Paris alone, to the national guard, who, supported by other troops, will make conciliations and save the two thousand encircled men.

You alone can make the pronouncement. You are the first of the first.[20]

The proclamation of the Republic on February 24 was the culmination of Michelet's dreams. However, he did not choose to become politically active in the new regime. In a letter to Noël, Alfred Dumesnil related Michelet's near appointment to a post in the cabinet:

Yesterday . . . the Republic was proclaimed at ten thirty at the Hôtel de Ville, but it had already been in everyone's hearts and on their lips. On the first list, posted in our quarter, M. Michelet was named to the Provisional Government. I led him to the Hôtel de Ville, but the congestion was so great that he could not get through into the assembly in order to find out the post of his nomination. In the official list which appeared this morning, he was not on it, having not appeared at the Hôtel de Ville. On the whole, it is preferable that he remain in his study. No one has greater moral authority in this country and he could best render his noble services if he abstained from taking an active part in the daily affairs of detail . . . [21]

In the first weeks of the Republic Michelet's home became a popular meeting area for intellectuals involved in the new government. "Our house has become a ministry," Alfred told Noël, "the crowd of curious visitors is endless. Masses of letters arrive each hour. Yesterday morning at six, some patriotic messengers invaded Michelet's dining room. It's amazing to see how suddenly we have become powerful!"[22] On March 4 Michelet attempted to implement his educational ideas by writing two of his friends in the new administration, telling them of the urgency "to enlighten the peasants by proclamations of the Provisional Government, read each day at the church and posted at the town hall."[23]

Throughout the exhilarating months of the Second Republic before the June Days, Michelet avoided political involvement and considered his function to be in the realm of education. Quinet had been nominated and would be elected to the Constituent Assembly, but Michelet did not want to enter politics. He told Alfred on March 3, "I want to remain where I am strongest."[24] A group from the Ardennes, the region of

Michelet's maternal origins, which he had lauded in *Le Peuple*, asked him to become their deputy to the Assembly. Immediately deciding to deny this request, Michelet wrote his aunt: "I want nothing for myself and desire to keep my independence with regard to the new government . . . I want to preserve the right to blame what is wrong, even in those who are my friends."[25] Politics by its very nature was divisive for Michelet. Elected officials had to take sides either supporting or attacking the government. Anything which separated France into parts, anything which prevented the harmony of souls, was anathema to Michelet's mission of uniting France. A partisan political life of charges and countercharges was a jejune method for realizing his aims. His role was far greater than being part of one of the many political factions. "The time required to carry out the functions of a deputy would force me to suspend my teaching, my history of France, and all my works."[26] As professor of history and and morals Michelet already had his desired position in the Second Republic. Therefore, he continued prescribing potions for national brotherhood in his books and lectures, while having Alfred take his place in the Ardennes elections:

> To my friends, known and unknown, who offer me their support. I accept your support not for myself, devoted at this moment to a sacred duty, the history of the country—but for my adopted son, my son-in-law, my only collaborator for eight years, P. Dumesnil-Michelet who is myself.
>
> His is worth more than you because he is young! Our dear and immortal Béranger was telling me the other day of the need for young men, new and with great strength. The new Assembly must represent by age, the rejuvenation of France.[27]

The professor of history and morals dramatically returned to teaching on March 6, 1848. Together with Quinet, who was lecturing for the first time in three years, they spoke in the large amphitheater at the Sorbonne. Three chairs had been placed on the stage, one of them for the absent member of the triumvirate, Mickiewicz. Michelet told a cheering audience that "this chair is that of Poland."[28] The return of Michelet and Quinet was an occasion for a joyful celebration, and, in this carnival atmosphere, Michelet remarked: "This is not a lecture, it is a fraternal salute. . . . We have come to congratulate the schools and to greet the Republic together."[29]

Michelet gave his one remaining formal lecture of the term on April 1, 1848. The foremost moral educator in France revealed to his auditors that he had played an intergral role in preparing the revolution:

> In looking back at my books and courses during the past five years, they prepared the revolution by diverse means, whether their tendencies were practical, political, or religious—I have nothing to regret, neither in my general method, nor in the special means by which I initiated the public to some frequently obscure ideas.[30]

In addition to his belief in the effect of his works, Michelet also thought that his personal representatives, the youth, had helped spread his ideas. "Young men . . . I called you this year to the greatest mission that one could offer to man, to the priesthood of pacification."[31] From the center of French education, the Collège de France, Michelet felt that his ideas for a moral revolution had been disseminated throughtout the country. He clearly seemed to think that he was in the center of the historical process and had personally been able to affect this process through the propagation of his thoughts. During this April 1 lecture he noted that the transformation of the new priesthood from the Church to the Collège de France had been completed. His students, having received his message, were part of this "priesthood." As a symbolic act, Michelet mentioned that a collection plate, which formerly was associated only with churches, had been started by his students at the Collège de France. The purpose of this collection plate was "not to profit religious tyranny, but for the humane idea of free brotherhood."[32]

The general euphoria after the February revolution began to diminish as the problems of the Provisional Government mounted. Ideological conflicts were eroding the already fragile authority of the government. Michelet closely followed the changing fortunes of this nascent regime, and his belief in a firmly established republic began to totter. On April 4, only three days after his enthusiastic and self-congratulatory lecture, he wrote in his diary, "Happiness and sadness: up until now I was active in the revolution; now I see it, I submit to it, I applaud it, my role is passive."[33] A festival of brotherhood on April 20 rekindled his hopes. "The festival of yesterday, I believe, founded the Republic on a solid base. Nothing has been more touching, more imposing."[34] The next week he voted for the Constituent Assembly, labeling his choices as: men of letters, economists, doctors, journalists, workers, merchants, and entrepreneurs.[35] The tumultuous invasion of the Assembly by dissatisfied radicals on May 15 prompted Michelet to write: "The rude and ugly event of May 15 brought me violently from the sky back to earth."[36]

Aware of the increasing breakdown of the government, Michelet devised more elaborate educational remedies to prevent an open confrontation between the educated and "the people." While politicians and pamphleteers of all ideological persuasions were arguing vehemently over the national workshops and other economic measures, Michelet wrote Béranger on June 16, 1848, of his more detailed plans for an aural and visual culture as a means of communicating with "the people." Despite the enormous public economic and social debates, Michelet felt that he was confronting the core of the problem:

I said in December 1847: the Press has not reached the people. In effect, you can see that right now it is on one side and the masses are on the other. It leaves a great number of men Bonapartists—that is to say, idolaters—and the majority of women, idolaters or Catholics.

The masses cannot read and do not want to read because it is tiring for men who are little accustomed to it. The Republic must act on the masses, to require reading which is impossible today. The newspapers, circulating libraries, adult schools, etc., work, but only in the long run. I want something which acts immediately. I only know three means. Others find them ridiculous; but you, who understand the people so profoundly, will perhaps judge them as the most immediately powerful means that one could employ.

1. Some clubs of public reading, where the best speaker reads for everyone a message in two parts, one centralized, emanating from the government, the other local, emanating form the region and which interests the peasantry by giving them useful information on the state of the market, career openings, etc.

2. The universal posting of announcements in large letters, very short ones, illustrated with colored figures which attract attention. The bulletin boards could alternate, that is, appear one day in one region, tomorrow in another.

3. A skillful colportage organized and composed by songwriters: a patriotic song skillfully employed as the organ of the Republic, as its

popular voice. Naturally, in Brittany, Alsace, and the South, it must adapt to the idioms and dialects . . .

This triple machine can scarcely be organized in its entirety by a government, but the latter can push and encourage it. It would be more successful it it functioned under the aegis of private interest . . . I would like to see a company or a centrally located republican bookstore, which would distribute bulletins, books, and songs, . . .

I feel that this is a pressing and urgent matter: to act energetically in order to inundate France with republican vigor and to substitute faith for idolatry; ideas for men; otherwise we will perish.

Judge me, correct me, I beg you. I know your profound good sense and I submit to it in advance. Show me other ideas. But in the name of God do something on this point, which is a matter of life or death.[37]

Michelet was prescient on the urgency of solving the class conflicts, because the June Days erupted a week later. In this revealing letter, not only did Michelet not propose any significant social, economic, or political changes, he did not even suggest literacy reforms. He merely wanted a moral and psychological sympathy for republicanism and France. Béranger's cryptic response was similar to his advice from the previous December: "Leave the people alone, they will find their way. In the new political setting they must do everything themselves; they will improvise their books, songs, and festivals. No one can do it for them."[38] Years later, Michelet apparently still felt that if his plan had been implemented it could have prevented the June Days, as he wrote on his copy of his June 16 letter: "This letter had no effect."[39]

The bloody class war in Paris known as the June Days abruptly crushed Michelet's hopes of national reconciliation. In four days of fighting beginning June 23 some fifteen hundred people were slain on the streets of Paris. Having throttled the uprising by June 26, the government troops began massacring the insurgents in the streets, in dark alleys, and in their homes. Some three thousand rebels were murdered in this brutal fashion while twelve thousand more were exiled to Algeria. During these June Days an insurgent, told that he was in front of Michelet's house, replied, "Who is Michelet?" Told this story, Michelet commented to his friend Auguste Préault, "I would no longer write *Le Peuple* today."[40]

Michelet's initial reaction to the June Days was to begin instantly his educational program. On June 27 he hurriedly jotted down in his diary, "I sensed the urgency to educate the people."[41] The next day he emphatically concluded: "Education! Education!—But May 15, but June 24 . . . No, I am not mistaken! Instinct is equal in power to reflection."[42] In July he tried to write a work on popular education, but discontinued it after ten days. "It is impossible for me to continue this work," he wrote Noël, but added, "France is always young, strong, immutable; we don't have to cry for her because of the acts of an imperceptible minority."[43]

Understandably, the gory days of June depressed Michelet. Alfred informed Michelet's cousin on July 14, "The cruel series of events in June has bled the heart of M. Michelet and stopped all his work, which is something a public event has never done to him before."[44] The June Days had stained the organic harmony of his beloved Paris. "Paris is now too sad . . . for me"; she, Michelet wrote in October, "is like a large sepulcher which needs a spark in order to revive."[45] Noël expressed the essence of Michelet's afflicition in a January 3, 1849 letter to Alfred. "M. Michelet has been wounded in his love for France. . . . A frightful breath of reality has exploded his fantasy."[46]

This temporary destruction of his ideal of France led Michelet to reflect occasionally that the schools, in particular the Collège de France, may not yet have the power and the influence which should be accorded to them. "I have been uprooted by two hurricanes: the rupture of June with the civil disorder and the conviction which followed that the schools were henceforth powerless."[47] The power of the universities was being undermined by the revival of Bonapartist sentiment. Childhood memories of Napoleon closing his father's printing press had forever instilled in Michelet an abhorrence for the Emperor and for the nephew. He thought, in September 1848, that this desire of others to recapture romanticized glories of the past would soon fade away. "France will pass, I believe, through a moment of Bonapartism in order to purify itself forever of this idolatry. All of this will leave, sooner or later, with Catholicism."[48] Louis-Napoleon, though, was elected President of the Second Republic in December 1848, and Michelet, like so many other intellectuals, would suffer as a consequence.

Despite both the "frightful breath of reality" which had punctured Michelet's vision of France in June and also the December triumph of

Louis-Napoleon, Michelet did not noticeably alter his fundamental ideals or methods. The civil war in June and the fervent support for Louis-Napoleon by the peasantry did not eradicate Michelet's personal conception of a future France. The only apparent difference between June 1848 and his social ideals for the next six years was his incorporation of another group, in addition to the youth, as an agent for bringing about the inevitable harmony of France—women. One main impetus behind his inclusion of women as a source of love and brotherhood was his November 8, 1848 meeting with twenty-three-year-old Athénaïs Mialaret. They fell deeply in love and married on March 12, 1849. "The purity and the wisdom of my young wife have clarified for me the important and intricate subject with which I am dealing in my course. No subject is more important. Right now women are the greatest obstacle to our social unity, to the strengthening of the Republic."[49] Women had to be freed from Bonapartist and Catholic sentiments in order to channel their love into the Republic. Then, women, as well as Michelet's young students, could help spread total love among all Frenchmen:

> The awful night of June 24 after the great light and hope of February, gave me the most terrible blow I have ever had. I tried to write a popular book but couldn't do it. I returned humiliated, sad, and somber to the impersonal work of my historical research. However, the vivid touches of my women, Mme Roland and Mme Condorcet, indicate sufficiently that if there was a remedy—if I was going to find a solution, it would be found in women, in love.[50]

Boosted by his ideas on women and on love, Michelet's diary and courses indicate that the failures of 1848 did not deter him from his original goals:

> I will combat the barriers which are in the cities and the classes of the cities. I am going to show the rich and the poor their common interests. I will give them a broad, inexhaustible foundation . . . the riches to be shared by reconciliation. Later I will penetrate more profoundly the individual soul, rediscovering in this soul the barriers and divisions which divide cities . . . factions, civil wars, tyrannies . . . If I succeed in pacify-

ing religions, cities, and the individual souls, I will then try to bring about what appears to be peace itself . . . love.[51]

Michelet saw himself thrusting his vision upon France in order to cure the ills of the country. His idea of action was not the kind involved with transitory cabinet posts or assembly seats. Instead, Michelet confined his actions around his complete belief in the power of the "word." "I speak of the barriers between the living, of those who do not love each other; hatred of race, hatred of class, hatred of people, hatred of the family."[52] These "hostilities of classes and peoples might end if there was a uniting of souls."[53] Moral and psychological evils, after all, could be annihilated through a rethinking of learned hatreds and a resurgence of innate love. "The history of death and destruction, that of hate is nothing other than ignorance and misunderstanding; it is a barrier of darkness which persists among men."[54]

The essential remedy was the same as before June 1848: "Education is the way."[55] Men and women were "divided as sciences," and Michelet wanted to "reestablish the unity" of which he had written in his 1825 *Discours sur l'unité de la science*.[56] On April 26, 1849, he lectured on his ideas for "a national French education."[57] In words reminiscent of Joseph de Maistre's famous statement in his *Considérations sur la France*, he told his auditors: "Everyone, Christians, philosophers, socialists, speak of man in general. But there is no man in general, there are only men in particular, there are only Frenchmen, Englishmen, etc."[58] And in this national education, Michelet wanted to use not only the power of the press but also his ideas on an aural and visual culture to harmonize the souls of both educated and illiterate under the aegis of France. "Our means [of education] are slow and insufficient . . . The printing press was a progress, the newspaper a progress, now we wait for the electric arts."[59] The possibilities of modern forms of communication would probably have made Michelet's imagination run wild, but for the moment he could only try to extend his previous ideas. After seeing George Sand's play *François le Champi* on April 2, 1850, Michelet wrote her of his own ideas on the "true theater":

The theater, the true theater, will revive the world . . . In my course of 1847-1848, which I published, I expressed the desire for a moral renovation aided by the theater. I still believe that the creation of a village theater, spread throughout the countryside, would be the most powerful means for bringing the people into contact with the true national spirit. Some patriotic proverbs under a very simple form would recall for them the life of our heroes; these proverbs would have a great effect in the country-side. The drama must be very simple . . . [60]

From his chair at the Collège de France, which he told his students in 1850 "was not only a magistrature, but a pontificate," Michelet continued to give sermons on his educational ideas which would naturally and easily prepare the flowering of love and the brotherhood of Frenchmen.[61] On March 6, 1851, the title of his lecture was: "The only base for teaching is *la patrie* itself." This was Michelet's last lecture, and it was altogether fitting that it was entitled with his central idea. For twenty-three years he had taught, thirteen of them in the highest educational post of morals and history in France. After March 6, 1851, one of his principal means of disseminating his ideas, the "spoken word," was taken from him forever.

Michelet's toubles with the administration of the Collège de France and with the government of the Second Republic had been accumulating for the past two years. Since 1849 Michelet had been continually harassed by the faculty, the administration, and the police. Undercover policemen attended his courses, while concocted copies of lectures were released by the government, and false accusations repeatedly assailed Michelet's character and intergrity. The correspondence between the administration of the Collège de France, the government, and the police, now preserved in the Michelet dossier in the archives of the Collège de France, overwhelmingly conveys the impression that the government of Louis-Napoleon felt that Michelet's course and the large number of students it attracted, constituted a very real threat to the stability of the regime. Lecturing under these controversial and tension-ridden circumstances only naturally increased Michelet's valuation of his own importance and the power of his ideas.

In February 1849 Jules Barthélemy Saint-Hilaire, the new director of the Collège de France, warned Michelet about the student disorders before each class, and he also posted a warning to the auditors to refrain "from tumult and shouting."[62] A new threat appeared on March 6,

1849. "The director again requests that the young men enter the Collège de France in an orderly manner. They should not disturb the tranquillity of this establishment by shouts or by songs. . . . The director hopes that the distressing scenes of the past days will not reoccur."[63] On the same day the prefect of police, at the request of Barthélemy Saint-Hilaire, ordered "thirty agents . . . to maintain order in the course of M. Michelet."[64] The police, both uniformed in the courtyard and under-cover in the classroom would continue their surveillance of Michelet's lectures for the next two years. During this whole period Barthélemy Saint-Hilaire wasted no opportunities to harangue Michelet. For example, when Michelet got married he was forced to cancel a class, and Barthélemy Saint-Hilaire promptly notified him that he had not acted in the "interests of the Collège de France."[65] At the same time, as Michelet informed Noël, colleagues such as Biot and Portets began making slanderous remarks about the material in his lectures.[66]

The constant pressure exerted by Barthélemy Saint-Hilaire on Michelet resulted from frequent government demands upon the director. The authorities wanted no disturbances. On February 8, 1850, the minister of public education wrote Barthélemy Saint-Hilaire: "M. Michelet's last course did not pass without disorder. I am assured that upon the professor's entry he was greeted with cries of long live the social and democratic Republic. . . . I hope, Monsieur . . . that you can explain this action to me."[67] Barthélemy Saint-Hilaire tried to carry out all of the requests of the minister of public education and of the government. The director of the Collège de France never supported the interests of Michelet and always defended the intrusions and policies of the government.

The final, and thoroughly successful, government campaign to close Michelet's course began in February 1851. The minister of public education requested Barthélemy Saint-Hilaire to obtain transcripts of each lecture, because of the "disorderly manifestations—provoked by words I can hardly believe were uttered—during M. Michelet's course."[68] One result of this letter was a distorted version of Michelet's February 27 lecture which made him seem like an atheist and raving revolutionary. On March 5 Barthélemy Saint-Hilaire asked Michelet to appear before the administration in order to discuss his course; that is, before the vice-president, the secretary, and himself.[69] Aware of his control of the situation, the minister of public education informed Barthélemy Saint-Hilaire, on this same day, that he was pleased "that the interests of this great establishment were preserved under your enlightened direction."[70] Later that day the minister asked the director to consider "the removal of the professor." Michelet's lectures were too provocative, according to the minister, because after the previous lecture, students had been incited to gather illegally in the courtyard, and someone had shouted "to the Bastille."[71]

On March 6, 1851, Barthélemy Saint-Hilaire requested fifty agents "dressed as bourgeois" to keep silence during the class and to prevent disturbances afterward.[72] The administration met with Michelet that day, informing him of the precariousness of his situation and notifying him that his colleagues had been summoned to vote on him. The director gave each professor a copy of the fabricated February 27 lecture "in order to prepare you for the meeting."[73] Quinet, taking Michelet's defense, wrote Barthélemy Saint-Hilaire: "De Sacy [a previous director] was an honest man, but you're just scum."[74]

Five days later, on March 11, 1951, by a vote of seventeen to four, Michelet's colleagues censured his teaching. Julius Mohl, one of the seventeen, wrote:

> . . . [his lessons were] deplorable rhapsodies, mostly sheer nonsense, striving for originality and attaining a sort of fantastic madness. . . . The fact is that we should have defended him, whatever might have been his opinions, if his lessons had not been an outrage to common sense. They were utterly indefensible on any account. I was very little flattered to have to vote for what they wished.[75]

On March 13, following a decision by the minister of public education, Michelet was formally suspended from teaching. Mickiewicz had been placed on a leave of absence. Quinet had refused to teach because his freedom was restricted, but only Michelet, in this highly unusual action, was suspended from, what had been historically, the most open educational institution in France. It was not until the following year on April 12, 1852, that a decree was promulagated by Louis-Napoleon, himself, formally expelling Michelet, Quinet, and Mickiewicz from the Collège de France.[76] The Emperor had silenced the father and now the nephew silenced the son.

Having lost his educational position, Michelet than proceeded to lose his historical post at the Archives Nationales. For twenty-two years he had been head of the historical section and had used the archives for his major works of history. The daily wandering among the dried parchments, followed by the feverish activity of bringing them to life again in his writings, ended in 1852. In the future, he would have to write without the benefit of the documents.

The pattern of Michelet's final years at the Archives was similar to that at the Collège de France. About the same time Barthélemy Saint-Hilaire became director of the Collège de France, Chabrier became head of the Archives. He too chided Michelet for wanting to miss work because of his marriage. Chabrier accused Michelet of not "understanding my situation"; too many days off would exceed the "the limits of article 42 of our rules," and he could not permit any infringement of archival regulations.[77] Their constant confrontations forced Michelet to spend less and less time at the Archives. On December 3, 1851, the day after Louis-Napoleon's coup d'état, Michelet and Chabrier had a violent political argument, Chabrier defending Louis-Napoleon and Michelet cursing his most bitter enemy. In the presence of a doorman Chabrier shouted," Go get me some pistols," and Michelet responded, "Go get the officer to arrest this old fool."[78] In his notes on his "rupture with the Archives" at the Bibliothèque historique de la ville de Paris, Michelet wrote of his "being forced to leave the Archives."[79] However, unlike the Collège de France, he did not wait around for an official decree from Louis-Napoleon. On June 4, 1852, Michelet refused to take the new oath to the government, *ipso facto* ending his career at the Archives Nationales. On June 12 he left his native Paris for Nantes and semi-exile.

After the coup d'état of December 2, 1851, Michelet accused, within his same world view, the men of letters for not reaching "the people." "I bear a grudge against December 2, I blame myself and all the educated class, writing or speaking to the men of letters, to the press, and to the Parliament. We have done nothing for the people and we are punished for it."[80] When Louis-Napoleon became Napoleon III the following December, Michelet wrote Alfred, "The Empire was proclaimed yesterday. Not a move, not a cry. The Bonapartists are thunderstruck by the impotence of their solitude."[81]

In Michelet's last contemporary social history, *Le Banquet*, written between April 24 and May 28, 1854, he again expressed his previous thoughts on and vision of France. Despite the civil war of 1848 and the personal calamities of 1851 and 1852, Michelet's social ideas were not altered. As he wrote in his diary on April 13, 1854, "The cruel experience of 1852 has not changed my doctrine."[82]

In *Le Banquet*, Michelet described more explicitly than formerly his idea of an aural and visual culture. This cultural orientation for communication, contrary to Béranger's advice, was still directed by the men of letters. "It belongs to the lettered, to those who have the time, the leisure, the study, the instruments of thought, the knowledge of the trials already passed through by the human race, to broadcast the way of advance and sometimes to prepare it."[83] Among the ideas suggested by Michelet were "sermons, stories, patriotic and sacred dramas" as well as books for the children.[84] His emphasis was on little, popular editions of everything, as if "the people" were children and could only understand a simply constructed and constantly repeated message. Little maps of the country "with three or four" central facts on the nation should be given to all of "the people."[85] This immediate and more emotional popular culture would awaken the historical sense of "the people" and show them that they were an integral part of France. "I have said: The press will always be . . . a secondary means of action in France. One can only act on this eminently electrifying people by the living way of oral communication, festivals, and entertainment spectaculars."[86] In his diary Michelet imagined an evening, using electrical effects, which would instantaneously instill the "word"—the emotion of patriotism and the love of France:

> What would be the effect of a chariot transformed one evening by an immense electrical light under the flag of *la patrie* and a sheaf of European flags; a chariot painted with the heroic images of the gods of France—while thundering at the same time would be an immense symphony of one hundred musicians to which responded the voice of the crowd—all of this illuminated and brightened . . . by the spoken word or the word in letters of fire, flashing during each pause and during each redoubling of the electric light . . . of printed songs in all colors, . . . or patriotic pictures, or metal-coated medals of our heroes . . . ?[87]

In addition to detailing his educational plans in *Le Banquet*, Michelet attacked all of the major Franch system-makers of the first half of the nineteenth century. The same day he began writing *Le Banquet*, Michelet told Quinet that France "is a religion, despite its fall and its miseries . . . I am devising a law . . . to explain that the disputes of our republican-socialist church are absolutely external . . . and only differ on secondary points of the new theology. We must understand . . . the unity of our glorious church."[88] Michelet, therefore, had to show the mistakes of Saint-Simon, the Saint-Simonians, Fourier, and Proudhon. Michelet's new church was "a communism of the heart," "a sentiment not a system."[89] It did not have "the hierarchy of Saint-Simon" where men divided into classes; it did not have the unharmonized "diversity of Fourier"; nor did it have the "anarchy of Proudhon" where all of the rich were excluded and the beautiful centralization of France was destroyed.[90]

The most grievous errors of these thinkers, according to Michelet, was to have neglected the unifying force of *la patrie*. Saint-Simon had the audacity to propose "the union of France and England."[91] Fourier wanted many little groups of association but not one only of France, while Proudhon advocated total decentralization. "*La patrie* has perished for them."[92] The Saint-Simonians and the liberal Catholics had likewise forgotten France. "M. Enfantin said: 'What is *la patrie*?'; M. Montalembert said: 'My country is centered in Rome.'"[93]

Saint-Simon, the Saint-Simonians, and Fourier had lost the true notion of *la patrie* because they had tried to slight the fundamental importance of the French Revolution. They were attempting to erect new societies after the crumbling of the old civilization. But the French Revolution had affected their thought unconsciously, and, according to Michelet, they were unable to interpret modern France correctly, because they had not fully comprehended the meaning contained in that momentous event. "The masters and immortal fathers of socialism, Saint-Simon, Fourier, really believed that they were proceeding by way of *absolute denial*, not seeing the narrow bonds which tied them to the Revolution, and misunderstanding the true mother who carried them in her breast; they, and all of the future."[94]

The "true mother," the French Revolution, only Michelet understood. It was "his" Revolution, because from 1846 to 1853 he had been writing his masterwork, *Histoire de la Révolution française*. From 1843, when he perceived that he was part of the new clergy, to *Le Peuple*, and then to *Le Banquet*, Michelet had been writing and expanding his social, moral, and educational ideas in order to foster a unitary, harmonized France. Despite the June Days, changes of regimes, and the loss of his teaching and archival posts, he had passionately maintained his unique vision of France. There was no major revision of his thought after 1848 or 1852, because he felt that the future essence of *la patrie* had already been revealed to him. He continually heralded the power of *la patrie* and its infinite capacity to overcome all internal hatred and class divisions. Nevertheless, Michelet's vision of France, her problems, and possible solutions to them, invariably differed from other intellectuals in Paris, because he had his own specific idea of *la patrie*. This particular meaning of *la patrie*—the origins of this omnipotent force—was only found in Michelet's interpretation of the French Revolution. In his *Histoire de la Révolution française* was revealed the true *patrie*.

# 11

## General Force of Things

While living amidst another tumultuous period of revolution and upheaval between 1846 and 1853, Michelet wrote his greatest history, *Histoire de la Révolution française*. All of the historian's imaginative and creative genius coalesced in this awesome re-creation of France's most cataclysmic period of history. The composition of this work, interrupting Michelet's chronological history of France—begun in the last, hopeful years of the July Monarchy, continued through revolution, civil war, coup d'état, and semi-exile—seemed to mirror, if only in miniature, the dramatic events of the French Revolution. Self-proclaimed replicas of Marat, Desmoulins, Danton, St. Just, and Robespierre filled the streets of Paris between February and June 1848, a scene brilliantly evoked by Flaubert in *L'Education sentimentale*. The collapse of the revolution and the return of Louis-Napoleon completed the cycle. In his diary Michelet often compared these events with similar occurrences during the French Revolution. Perhaps this era of shifting emotions in response to the constant turn of events, where the sensibilities of Frenchmen were rekindled and heightened by the memories of the past, also aided Michelet in his bringing to life the dead, but unburied, bones of his father's generation. Throughout these turbulent public and private years Michelet's historical craft was not impaired. Even in Nantes, after losing his jobs, his Ezekiel-like approach was as strong as ever. "I have discovered in these catacombs more than Cuvier found in fossils. I have found souls. I will re-create golden souls which had perished; which would no longer exist without me. I shall bring back to life amazingly tortured, but all the more instructive, souls."[1]

Michelet's *Histoire de la Révolution française* disappointed him because of its unsatisfactory sales, and disappointed the reviewers because of the content and interpretation. Lamartine's 1847 *Histoire des Girondins* was a far more popular work. Apparently buoyed by the sales, often into the tens of thousands, of his pamplets of the 1840s, Michelet decided to have six thousand copies of his first volume printed.[2] This proved to be a personal financial blunder since he, rather than his publisher Chamerot, financed the publication. A note of June 29, 1851, showed that at least 3,500 copies were still unsold.[3] When the number of copies that were misprinted, lost, destroyed, distributed among the press, and given to friends, are taken into account, it is doubtful that more than fifteen hundred copies were purchased. Although this was not a failure for a work of history, it certainly did not meet up to Michelet's expectations. The response of the press, meanwhile, was limited and reserved. Reviewers were unsympathetic with Michelet's brutal attack on Christianity and were perturbed by his lack of objectivity and careful analysis. One reviewer, Gustave Planche, blasted the book for creating false emotional states, for using history too much for polemical purposes, and for moving beyond the "real world" of the Revolution into "apocalyptic regions."[4] Editions of the next six volumes averaged 2,500 copies, a sharp reduction, but still none of them sold out. Four months after the appearance of the third volume, for example, Chamerot informed Michelet that sales were poor, with less than one thousand copies sold.[5]

Not until the last years of the Second Empire did Michelet's *Histoire de la Révolution française* become popular and receive the accolades of a new generation of intellectuals. Between 1868 and 1900 nine editions appeared, including a prestigious 1889 national edition approved by the Chamber of Deputies. In the last decades of the nineteenth century Michelet had become the standard source for the French Revolution. Aulard, an ardent admirer of Michelet, having been nourished on his histories, wrote in 1928 that:

> The influence of Michelet on Frenchmen in the second half of the nineteenth century is less perhaps than Jean-Jacques Rousseau in the eighteenth, but analogous. It has appeared to eclipse the wave of materialist history following Karl Marx. This form of history was only temporary. The greatest French socialist, Jaurès, if one reads his *Histoire socialiste de la*

*139*

*Révolution*, shows that he is still more of a disciple of Michelet than Marxist.[6]

Actually Jaurès claimed that his history was inspired equally by both Marx and Michelet:

> Our interpretation of history will be at the same time materialist like Marx and mystical like Michelet. Economic life, which has been the foundation and the spring of human history is essential, but beyond the succession of social forms, the thinking power of man aspires through a lifetime of thought to find intellectual harmony for the uneasy spirit and with the mysterious universe.[7]

The last forty years of French Revolution historiography have altered radically the assumptions of Jaurès and especially Aulard. Aulard's feeling that Michelet's influence was more permanent than Marx's and Jaurès's attempt to balance delicately the two, have both given way to variants of Marxist history. Social and economic history, secondary with Michelet, have become the twin foci for interpreting the French Revolution, while Michelet's complex psychological portraits of men and events have often been superseded by social class labels. Moreover, the rigors of twentieth-century scienfitic scholarship have revealed numerous errors of names and dates and unnecessary one-sidedness in Michelet's history, further eroding his credibility for many historians. Today, Michelet's *Histoire de la Révolution française* has been relegated to some, but far from all, bibliographies on the French Revolution—a strange resting place for one of the most artistic and remarkable works of French history.

When Michelet is recalled by modern historians it is generally in two areas: his idea of the class composition of the Revolution and his complete use of archival materials, most of which burned during the 1871 Commune. Both George Rudé and Albert Soboul, two of the most eminent contemporary scholars of the French Revolution, have praised Michelet's concept of "the people." In his study of revolutionary crowds, Rudé found that Michelet's use of "the people" during major events often corresponded to the facts.[8] Soboul noted the importance of Michelet's access to the documents and showed a great appreciation for his re-creation of the feelings and emotions of the revolutionary period.

Having handled the documents themselves, having obtained from eyewitnesses a living acquaintance with the Revolution, Michelet managed to capture the very soul of the people who had created it, with both their enthusiasms and their illusions. He speaks of the great hopes of 1789, the rage of the people who created the notion of the aristocratic plot, patriotic fervor in the year 1792.[9]

For source material, Michelet consulted the sixteen-volume *Choix de mémoires relatifs à la Révolution* edited by Berville and Barrière and published between 1820 and 1826; *Le Moniteur*; the forty-volume *Histoire parlementaire de la Révolution française* compiled by Buchez and Roux between 1834 and 1840 and containing newspaper articles, many of which were from *Le Moniteur*, pamphlets, mémoires, speeches, and transcripts of trials from the Commune and the Paris sections; the recently published mémoires of Lafayette, Bouillé, Busenval, Necker, and Grégoire; and the archives—the Archives Nationales, the archives of the Hôtel de Ville in Paris, the archives in Nantes, and Paris police records. While examining all of these sources, Michelet emphasized in his 1868 preface the central importance of the archives. His work "was born in the heart of the Archives."[10] The archives in Nantes had provided him with information on the Vendée. "For the Federations, I had hundreds of reports from cities and villages at the Archives Nationales. For the great tragedies of revolutionary Paris, the archives of the Hôtel de Ville opened the door to the Commune registers; and the prefecture of police provided me with . . . verbatim reports of our forty-eight sections."[11] Although Michelet may have used the other sources more than he cared to admit, especially Buchez and Roux, he is the only historian of the French Revolution to have utilized all of these archives.

In his *Histoire de la Révolution* Louis Blanc vehemently attacked Michelet for not citing his sources, for misquoting, and for using only part of a document, thereby altering the interpretation of an event. Michelet felt, however, ever since his appointment to the Archives Nationales in 1830, that his research was the most thorough of any historian. In 1854, for example, he wrote of Thiers's and Mignet's histories. "Remarkable books for their time, improvised by brilliant writers, but without sufficient study, without knowledge of the countless documents contained in the public archives."[12] His archival work,

Michelet recalled in 1868, allowed him to "judge day by day *Le Moniteur*, which MM. Thiers, Lamartine, and Louis Blanc follow too closely."[13] Blanc, Michelet's most outspoken detractor, was chastized for writing his history in London without the benefit of any of the archives.

Michelet acknowledged the criticism of his peers in 1868 for "having cited sources too rarely."[14] But, in response, he remarked that the archival material was followed chronologically, and anyone interested in checking the sources need only consult them. In his *Histoire de France* Michelet had previously defended the literary importance of historical writings over and above a dry cataloguing and presentation of speeches and documents. "A history being a work of art as much as of science, ought to appear removed from the machines and scaffolding which have prepared the construction of it."[15] Unfortunately Michelet's 1868 response to his critics, to investigate the archives themselves, became impossible three years later, as the majority of the archival materials in Paris perished in the flames of another civil war.

In addition to the archival research, Michelet possessed one further unique tool for reliving the Revolution—he had access to the oral tradition. Throughout the seven volumes of his history Michelet insisted upon the value of hearing the stories of key events told to him by witnesses of the French Revolution. His foremost storyteller had been his own father, who had seen and heard countless first-hand accounts of revolutionary events and political intrigues during his years as a printer in Paris. The daily political imbroglios were avidly discussed, beyond the ears of informers, by him and his closest friends. Furcy's death in November 1846, two months after Michelet began writing his history, left an immense gap in his son's life, as he lost, among other things, direct access to the Revolution. Furcy had "been tradition . . . especially for the Revolution."[16]

> But as "our thread of life is of a mingled yarn," while I enjoyed so much happiness in reviving the annals of France, my own peace has been disturbed forever. I have lost him who so often narrated the scenes of the Revolution to me, him whom I revered as the image and venerable witness of the Great Age, that is, of the eighteenth century. I have lost my father, with whom I had lived all my life,—forty-eight years . . . .

*142*

Many of these important questions, which have obliged me to fathom deeply the foundations of my faith, have been investigated by me during the most awful circumstances that can attend human life, between death and the grave,—when the survivor, himself partly dead, has been sitting in judgment between two worlds.[17]

In a chapter on his methodology at the end of the second volume, Michelet mentioned that he had read all of the books and manuscripts, but "in all matters of historical morality, had consulted above all the *oral* tradition."[18] This oral tradition had been passed on "by word of mouth of the people, by what they all say and repeat; peasants, men of the city, the elderly, middle-aged men, women, even children."[19] These people were often quoted in Michelet's history as authoritative sources on the crucial events of the Revolution. Despite all of the documents on the federations, Michelet had discovered their true importance "on the lips and in the heart of the people."[20] When he wanted to convey the psychological temper of August 10, he quoted "one of the participants . . . who is still alive, and who explained it to me clearly."[21] Michelet found an image of the Terror when he observed a survivor with a "sad and gentle expression on his face"; this man "always looked at the fireplace and never at me. . . . He spoke in a monotone. . . . What terrifying power Robespierre must have possessed."[22]

The oral tradition of the "the people" was an integral part of Michelet's approach to the French Revolution. In speaking of his methodology, Michelet, as in *Le Peuple*, reiterated that "born people, we went to the people."[23] "The people" already glorified by Michelet in his popular work on them, became his focus for his *Histoire de la Révolution française*. Michelet's intention was not to raise his favorite individuals on a pedestal nor even show the main events of the Revolution through the ideas and actions of men. Rather, Michelet sought to follow his amorphous idea of "the people" through the tortuous, but more fulfilling, paths of societal movement. "Every history of the Revolution until now has been essentially monarchical—either for Louis XVI or for Robespierre. This is the first republican version which has broken the idols and the gods. From the first page to the last, there has been only one hero: the people."[24]

"The people" were the "high and sovereign moral authority" of the French Revolution.[25] Michelet had never liked the idea of historians writing about individuals; that was the English way of philosophizing. The society and the nation, frequently represented by "the people" in the highest, most mythical sense, had always been Michelet's central concern in history. Now, with the French Revolution, he had to smash "the idols" of hero-worship and replace them with the less specific, but more universal nature of the Revolution. As in the *Histoire de France* when the movement of the nation transcended individual aims and actions, so, in 1789 did the movement of France, symbolized in "the people," supersede the desires of the leaders. This predominance of "the people," Michelet felt, allowed them to control their spokesmen and to generate the mightiest achievements of the Revolution:

> Another thing which this history will render most conspicuous, and which is true of every party, is that the people were generally much better than their leaders. The further I have searched, the more generally have I found that the more deserving class was ever underneath, buried among the utterly obscure. I have also found that those brilliant, powerful speakers, who expressed the thoughts of the masses, are usually but wrongfully considered as the sole actors. The fact is, that they received rather than communicated the impulse. The chief actor is the people. In order to find and restore the latter to its proper position, I have been obliged to reduce to their proportions those ambitious puppets whom they had set in motion, and in whom, till now, people fancied they saw, and have sought for, the secret transactions of history.
>
> This sight, I must confess, struck me with astonishment. In proportion as I entered more deeply into this study, I observed that the mere party leaders, those heroes of the prepared scene, neither foresaw nor prepared anything, that they were never the first proposers of any grand measure,—more particularly of those which were the unanimous work of the people at the outset of the Revolution.[26]

Michelet's approach to, research of, and interpretation of the French Revolution contrasted sharply with the other histories of the epoch. Perhaps the main meeting ground, a heritage from Burke and Maistre, was the assumption that ideas were the principal cause of the Revolution. It was not until Tocqueville's 1856 *L'Ancien Régime et la Révolution* that social and political factors were seen as more influential than Enlightenment thought. Beyond this general orientation, though, the causes, theories, heroes, and results of the Revolution greatly separated Michelet's *Histoire de la Révolution française* from those of Thiers, Mignet, Buchez, Carlyle, Quinet, Lamartine, and Blanc. None of these men were living witnesses to the French Revolution, but their seminal studies propelled the multi-leveled debate on the meaning and significance of that momentous period of history.

Written in the 1820s, Thiers's ten-volume and Mignet's two-volume *Histoire de la Révolution française* reflected the ideas of liberal, constitutional monarchists. Their comments on Louis XVI were often far from subtle strictures against the repressive policies of the Restoration governments. Absolute restrictions on liberties and freedoms, Thiers and Mignet seemed to warn, could lead to another trial of a king and another Terror. "Real liberty," Mignet concluded, had been achieved briefly during the Revolution, but was still the foremost unfulfilled objective for French government and society.[27]

Thiers's *Histoire de la Révolution française* was a political, military, and diplomatic narrative with only superficial suggestions for the causes and transformations of the Revolution. Legislative debates and resolutions in Paris were his central field of history. The bourgeois legislators played all the great roles of the Revolution, while Michelet's "people" were generally neglected or scorned. The storming of the Bastille was not the action of a loving people, as it was for Michelet, but rather the dangerous, uncontrollable attack of a "mob", of the "rabble."[28] The high points of the Revolution were the actions of the Constituent Assembly from 1789 to 1791 before the unleashing of the unruly, uncivilized popular forces. The idea of modern liberty had been formulated during the Revolution, but there was no lasting expression of it, as the Revolution inevitably proceeded into decay and collapse after the awakening of the lower classes. The positive contributions of the Constituent Assembly, the moderate, constitutional monarchist period of the Revolution, showed that liberty was possible in France, and, although it "has not yet come, it will come."[29]

> The Revolution, which was to give us liberty, and which has prepared everything for our enjoying it some day or other, was not itself, neither could it be, liberty. It was destined to be a great struggle against the old order of things. . . . But so violent a struggle allowed neither the forms nor

the spirit of liberty. For a moment, and but a brief one, the country possessed liberty under the Constituent Assembly; but when the popular party became so menacing as to intimidate public opinion; when it stormed the Tuileries on the tenth of August; when, on the second of September it sacrificed all those of whom it felt distrust; when on the twenty-first of January the popular party forced everyone to compromise themselves by soaking their hands in royal blood . . . when the popular party itself abdicated its power, and resigned it to that great committee of public welfare, composed of twelve individuals—was there, could there be liberty? No![30]


Mignet's history, although far briefer than Thiers's, was more scholarly and more theoretical on the political breakdown of the *ancien régime* and the necessity for a major transformation of society. However, the sentiments of Mignet and Thiers were similar. Once the Revolution began, each phase became inevitable. The Revolution became "as impossible to avoid as to guide it."[31] The Constituent Assembly and the genius of Mirabeau were the zenith of the Revolution, while August 10 "began the dictatorial and arbitrary period of the Revolution" with the popular classes destroying the initial movement for liberty.[32] Mignet's French Revolution ended with Waterloo, by which time liberty had been totally annulled. What was needed in the 1820s was a return to and expansion of the enlightened years of the Constituent Assembly.

After the July Revolution of 1830, French historians began to find new heroes and new high points for the years 1789 to 1794. The interpretative schema of Thiers and Mignet were too narrow and too limited for the next generation of historians who had little sympathy or belief in lasting achievement from a constitutional monarchy. The brief feeling of brotherhood in 1830 rekindled the desire for a free republic, and it was this theoretical aim which united Buchez, Quinet, Lamartine, Blanc, and Michelet. As with Thiers and Mignet, they saw in the French Revolution the germs and often the temporary fruition of their ideals for a future France.

While Frenchmen of the 1830s and 1840s treated their Revolution as a springboard towards a utopia, possible in their own lifetime, the great attack of the period came from across the Channel in Carlyle's 1837 *History of the French Revolution*. As the French historians sought to write more syncretic works and to find further beneficial aspects of the Revolution, Carlyle saw, from beginning to end, the senselessness and chaos of the revolutionary period. The *ancien régime* had been rotten, corrupted, and smelled of decay and decomposition, but the Revolution only substituted one form of anarchy for another:

> For ourselves, we answer that French Revolution means here the open violent Rebellion, and Victory, of disimprisoned Anarchy against corrupt worn-out Authority: how Anarchy breaks prison; bursts up from the infinite Deep,and rages uncontrollable, immeasurable, enveloping a world; in phasis after phasis of fever-frenzy——till the frenzy burning itself out, and what elements of new Order it held developing themselves, the Uncontrollable be got, if not reimprisoned, yet harnassed, and its mad forces made to work toward their object as sane regulated ones. For as Hierarchies and Dynasties of all kinds, Theocracies, Aristocracies, Autocracies, Strumpetocracies, have ruled over the world; so it was appointed, in the decrees of Providence, that this same Victorious Anarchy, Jacobinism, Sansculottism, French Revolution, Horrors of French Revolution, or what else mortals name it, should have its turn.[33]

Carlyle abhorred the doctrine of the rights of men and mocked the vain wish for equality. The Revolution was synonymous with chaos and anarchy. All of the acts from the Bastille to Thermidor were perpetrated by "the people" or "sans-culottism," who ignored all of the values of civilization in their bloody deeds of violence. "The people," in this very broad sense of encompassing nearly all participants, was Carlyle's focus, but his description of them and their merits was the direct opposite of Michelet's conception.

Religious interpretations of the French Revolution were central to Buchez's and Roux's introductions (but primarily ascribed to Buchez) in the *Histoire parlementaire de la Révolution française* and Quinet's 1845 *Le Christianisme et la Révolution française*. For Buchez, the former Saint-Simonian, the Revolution was a socialist and working class revolution with Robespierre the towering hero of the period. The ideas of the "Incorruptible" were the modern day equivalent of the doctrines of Jesus, in which early Christianity witnessed its fulfillment in contemporary civilization. "The Revolution is the final result and the most advanced state of modern civilization, and this civilization came entirely from the Gospels . . . all of the principles that the Revolution inscribed on its flag and in its codes; the words of equality and fraternity."[34]

Unlike Buchez, Quinet neither praised Robespierre nor perceived a worker's uprising in the Revolution. However, Quinet did discern in the first years, 1789 to 1791, the realization of the principles of primitive Christianity. Modern Catholicism, associated with the Jesuits, was a dangerous enemy for Quinet, but the early Church fathers, with their ideas on liberty and equality, were the marvelous discovery of the Revolution. "France and the Revolution offered the alliance of Catholicism; they were reunited . . . The similar developments and association of the primitive Church and of a rejuvenated nation, of the first Christian era and the new, of the principle and the goal, was a beautiful occasion."[35]

Appearing in 1847 along with two volumes of Michelet's history were Lamartine's eight-volume *Histoire des Girondins* and the initial two of Blanc's twelve-volume *Histoire de la Révolution francaise.* Both men, like Buchez, were apologists for various aspects and personages of the Terror. Lamartine did not glorify "the people" but instead wrote rapturously about the great figures of the Revolution such as Vergniaud and Robespierre. He lauded the Girondins and described Robespierre as "the entire incorporation of the Revolution—principles, thoughts, passions, impulses. Thus incorporating himself wholly with it, he compelled it one day to incorporate itself in him."[36] Lamartine did not deprecate the Constituent Assembly at the expense of the later years of the Revolution. As with Thiers and Mignet, the Constituent Assembly was one apogee of the Revolution. "The men of the Constituent Assembly were not Frenchmen, they were universal men . . . they were . . . workmen of God; called by Him to restore social reason, and found right and justice throughout the universe."[37] In contrast with his predecessors, though, Lamartine thought the Revolution progressed further in its accomplishments during the next couple of years. "After the month of April 1791; the march of the revolutionary movement advanced step by step to the complete restoration of all rights of suffering humanity."[38] The leaders of the Revolution, through their speeches, legislative acts, and forging of new institutions, instructed and aided "the people." These great men and not the collective force of "the people," as with Michelet, were Lamartine's main instruments and creators of the Revolution.

Although Louis Blanc was associated with socialism in the 1840s, his history dealt primarily with ideas and politics rather than economics. Three great principles, he thought, explained the origins and development of the French Revolution. The dialectical interplay between authority, individualism, and fraternity unveiled the profound novelties of the Revolution. Authority was the oldest principle, and it signified inequality, blind obedience, Catholicism, the monarchy, and political oppression. Individualism, dating from the ideas of Huss and Luther, became characteristic of the bourgeoisie in the eighteenth century. The first phase of the Revolution in 1789 was the overthrow of authority by individualism, with the proclamation of the Constituent Assembly signaling the triumph of the bourgeoisie. However, this stage of the Revolution was destined to fail, because individualism did not tie man to society; there was "no consideration that public utility should prevail over the religion of individual right."[39] With men acting out of self-interest, the only possible result was anarchy. Fortunately, though, another revolution had begun in the middle of the eighteenth century, when man was harmonized with society in the works of Jean-Jacques Rousseau.

This principle of fraternity, carried on by Rousseau's disciple, Robespierre, inaugurated Blanc's second revolution. From his very first appearance in 1789, Blanc lavishly praised Robespierre as the incarnation of harmony, unity, and fraternity. Unlike the egotism of the bourgeoisie, "Robespierre and the disciples of Jean-Jacques thought . . . that men are bound by a solidarity, a mysterious chain whose first link is fastened to the throne of God; that it is the happiness of the whole human family which furnishes the principles, rules, measure, and justification of rights."[40] Fraternity, evident in the actions of August 4, 1789, did not break through and crush its antithesis of individualism until three years later. The Robespierre reign of reason was the culmination of French history, which Blanc hoped would reappear the following year, 1848, when he personally became involved in another revolution.

Alexis de Tocqueville's 1856 *L'Ancien régime et la révolution* was the last major interpretation of the French Revolution of Michelet's generation. Tocqueville did not dramatize the Revolution nor sanctify "the people," but instead, placidly analyzed the evolution of the institutions from the *ancien régime* until the Napoleonic Empire. The thrust of the Revolution was political and social. "The aim of the Revolution was not, as once was thought, to destroy the authority of the Church and religious faith in general . . . it was essentially a movement for political and social reform . . . it sought to increase the power and jurisdiction of the central authority."[41]

Tocqueville's political and social analyses indicated to him that there was very little innovation during the Revolution. The institutions of the dying monarchy were crumbling, but, at the same time, the foundations of the new institutions had been erected before the convocation of the Estates-General. Although the revolutionary leaders thought of themselves as creators, Tocqueville thought they were merely reusing the structural remains of the past. "For I am convinced that though they had no inkling of this, they took over from the old regime not only most of its customs, conventions, and modes of thought, but even those very ideas which prompted our revolutionaries to destroy it; . . . they used the debris of the old order for building up the new."[42] Once the anarchy of the years 1792 to 1794 was ended (similarly to Thiers and Mignet, Tocqueville only admired the early years), it became easy for Napoleon to take over the centralized, administrative structure, begun by the *ancien régime* and fortified by the Revolution. However, Napoleon strengthened this centralization far beyond the wildest dreams of either a Louis XVI or a Robespierre. "Thus there arose, within a nation that had but recently laid low its monarchy, a central authority with powers wider, stricter, and more absolute than those which any French King had ever wielded."[43]

Tocqueville's calm dispassionate reasoning was stylistically antipodal to Michelet's intense personalization of history. Michelet's lyrical and frenetic dramatization of the French Revolution, although anathema to many scientific and positivistic historians, imbibed that period of history with a vitality and life worthy of a great playwright. The emotions and passions of men leapt from his hurriedly written pages. But this awe-inspiring work, what Gérard Walter called a "captivating enigma, an irritating miracle," was far more than a romantic re-creation of high hopes and battered dreams.[44] As in his *Histoire de France* and other works, Michelet's literary genius was combined in the *Histoire de la*

*Révolution française* with a refined philosophical and moral interpretation of history.

Michelet's lofty rhetoric and personal identification with the fortunes of France added luster and excitement to an all-embracing theoretical conception of the French Revolution. In order to derive the nature of this epoch he had to study not only the documents but also had to analyze his own mental framework, which had been so decisively influenced by this unique event. "I commune with my own mind. I interrogate myself as to my teaching, my history, and its all-powerful interpreter,—the spirit of the Revolution . . . . The Revolution lives in ourselves,—in our souls; it has no outward movement."[45] Michelet felt that in the Revolution, "France became conscious of herself."[46] Unlike Carlyle's hate-filled tirade against the ubiquitous evil, violence, and anarchy of the French Revolution, Michelet discerned the "utterly pacific, benevolent, loving character of the Revolution."[47]

Louis Blanc had formulated a triadic structure for his interpretation of the Revolution—authority, individualism, and fraternity—but for Michelet two world views explained the upheaval and transformation of French society. "I see upon the stage but two grand facts, two principles, two actors, and two persons, Christianity and the Revolution."[48] In his opening passages Michelet showed the theoretical differences between Christianity and the Revolution. "I define the Revolution,—The advent of the Law, the resurrection of Right, and the reaction of Justice."[49] Michelet contrasted the meaning of these key terms for the philosophy of a loving Revolution with the principles of the Middle Ages and *ancien régime.* This comparison was essential, according to Michelet, because the major question and departure point for an interpretation of the French Revolution was: "Is the Revolution Christian or Anti-Christian?"[50]

> This question, historically, logically, precedes every other. It reaches and penetrates even those which might be believed to be exclusively political. All the institutions of the civil order which the Revolution met with, had either emanated from Christianity, or were traced upon its forms, and authorized by it. Religious or political, the two questions are deeply, inextricably intermingled.[51]

*151*

Initially Michelet's solution to the problem of Christianity and the Revolution was complexly stated. "The Revolution continues Christianity, and it contradicts it. It is, at the same time, its heir and its adversary."[52] Grudgingly Michelet admitted that the "sentiment of human fraternity" was common to each of them.[53] But, beyond this single comparison, Michelet uncompromisingly revealed the glaring differences between Christianity, and what he considered to be the new religion, the Revolution. Since the early 1840s Michelet and been severing himself from his previous identification with and admiration of the Middle Ages and Christianity. In the *Histoire de la Révolution française* the full force of his complete break sprang forth in a bitter and scathing denunciation of the ideals propagated by Christianity. The loving nature of the Revolution arose from the ashes of harmful, burnt-out Christianity. By personally associating his own heritage with the Revolution, Michelet was able to dissociate himself totally from the values and morality of the Middle Ages and Christianity.

The Revolution, at variance with Christianity, founded "fraternity on the love of man for man, on mutual duty,—on Right and Justice."[54] Thus, even the one common sentiment of fraternity was antithetically formulated by the two religions. Christian justice was characterized by its very arbitrariness. Prior to the French Revolution, grace was selective, summarily excluding most Frenchmen—selective both from a secular viewpoint of the privileges of the various estates and the arbitrary power of the king in granting favors and from a religious viewpoint in the sense of salvation—only a few were saved. In the moral and religious overthrow of Christianity in 1789 and 1790, the previous secular legal standards and the relgious controls over men were shattered and replaced by the new religious principles of equal law and equal justice. The law became the same for all Frenchmen, engendering the crowning novelty of the Revolution, justice. With the end of selectivity, *all* men were saved, and fraternity could emerge between all Frenchmen. Justice "twice proscribed and banished" by grace and favor "burst forth" after six centuries of frustration "in the year 1789."[55] "The Revolution is nothing but the tardy reaction of justice against the government of favor and the religion of grace.[56] In a letter of 1854 Michelet recalled his philosophical differentiation of the two religions. "At the gravest moment of my life, the death of my father, I formulated the precise manner of the antagonism of the ancient faith and the new."[57]

Michelet's vision of the Revolution as a new religion replacing the old religion of Christianity sharply separated his orientation towards the past from his friend Quinet, Buchez, Lamartine, and even Tocqueville, who thought that the religious question itself was secondary to political and social reforms. As in his *Histoire de France* Michelet felt the necessity to attack the other historians in order to show the uniqueness of his own version. "Several eminent writers," he mocked, "with a laudable wish for peace and reconciliation, have lately affirmed that the Revolution was but the accomplishment of Christianity."[58] One of the worst offenders was Buchez and his colleague Roux who hypothesized "that the Catholic tradition perpetuated itself in the Revolution. In order to defend this paradox, one would have to believe that the Revolution . . . was identical to what it thought was the opponent; which is nothing less than to make the Revolution seem idiotic and imbecilic."[59] Immediately after the publication of Lamartine's *Histoire des Girondins* Michelet wrote him:

> I am committed openly, as you know, against the present Church for the Church of the future which I see appearing on the horizon. It would be impossible for me not to attack your tolerance of the old Church as you pass over its role and the crimes of the *ancien régime* and its guilty defenders who prevented the new Church from bearing fruit.[60]

For the first time, the ideas of Michelet and Quinet clearly diverged as Quinet persisted in viewing the Revolution as a rekindling and fulfillment of the ideas of early Christianity.

To buttress his philosophical and religious synthesis of French history Michelet reinquired into the religious nature of the Middle Ages. Instead of a France progressing slowly towards harmony and unity, Michelet now described a Nietzsche-like transvaluation of values and morals under the evil guidance of Christianity. Progress and freedom were totally retarded as man was forced "to entrust himself blindly to the hands of Grace."[61] As in *The Genealogy of Morals,* Christianity attempted to co-opt and invert the true meaning of moral precepts. For Nietzsche,

*153*

it was good and evil; for Michelet, liberty and justice. "I have lived too many centuries in face of thee (Christianity) throughout the Middle Ages, for thee ever to deceive me. After having so long denied justice and liberty, thou didst assume their name for thy shout of war. In their name thou didst work a rich mine of hate."[62] The priestly people plotted against humanity, manipulating the minds of people and forming phony "establishments of gluttony, termed Brotherhoods."[63] Their easiest prey were women and children. And in their wholesale propagation of an evil morality, agents of Christianity attacked and killed men of other beliefs, and then had the outrageous audacity "to baptize this pious assassination with the name of *justice of the people.*"[64] The reversal of values was only corrected with the new religion of the Revolution.

Fortunately, true justice was not crushed completely in the six hundred years before the Revolution. It always managed to survive, usually in the ideas of great intellectuals. In the eighteenth century "the government of grace" was assaulted by three men: Montesquieu, Voltaire, and Rousseau. Here, Michelet sided with all of his contempories, except Tocqueville, in suggesting that primarily ideas triggered the French Revolution. Montesquieu interpreted "the law," although Michelet did not like his English bias; Voltaire witnessed "right" and showed there was no "religion without justice, without humanity"; and Rouseau wrote that "Right is sovereign of the world."[65] These men, the theoretical vanguards of the Revolution, bequeathed the new definitions of law, right, and justice which would unite together and define the novel synthesis of the French Revolution. To be sure, economic problems such as famine and the squandering of money by the court accelerated the decline of the monarchy, but ideas generated the moral and religious transformation of French society.[66] With the proper meanings of law, right, and justice inaugurated by the new religion—the Revolution—grace and love became identical, and Michelet could now praise the true transvaluation of values:

> What is the old regime, the king and the priest in the old monarchy? Tyranny, in the name of Grace.
> What is the Revolution? The reaction of equity, the tardy advent of Eternal Justice.

O Justice, my mother! Right, my father! Ye who are but one with
God! . . .

O Justice, pardon me! I believed you were austere and hard-hearted, and
I did not perceive that you were identical with Love and Grace. And that is
why I have been no enthusiast of the Middle Ages, which have ever
repeated the word Love without performing the offices of Love.[67]

From the convocation of the Estates-General in 1789 until the climax
of the Revolution, the Festival of the Federation, on July 14, 1790,
Michelet followed the gradual fruition of his theoretical interpretation of
the Revolution. This period witnessed the birth and development of a
new religion. Michelet's imagery for the key events of this year was filled
with references to Genesis and Bethlehem. The origins of the French
Revolution were apparently as monumental and eternal as those of
Judaism and Christianity. Instead of Jewish prophets or Jesus formulat-
ing the doctrines, precepts, or tenets and epitomizing the central values
and beliefs of the new religion, Michelet discovered "the people" as the
fount and matrix of the new religion. The Estates-General marked "the
true era of the birth of the people."[68] Their life cycle, of birth and
growth, paralleled the biblical imagery for the first year of the Revolution. In another sense, "the people" became, for Michelet, the "world
spirit" of the revolutionary years. In them resided the varying fortunes of
the Revolution since they were at the center of history. Throughout the
Middle Ages, the Church, then various monarchs, and Joan of Arc had
imbibed, in his *Histoire de France,* the "world spirit." Now, the "world
spirit," having never left France, despite his reinterpretation of the past,
turned and twisted its way into "the people" as they moved towards the
culmination of the new religion, the Festival of the Federation.

The Jeu de Paume, resembling Jesus' birthplace, was the ideal building for beginning the new religion. It was "a miserable, ugly, poor, and
unfurnished building, but the better on that account. The Assembly also
was poor, and represented the people, on that day . . . It was like the
manger of the new religion,—its stable of Bethlehem!"[69] This unfurnished room permitted no hiding places "where the dreams of the past
can yet find shelter. Let, therefore, the pure spirit of Reason and Justice,
that king of the future, reign here!"[70]

The taking of the Bastille attained "what is morally the highest degree of order,—unanimity of feeling."[71] This was the first major act of "the people," and it was related by Michelet in Old Testament imagery. "A light broke upon every mind, and the same voice thrilled through every heart: 'Go! and thou shalt take the Bastille!' That was impossible, unreasonable, preposterous. And yet everybody believed it. And the thing was done."[72] Michelet's dramatic retelling of the storming of the Bastille within a religious framework conveyed the origins of the new faith. Not just a few Parisians took part, but everybody, all of "the people," felt the magnitude of the moment and acted as brothers. Even in George Rudé's modern, scientific analysis of the participants, after showing that only eight or nine hundred people took the Bastille, he then agreed with Michelet's general characterization. "Yet, in a wider sense, we may agree with Michelet that the capture of the Bastille was not just the affair of those few hundred citizens of the Saint-Antoine quarter who were most immediately involved, but of the people of Paris as a whole."[73]

Throughout the summer months of 1789 the National Assembly convened to discuss and reformulate the rights of man. For Michelet, the legislators, as representatives of the will of "the people," became the new religious and secular royalty. "The question was to give from above, by virtue of a sovereign, imperial, pontifical authority, the credo of the new age."[74] These legislators had to make legal what "the people" already felt on matters of right, law and justice. They were the prophets presenting their constituents with the legal codes of the new religion. "It was the philosophy of the age, its legislator, its Moses, descending from the mount, with the rays of glory on its brow, and bearing the tables of the law in its hands."[75] The Declaration of Rights guaranteed the new human morality based upon rights, duty, law, and justice. "The people" already knew and acted according to the standards of the new age. They had possessed these principles when they stormed the Bastille. In the countryside "the peasants did not need metaphysical formulae in order to rise in arms."[76] Nevertheless, although "the people," as bearers of the new morality, had precipitated the legal debates and constitution-making, the actions of August 4, 1789 symbolized the legal end of the old religion and the beginning of the new. "That 4th of August, at eight in the evening, was a solemn hour in which feudality, after a reign of a thousand years, abdicates, abjures, and condemns itself."[77] Late that night, the future unity of France, emblazoned with the principles of the Revolution, first appeared. "That night dispelled forever the long and painful dream of the thousand years of the Middle Ages. The approaching dawn was that of liberty! Since that marvelous night, no more classes, but Frenchmen; no more provinces, but one France!"[78]

On August 4 occured "the resurrection of the people"; it was "the first miracle . . . of this new Gospel!"[79] With the Revolution firmly established and "the people" aroused to their role, the course of events became impossible to change. Individuals tried to guide the Revolution or to change its direction, but the power of the new religion under the aegis of "the people" was unstoppable. The principles and forces of the Revolution in 1789 and 1790 trampled all opposition. "All were ignorant of the situation, all overlooked the general force of things, and attributed events to some person or other, ridiculously exaggerating individual power."[80] The "general force of things," embodied in "the people," was carrying the Revolution inexorably towards the Festival of the Federation.

The Festival of the Federation held at the Champ-de-Mars in Paris on July 14, 1790, was the pinnacle of the French Revolution. Local federations of brotherhood and of adherence to the new religion took place for eight or nine months before this, the largest celebration. For Michelet, the appearance of the various federations was "the stamp of originality of that period."[81] Initially, many of the small towns formed federations as a defensive measure against the resistance of nobles. As word of other federations resounded throughout the country, "the people" of France began to take the offensive and to relish in their new found harmony. The new Jerusalem gradually uniting them was "the Jerusalem of hearts, the holy unity of fraternity, the great living city, made of men. It was built in less than a year, and since then has been called *patrie*."[82] The capture of the Bastille had showed only the unanimity of Paris, but the federations manifested the unanimity of France.

Priests, nobles, and local parliaments attempted to forestall the increasing movement of unity, but they were unsuccessful. "The people" of France had abandoned egotism and had begun to act according to the high and mighty unselfish principles of the Revolution. The feverish momentum of the Revolution swept aside all dissenters or else ensnared them in the net of harmony. "The Revolution was so powerful in its nature, and so buoyant in its spirit, that every new event, whether for or against it, ever favored it ultimately and impelled it still faster."[83] The counterrevolution, the old faith, was helpless against the tide of the new religion. So overpowering did the new religion become in early 1790 that even the old faith was influenced by the collective psychology of the nation; by the "general force of things." "What rendered the counterrevolution generally powerless, was that it . . . possessed at heart, the philosophy of the age, that is to say, the Revolution itself."[84]

By quelling the counterrevolution, the Revolution saw that it was truly a religion. "And the counterrevolution, dissenting and discordant, attests the old faith in vain . . . It has no unity, no fixed principle . . . It staggers like a drunken man."[85] The new faith of the Revolution was the realization of the principles of France, and, as the great Federation approached, Michelet cautioned unbelievers in words reminiscent of Rousseau's application of the general will to the constitution of Poland: "One France, one faith, one oath! Here no doubtful man must remain. If you wish to remain wavering, depart from the land of loyalty, pass the Rhine, and cross over the Alps."[86]

The prime characteristic of the federations was their "spontaneous organization." The "world spirit" was in them alone during the first seven months of 1790. "That is history, the real, the positive, and the durable; and the rest is insignificant."[87] Legislators watched and followed, but did not lead the federations. By July 1790 the spontaneous, leaderless fraternal unions had removed all obstcles to unity. In his *Histoire de France* Michelet forecast the end of all *fatalités* and the ineluctable harmony of France. Now, for the first time, with the Festival of the Federation, Michelet perceived the concerted, selfless, unity of all Frenchmen; far transcending personal and regional differences. "Where, then, are the old distinctions of provinces and races of men? Where those powerful and geographical contrasts? All have disappeared: geography itself is annihilated. There are no longer any mountains, rivers, or barriers between men."[88] The jubilant fruition of this summit of French and world history had germinated originally because of the loving nature of the Revolution. For a moment, in July, "time and space, those material conditions to which life is subject, are no more."[89]

The General Federation in Paris was the moral symbol and embodiment of the new religion. Michelet's lifelong dream of multiplicity within unity was achieved on that day. Men of all classes, parties, religions, regions, fortunes, and origins were overcome by the emotion of *patrie*—of love, brotherhood, justice, and grace for all Frenchmen. "The whole possesses an extraordinary charm: the great diversity—provincial, local, urban, rural, etc.,—in the most perfect unity."[90] Despite a heavy rainstorm, hundreds of thousands of Frenchmen gathered together at the monument of the Revolution, the empty field of the Champ-de-Mars, to pledge themselves to the unity and harmony of "the Universal Church," the Revolution.

For Michelet, the description of this event was one of his most exciting moments as a historian:

> I am endeavoring to describe today that epoch of unanimity, that holy period, when a whole nation, free from all party distinction, as yet a comparative stranger to the opposition of classes, marched together under a flag of brotherly love. Nobody can behold that marvelous unanimity, in which the self-same heart beat together in the breasts of twenty millions of men, without returning thanks to God. These are the sacred days of the world—thrice happy days for history. For my part, I have had my reward, in the mere narration of them. Never, since the composition of my Maid of Orleans, have I received such a ray from above, such a vivid inspiration from Heaven.[91]

During the Festival of the Federation the vapors of love, justice, and law coalesced and enveloped all Frenchmen, as they experienced for a moment, the central core of the future France. "On that day, everything was possible. All divisions ceased; there was no longer either nobility, citizens, or people. The future was present. That is to say, time itself was no more. It was a flash of eternity."[92]

# 12

## And One Man In His Time
## Plays Many Parts

The unfolding of Michelet's dramatic version of the French Revolution had all of the trappings, including the pretentious bombast, of a great romantic play. The dominant imagery throughout the *Histoire de la Révolution française*, perhaps reflecting his current ideas on a new culture, was visual. Michelet filled his historical stage with vividly colored representations of the dramatis personae, despite his continual emphasis on "the people" as his only hero. Fortunately, his not wanting to personify the Revolution in men, as Lamartine had done, did not prevent Michelet from drawing portraits of innumerable individuals, groups, and clubs. "The people" were but one actor—and Michelet used that word frequently—in the initial rise, fulfillment, then slow, painful collapse of the loving spirit of the Revolution. Mirabeau, the Constituent Assembly, and Louis XVI; the Jacobins, Girondins, and Cordeliers; Marat, Danton, and Robespierre—each of them made their entrance and exit; enlivening the stage with the passion and drama of the Revolution. Each character went through his own development, ending, in most cases, in death. "The most tragic subject that history offers us, is certainly Robespierre. But it is also the most comic. Shakespeare offers us nothing comparable."[1] As with his depiction of Robespierre, Michelet often spoke of the Shakespearean quality of the Revolution, fully aware that this five-year upheaval, this tragedy in five acts, had outlived its prime participants. The chorus or "people" swayed with the rhythm of the Revolution, while the players moved forward to center stage when it was their turn to be at the forefront of history. Assemblies, clubs, and individuals may not have personified the Revolution, but, at the very least, they personified the varying moods of the Revolution. Without all of these richly woven characters, alternately dominating the action then receding to the background, Michelet's French Revolution would only have been a pale replica of its original self, but his imaginative and complex fashioning of this cast was probably the crowning achievement of this work.

Michelet's personal involvement with his characters was total. Statements such as, "I hope to kill Mirabeau tomorrow," were common in his diary and letters, as he concurrently composed the text.[2] In a posthumously published conclusion to the *Histoire de la Révolution française* Michelet passionately indicated his close attachment to the major individuals in his work:

> Throughout this work, which was my life and internal world for ten years, I made, on my way, among these re-created and reborn deaths, some very dear friendships which affected my heart. Then, when they were mine, when I had already lived with their genius and in exhilarating familiarity with them, I had to break them, to wrench them from myself. Can one believe that it didn't cost me anything to immolate Mirabeau? How much more I loved the Gironde, its glorious crusade for the liberties of the earth! . . . But my greatest heartbreak was to leave Danton. Who will ever know what it cost me to admit, towards the end, his moral fall, his equivocations, his fears, his duplicity?[3]

Danton was particularly difficult for Michelet to criticize. But, in varying degrees, Michelet felt that he had respect and compassion for all of the actors of the Revolution. "None of the great actors of the Revolution left me cold. Did I not live with them, did I not follow each of them as a faithful companion, to the core of their thought, and through their transformations?"[4]

By admitting Danton's "moral fall" and by following each individual "through their transformations," Michelet was adhering to his methodological ideas on describing men. From time to time in his *Histoire de la Révolution française*, Michelet stated that he always characterized individuals in a complex manner by illuminating both attributes and defects. His portraits of the leaders of the French Revolution were not static representations dependent upon religious, political, or social bias. Instead, Michelet consciously attempted to present the intricate, multi-leveled, and often contradictory, nature of each man. Michelet psychologized individuals, groups, and clubs. His individuals might mature, alter roles, or degenerate, and in each event or situation, a different aspect of their personality would emerge. Michelet captured the essence of his method in a passage comparing his historical portraiture to the style of Rembrandt:

> We have judged actions as they have occurred day by day, and hour by hour. We have noted our prejudices; and these have permitted us to frequently praise some men while blaming them harshly later. The forgetful and stern reviewer often condemns praiseworthy beginnings because he knows the ending ahead of time. But we don't want to consider this end in advance; whatever this man could do tomorrow, we will still mark to his advantage the good that he has done today; the bad will come soon enough: let him have his day of innocence . . .
>
> . . . It would be unfair for such a changeable creature as man to be stereotyped by one definitive portrait: Rembrandt made thirty portraits of himself, I believe, all resembling each other, all different. I have followed this method; art and justice counseled me equally. If one takes the trouble to follow in these two volumes each of the great historic actors, one will see that each of them has a whole gallery full of sketches, each one made at a particular time, according to the physical and moral modifications the individual had undergone. The Queen and Mirabeau appear and reappear, five or six times, looking distinctly different on each occasion. Marat appears in the same manner, under different aspects, all of them accurate, though dissimilar. The timid and sickly Robespierre, scarcely seen in '89, is drawn in November '90, in profile, at the rostrum of the Jacobins: we drawn him frontally (in May '91) in the National Assembly, with a rather masterful air, dogmatic, already threatening.
>
> We have then dated carefully and minutely, the men and the subjects, and the moments of each man.
>
> We have already stated and repeated a word which has remained prominent in our mind and which has dominated this book: *History is time.* [5]

Frequently, Michelet studied paintings of revolutionary leaders, hoping to sense their various internal forces and moral dimensions. Through these pictures, writings, and actions, Michelet tried to describe the "moral modifications" and variety of poses of each individual, thereby unraveling and evincing the maze-like threads of "the inner man."[6]

One result, Michelet often surmised, from his method of carefully dissecting the many parts of individuals, was the dilution of their supposed greatness. At the end of his work, Michelet wondered whether he had "reduced, because of the extraordinarily thorough anatomy of people, the grandeur of heroic men who, in '93 and '94, sustained the faltering Revolution through their indomitable personalities?"[7] In his questioning Michelet seemed to fear that his psychological studies of the attributes, weaknesses, and mistakes of the leaders, automatically lowered their stature for himself and for his readers. Since Michelet, in all of his writings, preferred units of wholeness as a goal or final value, his assumptions of individual reduction were, at least, personally valid. Individuals united with France, the ultimate amalgamation of unity and fullness, only in their highest and most selfless moments. Michelet realized that inner divisiveness and inability to merge totally with France became apparent when he revealed the faults and contradictions within a man. Individuals were "secondary" in relation to France in Michelet's philosophy, and the further evidence of a man's lack of unity could only diminish his importance.[8]

"The people," the hero of the *Histoire de la Révolution française*, were the large, amorphous unit of wholeness. A thorough description of them unearthed neither divisions, duplicity, nor disharmony. Who were "the people," Michelet's hero, who apparently communicated rather than received the ideas of the Revolution? How did they act? As in *Le Peuple* Michelet did not define "the people" precisely. Most often, they seemed to be the illiterate. When speaking of some workers, for example, Michelet added: "Several are already literate rather than people."[9] While the composition of "the people" was not analyzed by Michelet, he did scorn those historians who attempted to categorize "the people" or separate them from the rest of society. France simply could not be divided into "property-holders and non-property-holders, or between the rich and the poor" as "the authors of *Histoire parlementaire*" had done.[10] Contemporary social interpretations, Michelet felt, while perhaps relevant to the France of 1848, were not at all applicable to the Revolution. Buchez, Roux, and other socialists had confounded grievously the nineteenth-century concept, "the working class," with "the people." "The big cities, the working class, absorb all of the attention of the authors of the *Histoire parlementaire*. They forget one essential factor. This class was not yet born."[11]

Another type of mistaken assumption, this one advanced by Blanc, was the dualism of French society. In positing two revolutions, the individualistic-bourgeois and then the fraternal-people phase, Blanc had tried to separate revolutionary France into two hostile groups. Michelet noted, however, as he had in *Le Peuple* for the France of the 1840s, that "the people" and the bourgeoisie could not be distinguished distinctly for the French Revolution. France was only one; at least that was her aim, and any interpretation, like Blanc's, which prevented this goal *ab initio* was incorrect and anathema to Michelet.

"The people" in the *Histoire de la Révolution française*, as in *Le Peuple*, represented, in the highest sense, France. They were a unit of wholeness which could not be divided, because their major moments of participation in the French Revolution were only during the culminating events reflecting French unity. When "the people" symbolized France, they could not, as in Rousseau's idea of the general will, err. In fact, during the Festival of the Federation, there were no people, only Frenchmen.

In addition to the Festival of the Federation further high points for "the people" and for France were: the storming of the Bastille, the October 1789 march on Versailles, the preparations for war in 1792, and August 10, 1792. In each instance, the qualities and characteristice of these events were similar. These key moments of the Revolution had all arisen "spontaneously" and had been led by "the people." After any one of these periods, the Constituent Assembly or some other body may have made new laws, but the psychic reality of the situation had already been expressed. Everyone took part in these instinctively impelled actions. As with the federations, after they had gained momentum, "all" men became involved. In the taking of the Bastille "all of Paris" participated; the decision of October 6 "was unanimous" among those who went to Versailles; the main influence of the war movement was in "the people," "everyone finding the sentiment for it in himself"; August 10 "was a great act of France . . . .It wasn't done, as has been said, by the rabble, but truly by the people, by which I mean a mixed mass of all kinds of men: soldiers and civilians, workers and bourgeois, Parisians and provincials."[12] When "the people" acted as one with France they were comprised not only of the illiterate, but of all Frenchmen, as on July 14, 1790 and August 10, 1792. And Michelet described with impassioned pleasure these rare occurrences when "the people" manifested wholeness and unity.

Since "the people" were Michelet's symbol of France, no negative aspects could be ascribed to them. They were all present during the majestic attainments of the Revolution, but were *never* involved in the nadirs. Both quantitatively, in numbers, and qualitatively, in actions, Michelet was emphatic in showing "the people" unrelated to the horrors of the Revolution:

> A thing to be told to everybody, and which it is but too easy to prove, is that the humane and benevolent period of our Revolution had for its actors the very people, the whole people,—everybody. And the period of violence, the period of sanguinary deeds, into which danger afterwards thrust it, had for actors but an inconsiderable, an extremely small number of men.
>
> That is what I have found established and verified, either by written testimony, or by such as I have gathered from the lips of old men.
>
> The remarkable exclamation of a man who belonged to the Faubourg Saint-Antoine will never die: "We were all of us at the 10th of August, and not one at the 2nd of September."[13]

All of Paris was aroused on July 14, 1789; all of France on July 14, 1790; August 10 was an act of all Frenchmen; but during the September massacres, "the people" stayed away while "three or four hundred" misfits bloodied the good name of France.[14] Only the great events had a large number of actors, while the violent, harmful events had not only a small amount of individuals, but also none of them even belonged to "the people." For one Michelet summit, the 1792 élan for war, he described the dramatic, tearful meeting of Frenchmen, embracing each other as brothers and expressing their immense faith in fighting together for France—a meeting, according to Walter, which did not exist except in "the unquenchable imagination of Michelet."[15]

Although Michelet glorified "the people" he did not think they aspired to equality during the Revolution. Lamartine had written of the desire for equality among "the people"; an interpretation Michelet opposed.[16] Liberty, far more than equality, appeared to Michelet as the fundamental aim of the French people during the revolutionary period. Occasionally during 1789 and 1790 debates on equality, Michelet would interject his own opinion to show disfavor with the propagators of equality. In his judgments Michelet would reveal not only a realistic hesitancy towards permitting "the people" to vote, especially after having witnessed the election results of December 1848, but also an attitude, unlike his formal, methodological statements, in which "the people" apparently did not know what they were doing or how to act. In a passage written in 1847, or before the peasantry all voted for Louis-Napoleon, Michelet questioned the wisdom of allowing the majority of "the people" to vote:

> On the 22nd of October, the Assembly decreed that nobody could be an elector unless he paid in direct taxes, as proprietor or tenant, the value of three days' labor.
> With that one line, they swept away from the hands of the aristocracy, a million rural electors.
> Of the five or six hundred electors produced by universal suffrage, there remained four millions four hundred thousand proprietors or tenants.
> Grégoire, Duport, Robespierre, and other worshipers of the ideal, objected, but in vain, that men were equal and ought therefore all to vote according to the dictates of natural law. Two days previously, Montlosier, the royalist, had likewise proved that all men are equal.
> In the crisis in which they then were, nothing could have been more futile and fatal than this thesis of natural law. These Utopists thus bestowed a million electors on the enemies of equality in the name of equality.[17]

Rejecting the thesis of the drive for equality among "the people" and even manifesting a personal disapproval of this desire was only one instance when Michelet showed his distrust of "the people." Another area of discord appeared during the trial of Louis XVI when he questioned the wisdom of "the people" as a moral judge. In this broad, reflective passage Michelet's ambivalence towards "the people" and their instinctive, anti-intellectual qualities, again emerged:

Yes, throughout the centuries, the voice of the people, on the whole, is undoubtedly the voice of God; but for one occasion, for one place, for one particular affair, who would dare claim that the people are infallible?

In judicial proceedings especially, the judgment of the great crowds is singularly fallible. Take some juries with a few men of the people and quickly isolate them from the passion of the day; they naively follow good sense and reason. But the people as a whole, are the least certain, perhaps the most dangerous of judges. A great risk, foreign to all reasoning, rides on these violent and uncertain decisions; no one knows what will come from this immense urn in which storms lie buried. Civil war will come from them sooner than justice.[18]

Despite the frequent admission that "the people" were his principal hero and his leading actor for the Revolution, a strange contradiction surfaced in this section on the sagacity of "the people." Although "the people" generated the high points of the Revolution, usually through their instinctive wisdom, Michelet did not want them to acquire equality nor did he trust them to take part in the judicial process during the Revolution. In these cases, reflection and intelligence, not spontaneity and immediacy, were the superior attributes.

Aside from "the people" there were numerous other players of the revolutionary period. Although Michelet denied it, did he have any other heroes? Despite his methodological statements, did certain privileged leaders speak for "the people"? As in *Le Peuple* there was a continual tension in the interaction between the men of instinct and the men of reflection, where only the genius approached a synthesis of the two, thereby merging with France. Were there any geniuses during Michelet's French Revolution who combined the wisdom of the educated and the spontaneity of the illiterate and who spoke not only for "the people" but also for the new religion and France? Only a genius could escape from the divided and secondary nature of individuals and achieve fullness through representing France, undivided. The true genius, in a Hegelian sense, would have to appear continually in the forefront of history, and for Michelet, this was no mean task.

The question of heroes, a perennial focus of debate, was paramount among the historians of Michelet's generation. Blanc's apology for Robespierre and Michelet's for Danton began the major historical controversy over the great men and visionaries of the Revolution. Michelet praised Danton as well as Desmoulins, Chalier, and the Paris Commune. Was Danton, as Blanc suggested, Michelet's real hero, instead of "the people"? Did Danton fulfill the criteria Michelet established for a hero of France?

A Michelet hero had to symbolize the new religion of the Revolution. Therefore, men or groups could not have divided loyalties, nor represent an external force or internal antagonist. Moreover, even if committed to the new religion, a hero could not be a partial representative of France, namely, by speaking only for some Frenchmen or by espousing such causes as decentralization theories. Mirabeau, the National Assembly, the Jesuits, England, the Vendée, Louis XVI, the Girondins, and Robespierre were the best examples of these mistaken or incomplete visions. Danton, the greatest individual of Michelet's *Histoire de la Révolution française*, possessed none of these defects. Internal threats and external obstacles were the foci for many of Michelet's chapters, as the omnipresent heretics attempted to extinguish the fresh flames of the new religion.

During the 1920s Mirabeau was seen as the premier hero of the French Revolution. Thiers and Mignet portrayed him as the epitome of Enlightenment thought. Even Carlyle stopped his tirade against the Revolution long enough to praise Mirabeau as "the chosen man of France . . . who shook old France from its basis; and, as if with his single hand, has held it toppling there, still unfallen. What things depended on that one man!"[19] With Mirabeau's death "the French Monarchy may now therefore be considered as, in all human probability, lost; as struggling henceforth in blindness and will as weakness, the last light of reasonable guidance having gone out."[20] By the 1840s, however, the exalted position of Mirabeau was no longer accepted, and he began to lose forever, to new heroes, the prestige that once was his alone. Blanc could not resist emphasizing Mirabeau's sudden accumulation of wealth during the Revolution. In attacking Mirabeau, Blanc facetiously noted: "He was a man to give heroic proportions even to baseness."[21]

In theoretical terms conforming to his philosophy of the Revolution, Michelet deflated the exaggerated greatness of Mirabeau. Mirabeau, according to Michelet, was tragically caught between the two religions. "He wanted to save two things—royalty and liberty; believing royalty itself to be a guarantee of liberty."[22] Unfortunately, Mirabeau was not far-sighted enough to realize the fundamental incompatibility of the old and new faiths. A Michelet hero must have a unitary vision, for individual genius was worthless if "in that man ideas are warring together, if principles and doctrines carry on a furious struggle in his bosom."[23] Mirabeau was this type of genius. He was "contradiction personified. What was he in reality? A royalist, a noble in the most absolute sense. And what was his action? Exactly the contrary; he shattered royalty with the thunders of his eloquence."[24] Mirabeau's attempt to straddle two differing world views was doomed to failure. Initially, he led the National Assembly into the bright, but unknown sunshine of the future, but uncertainty and doubt cast him "back upon what was called the old order—true anarchy and a real chaos. From that fruitless struggle he was saved by death."[25]

If Mirabeau, one of the great representatives to the National Assembly, or what was later called the Constituent Assembly, was divided between two competing world views, then the other members certainly had to have comparable or even more serious theoretical misunderstandings. The National Assembly was not a homogeneous body, committed to the principles of the new religion. All types of views and ideas were present. "Created before the great Revolution which had just taken place, it was profoundly heterogeneous and confused, like the chaos of the *ancien régime*, whence it sprang."[26] This form of heterogeneity was distasteful to Michelet, who wanted all of the legislators to represent the new principles of France. Because of this harmful conflict of viewpoints, Michelet often described the Assembly as "floating," "divided," or "wavering." Other groups, most notably "the people," through their feelings and actions, forced the Assembly to make new laws. Followers rather than leaders, the National Assembly representatives, nevertheless, served the useful function of "the recorder of France."[27] Often, in their debates, the legislators were unable to come to a consensus or to make a decision. Michelet's methodological device for arousing the Assembly from their torpor was to have a member dramatically stand up and set forth what Michelet considered to be the desired course of action. Suddenly, the Assembly would become quiet. Realizing that he was expressing the opinion of "the people", of "all" Frenchmen, the legislators would accept his position immediately. In this manner, the ideas and emotions of "the people" were made known, then accepted, and recorded as the law of the new France.

Mirabeau and the National Assembly were caught between the two faiths, but the Jesuits, priests, Vendée, England, Europe, and Louis XVI were the persisting tentacles of the old religion, trying to hold onto a vestige of the past. These internal and external threats to the new religion continually attempted to thwart the progress and success of the Revolution. The Jesuits and England were long-time enemies of France, who merely continued their antagonistic methods. Europe was a new opponent. In the first years of the Revolution, France had opened up her arms to the world in love and brotherhood, but had been rejected by, what Michelet perceived to be, the anachronistic monarchical regimes of Europe. England, the great power of Europe, actively and successfully convinced her fellow nations of the evil and corruption that had befallen France. Therefore, France, despite the loving nature of her new faith, was forced to go to war with Europe.

Fear and hatred continued to be widespread in the new France of 1789 and 1790. One principal cause of this unwarranted fear was the false propaganda circulated by the Jesuits and their blind spokesmen, French priests. The bourgeoisie, meanwhile, copied the English in their individualistic, egotistical ways, devoid of self-sacrifice. "To the simple, credulous crowd, to the woman and the peasant, the priest has given the opium of the Middle Ages, troubling the mind with wicked dreams. The bourgeois had drunk English opium with all its ingredients of egotism . . . and liberty without sacrifice."[28] In Avignon in 1791, the major battle was between France and the priests. Throughout the country confrontations ensued, pitting the advocates of the new religion against the remnants of the old.

The best example of priest infiltration and control was afforded by the famous counterrevolution in the Vendée. For Michelet, Vendéen peasant attacks against the Revolution were the result of a "cruel misunderstanding" as well as "unbelievable ingratitude, injustice, and absurdity."[29] Much like his pamphlet on the Jesuits, Michelet described the manipulation of peasants and women by the evil priests. This harmful control of thoughts and emotions led these naive peasants and women to become, unknowingly, agents of the counterrevolution. These misled "people" had not been informed that the Revolution was the new and true religion. Moreover, this lack of communication, Michelet explained, between the center of the Revolution in Paris and the Vendée enabled the counterrevolution to succeed. Isolation from the Revolution had kept the Vendéens unaware of its loving nature. If "the people" had known of the new faith, they would have embraced it immediately, rather than tragically attacking "France":

> The Vendée, whatever one may think, was an artificial creation, cunningly prepared by a skillful worker. In this obscure and remote corner of the world, without roads, the priests found a strong element of resistance in a people naturally opposed to all centralized authority. With the aid of women, the priest could slowly, at his leisure, create a bizarre and unique work of art: a revolution against the Revolution, a republic against the Republic.
>
> . . . The Vendéen, enclosed, blinded, in his own savage thicket, could not see the movement flowing around him. A momentary glimpse would have discouraged him and he would not have fought. Someone should have taken him to a mountain peak, where he could have surveyed and seen the momentous events taking place in the distance. He would have made the sign of the cross, believing himself at the Last Judgment and said: This is the work of God.[30]

In the person of Louis XVI the internal and external threats coalesced. Michelet believed, as did his fellow historians, that Louis XVI was guilty, but probably should have been exiled rather than guillotined in order to show the humanity and mercy of the Revolution. In his last years, Louis XVI had kept in contact with the enemies of France, the European monarchs, in the hope that they would help restore him to his throne. This continual plotting of Louis XVI against France, and therefore, against the Revolution and the new faith, was a criminal act of the first magnitude. By fostering intrigues against the France of love, justice, and law, Michelet's Louis XVI was guilty of the heinous moral crime of attempting to kill a nation. "A person is a holy thing. But as a nation takes on the attributes of a person and becomes a soul, its inviolability increases in proportion. The crime of transgressing against the national personality becomes the greatest of crimes."[31]

Aside from all of the poisonous arms of the old religion, individuals and groups attempting to unite with the new religion unknowingly infected the Revolution with deadly viruses. The Girondins in 1793 went counter to Michelet's whole philosophical views of France by supporting decentralization theories. Michelet had always fervently believed in the necessity of French centralization. In his *Histoire de France* each monarchical act leading to further centralization was unquestionably recognized as beneficial to the country. No Proudhonian concepts of small, separate, and autonomous regions of France pierced Michelet's consciousness. Centralization had given France the unique ability to harmonize totally. Administrative centralization of the Middle Ages, now seen as insufficient by Michelet, was enhanced during the Revolution by fraternal and moral centralization. The Festival of the Federation was the momentary realization of this multi-leveled centralization— administrative, social, political, emotional, and moral—which Michelet felt would be repeated in the nineteenth century. Without this vision of the future, the Girondins, although "united in heart," were drawn into an "involuntary federalism."[32] The Girondins had forgotten that France could never "accept the weak federative unity of the United States or Switzerland, which were only systems of voluntary dissension."[33]

Decentralization theories, if accepted during the Revolution, could only have led to further disunity and decay. Forgetting that "unity is the eternal dream of humanity," the Girondins hastened their own downfall by following the opinions of their new, rightist members—advice contrary to the true nature of France and of the Revolution.[34]

> The regional directors, the local nobles, the rich, all the lukewarm part of the republican party including disguised royalists, called themselves Girondins. Their common attitude, infinitely dangerous, was to loosen the nerve of the Revolution, to diminish central influence, and to increase local influence in themselves. Basically, these men were the enemies of unity.[35]

The heroic Girondin leaders, many of them men of letters, who had founded the Republic, had led the war preparations against Europe, and had started the tenth of August, had now evolved to the unenviable position of defending a motley group of supporters opposed to "the unity of *la patrie*."[36] Their only other alternative, at the time, was to have reconciled themselves with the Mountain and "vote for the revolutionary Tribunal and the Terror. . . They preferred to perish."[37]

The greatest internal dividers on the side of the Revolution were the Jacobins, personified in Robespierre. Michelet's rancor towards Robespierre was chided in an unremitting sally of charges in Blanc's *Histoire de la Révolution française*. Blanc's incessant and vituperative responses to Michelet's interpretation of Robespierre, Danton, and the French Revolution, were scattered throughout his twelve-volume work. A total of over one hundred pages in his text and footnotes were devoted to correcting Michelet's errors of fact and of explanation. Blanc's most common method was to write a six or eight-page appendix after each major subject, listing Michelet's textual errors, his unsubstantiated forays against Robespierre, and his self-deceptive praises of Danton.

Blanc's thesis was monotonously the same. Michelet had singled out Danton during the high points of the Revolution and had accused or implied Robespierre to be responsible for the most hideous aspects of the Revolution. Blanc's own interpretation was precisely the reverse. For example, with the September massacres, Robespierre was implicated by Michelet as an instigator, whereas Danton was absolved completely of preparation or participation. For Blanc, the facts proved just the opposite.[38] Although agreeing with Michelet's basic analysis of August 10, Blanc showed Danton's role to be minimal not central, and stated that Michelet's hatred for Robespierre had prevented him from seeing the pivotal position he had had during this period.[39]

Blanc's unparalleled obsession with proving the incorrectness of Michelet's work, reflected, in part, the fundamental differences of interpretation between these two men. For Blanc, Robespierre, as leader of the second revolution, spoke for "the people," and represented the highest attributes of *patrie* and brotherhood. Michelet's Robespierre, although occasionally aiding the Revolution, did not speak for "the people" and did not further the principles of the new religion—love, justice, and law. Instead, Robespierre reverted in the last months of his life to the ideas of the *ancien régime*, by becoming a "priest" and by artibrarily condemning to death his fellow Frenchmen. Blanc's Robespierre was at the forefront of the Revolution, a shining visionary of the future, while Michelet's Robespierre blocked the progress of the new religion and its principles by turning into an agent of the counterrevolution, and reviving the discredited and injurious principles of the old religion.

Blanc described Robespierre and the Jacobins as the incarnation of Rousseau's ideas on unity and brotherhood, but Michelet began his version less propitiously. The Jacobin headquarters were indicative of the closed and conspiratorial nature of this club:

> I prefer—by the yellow glare of the lamps glimmering through the fog on rue Saint-Honoré,—to follow the dark, dense crowd all wending in the same direction to that small door of the convent of the Jacobins. It is there that the agents of the insurrection come every morning to receive orders from Lameth or the money of the Duc of Orleans from Laclos. At this hour the club is open. Let us enter cautiously, for the place is poorly lit.[40]

As the Revolution progressed, Michelet's imagery of this dark meeting place become more Nietzschesque. At the entrance "one's mind was disturbed and one's heart became ill at ease";then members descended "a somber stairway"; "everything was narrow and shabby . . . There was no air down there; it was difficult to breathe."[41] In the Jacobin clubs there were no men of "the people." While Michelet agreed with Blanc and Lamartine that Robespierre became, perhaps, the most popular man among "the people," he felt, unlike his contemporaries, that Robespierre did not understand nor speak for "the people." Out of touch with the heartbeat of the Revolution, the Jacobins increasingly assumed the character of a priesthood, while Robespierre "gradually became the head of this clergy."[42]

The Jacobins represented diverse opinions in the beginning of the Revolution, but, more and more, they lost their individual independence while one man, alone, thought and reasoned for them. "I perceive at the summit of this prodigious edifice of one thousand associations the pale head of Robespierre."[43] What kind of man had come to speak for the mental and emotional frame of mind of the Jacobins? "Boring" and "monotonous" were Michelet's common images of the personality of the "Incorruptible."[44] He was a sickly, dull, and lifeless man who kept secret his outrageous plots against the person of France. No man of feeling could get close to this austere individual; only colder, more heartless people such as St. Just could enter into this chilly world. This frequent seclusion in an emotionless world isolated Robespierre from the "popular instinct."[45] Nevertheless, in trying to maintain his policy of giving all sides of a man, Michelet admitted that Robespierre exerted "great moral authority."[46]

In 1792, before their support of decentralization theories, the Girondins, in Michelet's opinion, were the primary advocates of war against all external enemies. The Jacobins, on the contrary, feebly acceded to the war effort, because they preferred to begin an internal war against all of their enemies within France. "The Gironde wanted external war . . . the Jacobins, internal purification, the punishment of evil citizens, and the crushing of all resistance by means of terror and inquisition."[47] On this issue, Blanc blasted Michelet for "mutilating and falsifying history," because the facts proved that Robespierre was not against the policy of foreign war.[48] However, for Michelet, the Girondins in 1792 understood the spirit of the Revolution, of unity and transcendence of internal conflicts through mutual love of France. The Jacobins, though, did not grasp the higher unity of *patrie* and proceeded as if they, alone, represented the brotherhood of France. In Michelet's world view, schemes of internal purification, as well as decentralization theories, were divisive, retrogressive, and contrary to the principles of the new religion. All Frenchmen, after coming into contact with the Revolution, would eventually accept it with open arms; there was no need to punish dissenters through violent internal purges, the Jacobin and Robespierre position of internal rather than external war, further manifested, for Michelet, their foreignness to the "popular instinct."

Fortunately, the Girondin position prevailed temporarily, while the Jacobins continued to support the Revolution. However, as the unity of the Revolution began to fade and decompose, the artificial associations of Jacobins increasingly gained control of the country and of the Revolution. "For lack of a natural association which gave to the Revolution living unity, it was necessary to have an artificial association, a league, a conjuration, which gave it at least a kind of mechanical unity."[49] The "positive force" of the Jacobins was their support of the Revolution, but their "negative force" of "political and moral censure" overrode their previous contributions. By 1793 the inquisitorial spirit of the Jacobins had gained the upper hand, proliferating fear, hatred, and terror throughout the country. Under the evil rule of Robespierre and the Jacobins, all of the principles of the Revolution were abrogated; "all Frenchmen," who in July 1790 had embraced in love and brotherhood, were now, "after fifteen months of Jacobin reign, . . . suspects."[50]

As Michelet's Robespierre unleashed his bloodthirsty horde against other supporters of the Revolution (Blanc and Lamartine, who opposed this thesis, suggested, as do most modern commentators, that Robespierre tried to be a moderating force during the Terror), he also reinstituted the forms and customs of the old religion. Under the title "Supreme Being," Robespierre brought back the corrupt doctrines of the Middle Ages. During, what Michelet called, his "papacy," Robespierre filled the Jacobin clubs with priests and tried to forge for himself the image of the new "messiah." This ostentatious mimesis of the past did not convert "the people," who were in tune with the true Revolution. Robespierre's elaborate Festival of the Supreme Being on June 8, 1794, was a failure; his appearance before "the people" was "met by a silence of death."[51] As Thermidor approached, Robespierre sank more and more into a self-made quagmire. Unwittingly, this "great moral authority" had led the Revolution into the avaricious arms of the ancient faith; the priestly religion maintained by internal repression and violence. The cyclical nature of the revolutionary years became apparent for Michelet in retracing January 1794 when "the mass, the vespers" returned and was heard on "rue Saint-André-des-Arts . . . which is near the Pont-Neuf, that is to say, the center of Paris."[52]

In one of his many derogatory footnotes, Blanc accused Michelet of deluding himself by thinking he had written the first republican history, when, in reality, Danton had been his only "idol."[53] Michelet, replying to this attack in an 1869 preface, denied having "taken Danton for a hero."[54] For evidence, Michelet assumed his typical methodological pose, recalling his juxtaposition of the varieties of Danton's behavior, which had included Danton's disastrous equivocation before Robespierre. "It is especially his fatal softness in November '93 that I have never been able to pardon. I looked unfavorably upon his cowardice."[55] After this example Michelet dismissed Blanc's criticism, and he reiterated that "the people" were his only hero. But Blanc's charge had stung, for it questioned Michelet's central premise. Reading the *Histoire de la Révolution française*, without accepting literally the methodological statements, perhaps as Blanc did, makes one wonder whether Danton was in fact Michelet's idea of a hero?

The atmosphere of the Cordeliers emitted all of the freedom and openness that had been lacking in the headquarters of the Jacobins. Honesty, passion, and emotional intensity characterized their discussions. "Their genius, entirely instinctive and spontaneous . . . distinguishes them profoundly from the calculating enthusiasm and the moody cold fanaticism which characterizes the Jacobins."[56] The instinctive quality of the Cordeliers allied them naturally with "the people." Unlike Robespierre, who albeit was popular among "the people," the Cordeliers associated with, listened to, and understood "the people." "It was the originality of the Cordeliers to be and ever remain mixed with the people. . . . They believed in the people and had faith in the instinct of the people."[57] Marat and Desmoulins were two of the most potent forces behind the Cordeliers, but as far as contact with "the people," intellect, or emotional strength were concerned, neither of them could equal the power of Georges Jacques Danton.

For an image of Danton, Michelet studied a portrait begun by David and completed by disciples:

> What is most frightening, is that he has no eyes; at least, they are scarcely perceptible. What! is this terrible blindman to be the guide of nations? . . . What we read here is obscurity, dizziness, fatality, and absolute ignorance of the future.
>
> And yet this monster is sublime. This face, almost without eyes, seems like a volcano without a crater,—a volcano of fire,—which, in its closed furnace, turns over and over the conflicts of nature . . . How awful will be the eruption.
>
> In that hour, an enemy, frightened at his language, but doing justice, even in death, to the genius that has blasted him will describe him with these everlasting words: the Pluto of eloquence.[58]

Later, Michelet described Danton's appearance as "half bull and half man," who "in all his majestic hideousness was a tragic mask to trouble any heart."[59] This monster with overflowing passion, knew no hatred; he only loved. He was "the greatest genius and probably the most penetrating intellect of the Revolution."[60] Through Danton, the instinct of "the people" combined with the wisdom of the educated in love, harmony, and brotherhood.

*177*

Michelet's captivation with Danton was not shared by Blanc, who castigated him at every opportunity, as Michelet had done with Robespierre. But, even Lamartine, whose admiration for Robespierre irked Michelet, vehemently assailed Danton's character and motives. Danton's known involvement in large-scale bribery and personal acquisition of wealth during the Revolution were mentioned by Michelet but only so that he could deny them. Lamartine, however, like Blanc, saw them as symptomatic of a complete moral vacuum:

> Ambition was his whole line of politics. Devoid of honor, principles, or morality, he only loved democracy because it was exciting . . . His sole genius was contempt for honesty, and he esteemed himself above all the world because he had trampled under foot all scruples. . . . His contempt of the people must incline him rather to the side of tyranny. . . . His most revolutionary movements were but the marked prices at which he was purchasable. . . . He was bought daily and next morning was for sale again. . . . Immorality, which was the infirmity of his mind, was in his eyes the essence of his ambition; he cultivated it in himself as the element of future greatness. He pitied anybody who respected anything. Such a man had of necessity a vast ascendency over the bad passions of the multitude. He kept them in continual agitation, and always boiling on the surface ready to flow into any torrent, even if it were of blood.[61]

Diametrically opposed to the opinions of Lamartine and Blanc, Michelet retold Danton's career within the context of leading player of the Revolution. Michelet's Danton was the most creative thinker of his times and the greatest mediator between political parties. During the debate on going to war, for example, "Danton, as always, was the most original."[62] In the controversy over decentralization theories, Danton, as he had often done in the past, arbitrated between the Girondins and Jacobins. For the high points of the Revolution, such as August 10, Danton managed to be at center stage, frequently speaking for "the people," although Michelet insisted in a footnote that no one, not even Danton, was the author of that event.[63] Financial indiscretions attributed to Danton were exaggerated, distorted, or incorrect in Michelet's characterization. While an honest Danton was present at the important events of the Revolution, he wisely avoided and was uninvolved in the cruel acts of the period. Lamartine described one of these violent periods, the September massacres, in a different tone than Michelet. "If a drop of blood stains the hand of a murderer, oceans of gore do not make innocent the Dantons! The magnitude of the crime does not transform it into virtue."[64]

Danton was able to fill this dual role of creative intellect and successful mediator, because, for Michelet, he, alone of the revolutionary figures, was capable of understanding all men and feeling all passions. "Danton, in whom life was so powerful, through whom vibrated all life, always had under his hand a vast keyboard of men whom he could play; men of letters, servants of execution, fanatics, intriguers, sometimes heroes even; the whole immense and varied scale of good and bad passions."[65] Danton was the consummate actor of the Revolution, filling any role the script required. But there was method in Danton's uncanny ability; all of his skill was devoted to the principles of the Revolution—love, justice, right, and brotherhood. This former minister of justice was "the great artist of the Revolution who took all of the parts of the pure and impure elements, good and evil, virtues and vices, and threw them together into meaningful matrices, he made surge from them the statue of liberty."[66] Because of Danton's genius for penetrating into, understanding, and expressing all passions and feelings, "all history was in him."[67] It was Danton "who made the supreme effort for the unity of *la patrie*."[68] His lofty qualities and commitment to the principles of the new religion made him, during the crowning moments of the Revolution, as had been the case with "the people," synonymous with France. "Danton was . . . the voice even of the Revolution and of France."[69]

Michelet balanced this worship of Danton, he felt, with a blistering assault upon Danton's cowardice in 1793 and gradual turn into the arms of his betrayer, the Jacobins. Beginning in April 1793, Danton's attitude was "deplorable."[70] He was probably the only person "who could have saved the Republic but instead the parties each did their best to destroy him."[71] The Girondins had initially forced Danton to retreat, because of their calumnious accusations that he had connived in traiterous activities with Dumouriez. With his mediating position threatened, where he had stood above all parties and all internal power struggles, Danton foolishly sought support with the Jacobins. On April 13 Danton went against his basic principles, an unpardonable crime in the eyes of Michelet, by agreeing with Robespierre to abandon the war in Europe and thereby tacitly sanctioning the shifting of the battle to the inner confines of France. By the summer of 1793, the Jacobins, through the voice of Robespierre, wanted to destroy the Girondins, who were increasingly allying themselves with royalists. Danton, whose position was always the pacification and reconciliation of the internal divisions of France, was theoretically against stringent measures, but, having already compromised himself with the Jacobins, his strength to resist and his power to block large-scale massacres, had lost their former force. The hate-filled side of the Revolution personified in Robespierre now prevailed over the loving side, personified in Danton. By the fall of 1793 Danton, whose power had been eroded through indecision and equivocation, blindly followed the dictates of the "Incorruptible." It was pathetic "to see Danton speaking against Dantonists," while "begging the favor of his" Jacobin enemies.[72]

On April 5, 1794 (16 Germinal year I), the "voice of the Republic" was guillotined. In recounting the trial and Danton's last moments, Michelet poured forth all of his sympathies for this giant of the Revolution. Michelet again reiterated that Danton had been totally blameless and uninvolved in the conspiratorial actions of the Orleanists and Dumouriez. In the spring of 1794, not only Danton and the Dantonists, but also Chaumette and the Paris Commune perished. Michelet had lavishly praised the Commune while neglecting the atrocities committed in its name. The end of the Republic and Revolution "dates for us, not from Thermidor, when it lost its formula, but from March and April," when the bearers of the principles of the new religion were fatally silenced; "when the genius of Paris disappeared with the Commune, when the Mountain collapsed under the terror of the right, when the speaker's platform, the press, and the theater were razed in the same blow."[73]

Predictably, Blanc and Lamartine did not show Michelet's sadness at Danton's end. For Blanc, Michelet's blind love for Danton prevented him from understanding the complex, irenic position of Robespierre.[74] Lamartine offered, with theater imagery as in Michelet, an interpretation suggesting that Danton lacked the very qualities that Michelet felt he had possessed more than any other man of the Revolution:

> Thus died on the stage, before the multitude, the man for whom the scaffold was also a theater, and who desired to die applauded, at the close of

the tragic drama of his life, as he had been at the beginning and in the middle. His only deficiency as a great man was virtue. He had its nature, cause, genius, exterior, destiny, death, but not its conscience. He played the great men, but was not one. There is no greatness in a part—there is greatness only in the actual faith. Danton had the feeling, frequently the passion of liberty, but not the faith, for internally he professed no worship but that of renown.

The Revolution was with him an instinct and not a religion. He served it as the wind serves the tempest, by elevating the foam and sporting with the waves. He only understood its movement and not its direction. He had its intoxication rather than its love.[75]

In probably his greatest tribute to any individual of the revolutionary period, Carlyle evinced sympathies for Danton on the same order as Michelet's. Considering the venom protruding from Carlyle's text on the Revolution as a whole, this passage stands out with a particular poignancy:

> So passes, like a gigantic mass, of valor, ostentation, fury, affection, and wild revolutionary force and manhood, this Danton, to his unknown home. He was of Arcis-sur-Aube; born of "good farmer-people" there. He had many sins; but one worst sin he had not, that of Cant. No hollow Formalist, deceptive and self-deceptive, ghastly to the natural sense, was this; but a very Man: with all his dross he was a Man; fiery-real, from the great fire-bosom of Nature herself. He saved France from Brunswick; he walked straight his own wild road, whither it led him. He may live for some generations in the memory of man.[76]

For Michelet, "the great dream of Danton was an immense table where reconciled France would sit together in order to break the bread of brotherhood, without distinction of class or party."[77] Danton and his colleagues had overthrown the throne and created the Republic, had saved the Revolution by organizing it around justice, and had exhibited model behavior as citizens of the new faith by "hating no one and loving each other until death."[78] Such was the last scene of all, that summarizes and ends this strange eventful history. As mediator of the new religion, Danton spoke for "the people" and approached an internal synthesis of the instinct and reflection duality. He had had his moments on stage as the pure embodiment of *la patrie*, but his moral fall of 1793 showed that, as an individual and not an abstract group, he was still susceptible to weakness and divisiveness. Not completely harmonized nor full, Danton was unable to resolve the tension between the educated and the illiterate or between classes, except on occasions. Danton was a genius, but only a near hero for Michelet. After Joan of Arc he had come closest to resolving in himself the dichotomies of man's nature and the varieties of classes in order to become forever one with France. Having been able to play all the parts of the new religion and having represented all of its principles, Danton made his lasting mark on France. At his guillotining Michelet quoted a "patriot," who exclaimed: "They have decapitated France!"[79]

# 13

## Great Expectations

Preconceptions of time and history in Michelet's world view, depicted in his *Journal* and books from 1843 to 1854, seem to prefigure, in part, Nietzsche's satirical portrait of "historical men" in *The Use and Abuse of History*. For Michelet's intoxication was with history; it contained all of our knowledge about man and society. In order to understand the present state of civilization, we must be aware of what had transpired in the past. There was an extraordinary progression in historical direction in Michelet's vision, which led to the present and embodied all the possibilities for the next stage in history. While Nietzsche's man had to break free from history in order to act, Michelet's man could only act positively in the present and future after having imbibed and kept in view our knowledge of the past. The failure and evil of the French Revolution, Michelet felt, was "in having lacked trained men who knew the past and understood it."[1] Therefore, those men who acted with a greater vision of the past and with a greater sense of historical time would be morally superior to those oblivious of their historical heritage. Michelet saw himself in the center of this historical process—charting, prodding, and educating his fellow Frenchmen more quickly towards their historical destiny. His professorship enabled him to spread his ideas—ideas that had been most fully formulated in his *Histoire de la Révolution française*, as he had revealed "France to herself." Until this work France had been in "the shameful condition of an idiot who had forgotten herself two or three times, not knowing a word of her past and no longer even responding when asked her name. . . . How can one act, when one doesn't know what one is and what one was?"[2]

*183*

The destiny of France foreseen by Michelet—of total brotherhood and total love, unfettered by the class wars of his day—had been manifested during the Festival of the Federation. On July 14, 1790 the development of France "passed infinitely beyond antiquity and Christianity."[3] Unfortunately, the principles of love, justice, and law were crushed in the wake of the Terror and the Napoleonic Empire. But what had been true for the brief period of federations, became Michelet's evidence of France's true principles and true spirit, forever. It was to the task of regenerating these principles indefinitely that Michelet, the educator, devoted himself from 1843 to 1854. "Because of all the evils of this country, the most serious, in my opinion, is when the individual loses consciousness of himself, of his nature, of his mission, of his role in the world, the historic consciousness of his true past, the name even of *patrie*."[4] In his vision, "progress," in the highest sense, was the flowering of France's autochthonous principles, whose initial appearance he had heralded in the first years of the French Revolution.

Between 1843 and 1854 Michelet's sense of the tempo of history had a direct bearing on his views of the past, present, and future. There had been a steady progression in history through time—epochs had risen and succumbed, while a new society and religion, modern France, still reverberated from the pains of passing into adulthood. The French Revolution had clarified the principles which her citizens should learn, emulate, and live by in the future. In 1789 and 1790, the joyful years of birth and development, time had passed quickly and smoothly. There were no sudden shifts of tempo but only agreeable accelerations of speed during the apogees of these years, when history entered the realm of blissful, flowing harmony. By 1792 and 1793, though, there had occurred a conscious change in Michelet's structure of his work. "I have begun already," he wrote Noël, "by changing the rhythm of my history. Long chapters are no longer possible; only short, hurried sections, one quickly following the other. The dominant phenomenon of the Terror is the amazing passage of time."[5] The disintegration of the Revolution and the haphazardness of Michelet's chapters were paralleled by his sense of the tempo for these years. Time moved rapidly as in 1789 and 1790, but now it rarely flowed. It became chaotic, jerky, and too disjointed to enable the previous rhythm and harmony of the Revolution to reappear.

This speedy, directionless passage of time led into and reflected the disorder and convulsions of Thermidor.

During these eleven years the great evils of French history for Michelet were the Middle Ages and the Napoleonic Empire. The former had opposed the birth of the true France, and the latter had impeded the natural flow of France to maturity. The sense of time Michelet associated with these vice and hate-ridden periods was quite slow, if not static. The constant movement and dynamism that he had discerned during the French Revolution, even during periods of the last years, were totally absent from the Middle Ages and the Napoleonic Empire. These two periods "languished"; there was a "somber monotony . . . the waiting without hope, without desire, if not that of death."[6] Time virtually came to a standstill. The slowness of the time also reflected the tone of the auditory and visual senses; during the Napoleonic Empire "all was dark. Dark was France! Light only shined outside of France."[7] In this epoch where Michelet's father's press was silenced, "no one spoke; there was profound silence."[8] It was terrible to be alive during these periods when time and history trickled from the giant rivers into tiny, jagged tributaries.

While time stopped amidst silence "the principles of the Revolution, which give way to these grand wars, were perfectly forgotten; most people didn't know why they were fighting . . . nobody took life seriously. Anything that took the future into account was neglected."[9] With "the principles of the Revolution" abrogated, Frenchmen were forced to live without the wonders of the press, without equality, without love, and in effect, without history. This ephemeral vision, in essence, revolved around the love of one man, Napoleon, rather than the equal love of all men under the aegis of France.

Once emancipated from the Napoleonic Empire, Michelet's sense of time quickened. The days of his own period returned to that lively pace of the French Revolution, and then began to attain and further the accomplishments of the Festival of the Federation. The tempo of history was carrying France towards her goal in Michelet's own lifetime. Since 1843 he had been feeling profoundly "modern," welcoming the present and future while bidding adieu to the sordid intrigues of the Middle Ages. It was a "hectic life where days quickly follow days" as France had

*185*

now recovered from the loss of vitality suffered at the hands of Napoleon I, Restoration governments, and the disappointing July Monarchy.[10] Much like 1789, Michelet wrote in his 1847 introduction to his *Histoire de la Révolution française*, "The world is waiting for a faith, to march forward again, to breathe and to live."[11]

With the approach and then success of the February revolution, the tempo of time multiplied rapidly. Michelet "sensed the necessity to see Quinet" in order to discuss the progress of events and plan future strategy.[12] Returning triumphantly to the Collège de France on April 1, 1848, he told his auditors: "A century has passed in a month."[13] The February revolution, in addition to this increased speed of time, had brought back the flowing, harmonious rhythms of 1789 and 1790 and, correspondingly, the principles of France. This quickened movement needed guidance and direction in order to prevent a return to the chaotic, pulsating days of 1793 and 1794. Michelet's course of action—education—became more urgent, not only because of the possibility of its success but also, perhaps, due to his fears of another Terror and collapse of another revolution. With the "word" spread forcefully and continuously perhaps nothing would impede the mellifluous union of time and history.

Tragically, the attempt to unite France failed. After the bloody June Days, Michelet's sense of time again slowed down; there was occasional "languish" and the realization that "patience" was needed in achieving France's quest. Unity would no longer be accomplished in his lifetime. In a higher sense, the brisk, but smooth, passage of time for Michelet always brought abundance, consolation, progress, and the fulfillment of France's principles; it was only when time halted or, conversely, went out of control, that it forestalled the ripening of an epoch.

In addition to his ideas paralleling the tempo of time in history, Michelet had moral attitudes towards immediacy. The "moment" was Michelet's word for the smallest unit of time in history. "Moments" cannot be defined as an exact unit of time, but, as always in his total historical vision, Michelet had something very specific in mind when he used the word "moment":

> The aim of life? . . . to be rich? to be old? All this is just an end. It is not a goal.

186

Extend the horizon, enlarge and universalize each moment of life, make each moment be a goal of sorts, so that each day you should be able to say: If death comes tomorrow, at least I have lived today. This thought must dominate and be the direction which one gives to a child and the direction which a young man gives to himself. It is a great misfortune that the child daily receives only dry, boring instruction, in view of the future results and future happiness. And there is another great misfortune that the student many times devotes himself so exclusively to the special study of his future profession that he forgets, along the way, that he is a man, dividing his life between his vocation and his pleasure, without anything to reserve to the general thought of duty, of country, of humanity, of the past, and of the future.[14]

The "moment" was totally bound up with history—it was the inner heartbeat of the vast sweep of history, not a time to spontaneously abandon the principles and ethics of the past. Without the complete picture of past and future, present actions lost all semblance of morality; men did not conform to the principles of their age. This is one reason why Michelet fulminated against the Napoleonic Empire. Time moved slowly and people "did not take life seriously," because they had tiny, puny visions of history.

Intrinsic to his use of the "moment" was Michelet's assumption that different kinds of lives were led in different periods of history. An individual could live maximally in some epochs or short time spans, while being unable to live maximally in other periods of history. Therefore, the "general force of things," the flow of time through history, which brought abundance and progress, had to be conducive to allowing people to think of the larger units of *patrie* and society. Michelet revealed in his histories that there had been very few supreme "moments" when everyone, or even a few people, were constantly preoccupied, let alone united, with the society and country, without regard to their own selfish motives and daily, private actions. Aside from the era of Joan of Arc, the three main maximal periods of French history were 1789 and 1790, July 1830, and the years 1843 until June 1848. During these expressive periods of plenitude, the impact of the "moment" was so overpowering that these "sensations of eternity," as Freud might have called them, were difficult to escape. The Festival of the Federation, the greatest "moment," was not subject to linear, historical time, because the flow of history was so perfect, that past, present, and future had temporarily merged into eternal time, that rare union of quantitative time and the qualitative "moment."

If someone was not alive during these climactic periods of history, then, within the context of Michelet's use of the "moment," the individual could not have lived a maximal life; he would have been too weighed down by the lack of history and lack of vision of his age. For example, in the Napoleonic period, no one, not even Michelet, could have experienced a great "moment," because men were too imbued with the individualistic, egotistical, immoral, and historyless temper of the time.

Michelet's unit of time, the "moment," provides one philosophical support for his apparent belief that he was at the center of history and could personally affect the historical process. No one more than Michelet had universalized "each moment of life" or thought continuously of his country, "of the past and of the future." Unlike Danton, Michelet was a true hero of France, because with his overwhelming historical knowledge, he would never tragically sacrifice his principles and the principles of France. As chronicler of the major "moments" and men of history, Michelet had experienced *all* of the great "moments" of France. He had cried over Joan, had stormed the Bastille, had witnessed the debate and signing of the Declaration of the Rights of Man, and had joyously relived the love and brotherhood of the Festival of the Federation. "How am I not the true priest," he exclaimed in 1847, "I who held this year the saint of saints on the altar of the Federations?"[15] As professor of history and morals at what he believed to be the central educational institution in the central city of the central country of the world, he attempted to alter the course of history. One backdrop to all of Michelet's contemporary writings during this period was his own belief in the exalted importance of his position and his desire to spread his fully synthesized ideas for a moral and psychological revolution. His greatest plan for inducing a full "moment" for all Frenchmen during the exciting months of 1848, according to one disciple, was to hold a huge Federation composed of "seventy delegates of the National Guard from each region: multiplied by eighty-five, this would be around six thousand men . . . marching together . . . through Paris" showing "fraternity in action, the embracing of France by France."[16]

Michelet had what he considered to be the greatest and largest historical vision—it covered all of historical time—and in this sense he was morally superior to all men, whose visions of history covered smaller spans of time or who were historyless. "The life that I have in me is not my life, it is the thought of the centuries. The source is not mine, it is the common source of the world and of history which has come from God . . . It is that of the human race, of action and of universal passion, the great river of life, of work, and of suffering."[17] If he failed in the "moment" to unite his countrymen, he could constantly console himself by knowing that his "moment" was the highest moral act.

Historians and intellectuals such as Michelet in Paris during the first half of the nineteenth century often, and with some reason, placed a high value on their own importance. Educated Frenchmen of these generations were both intoxicated with history and accorded their best historians rewards and renown probably not previously nor since matched. Guizot and Thiers alternately governed the July Monarchy; Michelet, resident historian at the Collège de France, was well-known throughout France; Lamartine became head of the Provisional Government, while Blanc played a significant role in that brief regime. Historians led the country while numerous intellectuals felt and acted, often in a Saint-Simonian sense, as if they belonged to the moral class directing and controlling French society.

These historians, particularly those in positions of distinction, believed in the power of ideas to change society. It was commonly assumed by Michelet and other Parisian intellectuals that the works of Voltaire and Rousseau were the biblical sources, causes, and inspiration behind the French Revolution. For Michelet, men made history, and, although "the people" may have been his hero, he considered the ideas of Voltaire and Rousseau to have been the most powerful forces igniting the new religion. Thus, in the months preceding and after the February revolution, it seems that Michelet, among others, unquestioningly accepting the thesis that men and ideas had caused one revolution, felt that he personally could and then did cause another revolution. For several months Michelet thought he had succeeded in his mission. Despite collapse, the groundwork had been laid, and even after June 1848, one fellow historian, Augustin Thierry, wrote Michelet, praising him for revealing the true principles of France, which he expected would directly "contribute" to and become part of the foundation for the future progress of the nation.[18]

The failure of France to ripen perpetually after February 1848 did not change Michelet's belief that time would bring fulfillment through history. The "moment" looked not only to the past and present in its magnificent sense of time, but also to the future. The future aim of France was "unity, the unity of heart in the diversity of characters: all in one yet each remains himself. How is this unity attained? Brotherhood is the means and the goal."[19] Accordingly, France would reach her goal of multiplicity within unity based on the unique principles Michelet saw in her history: unity, brotherly love, equal law, and equal justice. But in order to achieve this ideal society, the educators of the country continually had to make fellow citizens aware of France's historical principles, for a "society indulging in the ignorance of its own principle, to the unconcern for the future, a society which does not ceaselessly create the society of tomorrow . . . will only survive by accident."[20] Despite setbacks and the revival of Bonapartism, Michelet did not question progress, and consequently devoted himself to propounding the principles of this great France, so that the future would produce a galaxy of individuals such as Joan of Arc and a myriad of events such as the Festival of the Federation. "Passing my life between the pains of the past and the present, between the two abortions of the Republic; my faith is not shaken from it."[21] The shining "moments" of the past would be recaptured and magnified a thousandfold.

In this organic, stadial formulation of the history of France Michelet focused on his agency for the next stage of history. He looked to the man of the future and wondered "where then occurs the gestation of what is going to be? In you. You-yourself are that receptacle where the past deposits the germs of the future . . . be like a pregnant woman who puts all of her fruit in view."[22] By "you" Michelet meant the youth—the students who were educated directly by him on the basic principles of France. These students, the educated youth of France, passed through the Collège de France and were impregnated by the wisdom of Michelet's total vision. The fruit of this vision, easily communicable, would be placed in clear view for the next generation. The principles of France would protrude through this exhibition and help spread the "word" more quickly. This future proliferation would speed France increasingly onto her destiny—Michelet was totally convinced that this maturation "must come sooner or later":

> I have a fixed, rational order according to which things normally must happen. The events can change this order, but it is no less according to reason. This order is that brotherhood must precede the laws, that a better code of laws must then follow it; the result being the expression of brotherhood. Therefore without waiting for a political revolution and the actions of the state, we must in the measure of the liberties that we still have, begin today the work of brotherhood, and that this beginning must be made by the young man; he has the time, the temperament; he is still undeveloped.[23]

The students that came to Michelet were still "undeveloped" because they were, as yet, uncorrupted by the class hatreds of France. The youth were the malleable section of the life cycle. While their parents were lost in tiny, dark visions of envy and fear, these students came into contact with and then immediately embraced the grand, moral vision of Michelet. From the seeds to the placing of the fruit on view, the youth would carry forward both the torch of France and the torch of Michelet's own personal concern for posterity and for the continuation of his ideas. "I blur together in the same hope," he confided to his students, "the immortal, infinite progress of my soul and the limitless progress of my *patrie*."[24]

# 14

## *Woman, the Gentle Mediator Between Nature and Man*

The last volume of Michelet's *Histoire de la Révolution française* was his twenty-seventh published book in twenty-nine years. Many fifty-five-year-old men might have slowed down at this point, especially after having concluded a huge and exhausting study of the French Revolution and after having lost easy access to the archives. Michelet, however, increased the rate of his writing, although not the quality of it, during his last twenty years. From 1854 until his death in 1874 he wrote twenty-six more volumes, averaging some four hundred pages in length. Eleven final volumes of his *Histoire de France* and three of his *Histoire du XIX<sup>e</sup> siècle* comprised more than half the total, but, at the same time that Michelet was composing these histories, he was writing other works on vastly different subjects.

Between 1854 and 1869, nature and women rivaled history in impor-tance in Michelet's *œuvre*. Some of these works on women blended with Michelet's knowledge of history, such as his imaginative *Les Femmes de la Révolution* or his bizarre *La Sorcière*. Sections of *L'Amour* and *La Femme* were written within the context of the moral reform of society, a theme from his pamphlets and lectures of the 1840s and early 1850s. But most of *L'Amour* and *La Femme*, in addition to his four volumes on nature, revealed a distinct world view not only different from the world of Michelet, the historian, but often diametrically opposed to it. Moral fulfillment for the individual and progress for society through time and history were replaced in Michelet's studies of nature and of the ideal woman by a timeless and historyless utopia. Nature had been discussed extensively by Michelet in the 1830s, but generally as a negative element in his philosophy of history. One main exception was his following of the contemporary Cuvier and Geoffrey Saint-Hilaire controversy. Modifications in his analysis of nature and of the importance of women increasingly emerged after his marriage to Athénaïs Mialaret in 1849. Frequently, Michelet explained his interest in and outlook on these subjects in the 1850s and 1860s as a direct influence from his wife. Furthermore, the Parisian political, social, and intellectual climate during these two decades contrasted considerably with the temper of the 1840s. Either from desire or as a means to escape political pressures, many eminent writers turned to subjects such as nature, which were devoid of political and social content. Michelet's works on women, love, and nature were his most popular works, even more widely read than his controversial pamphlets of the 1840s. These best sellers, often totaling forty and fifty thousand copies sold, astounding sales for his day, were staid, conservative works, perhaps even anachronistic. These were not the radical, polemical works of a historian *engagé*, as in the 1840s, devoured by an aroused citizenry concerned about political, religious, and social injustices. The bourgeoisie, not "the people," bought these books, and Michelet's letters and *Journal* showed his ecstasy over his success. Ironically, Michelet reached his greatest readership through these works on love and nature, which were completely removed from a historical context.

While writing a short biographical sketch of his wife in 1861 Michelet recalled the circumstances of their initial romantic moments in late 1848 and 1849: his position at the Archives was becoming more precarious with the death of Letronne and his replacement by the "evil" Chabrier, the administration of the Collège de France was becoming increasingly reactionary under a new director, and his books were being placed on the Index. Therefore, Michelet continued, it "was a blessing from heaven or rather a predestination, to meet precisely on the eve of these tragic days such a brave and innocent young soul," for she saved him from being crushed by the loss of his jobs and the collapse of his dreams for France—"December 2 came after the June Days, it would have been too much. The pain that time would have killed me."[1] For Michelet, Athénaïs rescued him from emotional distress during this turbulent four-year period of his life. This was the beginning of an extraordinarily intimate twenty-five year marriage. Prior to this, except for a brief period with Mme Dumesnil, Michelet had never devoted much of his time nor energies to other people, preferring either from choice or necessity to remain immersed in his work. Michelet's relationship with Athénaïs altered this previous pattern of his existence. She became his primary occupation, the recipient of his boundless affection and concern, for the last third of his life.

Twenty-eight years younger than Michelet, Athénaïs was born October 17, 1826, at Lêjoac near Montauban, the fourth of six children of Yves-Louis Hippolyte Mialaret and Marguerite Emma Becknell. On the eve of the French Revolution fifteen-year-old Yves-Louis went to Saint-Domingue, or present-day Haiti, where, while teaching, he became private tutor for the children of Toussaint Louverture, one of the leaders of the independence movement. After returning to France he held a series of teaching and governmental posts, eventually assigned to Elba Island in 1812, where he would cross paths with Napoleon. Condemned to exile in 1815 because of his Bonapartist sympathies, he fled to Louisiana where he tutored and then married the daughter of an English family in 1820. Five years of farming success convinced Yves-Louis to return to France where he could live leisurely from his savings. Several years after Athénaïs's birth, however, he became restless and returned to America with one of his sons for further adventure. He never saw his family again, remaining in the New World and dying of typhus in Cincinnati in 1841.

Similarly to Pauline, Athénaïs was raised without a father and by a mother whom she considered to be cold and heartless. Placed in a series of pensions and convents, Athénaïs was able, unlike Pauline, to improve her situation through her intelligence and ingenuity. A teaching certificate for elementary schools and the aid of friends enabled her to become private tutor for the children of Princess Cantacuzène in Vienna in December 1846. Her mother had told her frequently to become a nun, a life Athénaïs considered, but her experiences in Vienna, according to Michelet, turned her against the corrupted and sick world of Catholicism. In Vienna, as Michelet related in his *Mémoires d'une jeune fille honnête*, Athénaïs was shocked by the promiscuity, slovenliness, and materialism of the nuns and priests. Cases of young, naïve nuns becoming pregnant were common. Scores of prostitutes walking the streets in Paris and London, surmised Michelet, were "nothing in comparison with the debauchery in Vienna."[2]

While bewildered by Vienna, uncertain about her previous religious convictions, and unsure about her vocational direction, Athénaïs happened to read Michelet's *Du pretre, de la femme et de la famille*. Inspired as never before by the lofty, impassioned, and consoling prose, she wrote to the famous historian on October 23, 1847, telling him that she had lost her father at fourteen and since then had desperately needed a guide. Overcome by his moral wisdom, Athénaïs implored Michelet to "take the place" of her father and to "speak to me as you do to your own child and to give me advice, because I know that I will never be the same again now that I have read your book."[3] Responding the following week, Michelet recommended that she seek peace and consolation through the reading and contemplation of classic works such as Shakespeare, Dante, Plutarch, the Bible, and even sections of his own *Histoire de France*.[4] Their correspondence continued spasmodically through their respectively viewed revolutions of 1848, each of which they reported to the other.

In September 1848 Athénaïs informed Michelet that she was coming to Paris soon and asked for his aid in finding her a teaching post. On November 8, 1848, Athénaïs arrived in Paris and at four o'clock that afternoon met her future husband. The romance, as viewed through their letters, blossomed immediately. Less than a month later the comments of Michelet, who was already rapturously in love, appear to have overwhelmed this twenty-two-year old provincial woman. She wrote Michelet on December 2: "I have been troubled since our walk. . . . In spirit I am still a child who is trying to find herself . . . You tell me that this is already more than enough, that with me you will be uplifted, stronger, and more creative . . . But what if all this is only an illusion of your tenderness?"[5] The suddenness of their relationship and the obvious disparities in their ages and life experiences continued to make Athénaïs uneasy. Conversely, Michelet was absolutely and unequivocally committed to her. For him, love had superseded all possible problems. By her letter of December 13, Athénaïs, although still uncertain, showed her willingness to try to satisfy his principal needs. "First you ask me to bring you peace of mind; then you lay bare your soul, prostrated, exhausted . . . You make me extremely uneasy. Yes, of course I will help bring you harmony. . . . I will do everything possible to bring you happiness."[6]

Throughout his letters, and repeated in Athénaïs's responses, Michelet wrote of his personal desire for "harmony." He recalled his lack of harmony and unity as a child and as a professor. Instead of becoming involved in personal relations, he had chosen, in the 1820s "humanity," where nothing was personal and individual relations were secondary. In his letter of January 3, 1849, Michelet posed the same questions that he had in his diary in the 1820s and 1830s, and this time he asked for love and harmony with another human being, with Athénaïs, rather than with "humanity" or "France":

> Ah, that you can think that I was a genius! . . . Well, friend, if I was, remember, that it was from having *sensed* the people and from having known, before all else, that the secret of life, its mystery, was in the midst of crowds.
>
> What results from this is: 1) That in keeping myself free from individuals, not following anyone and not helping anyone, I have not lived in the right circumstances and have *remained poor*; 2) Furthermore, living with the universal breath of France, with the great popular soul, I have nearly always lacked individual attachments and, having given little to myself, I have gone through life without or *nearly without love*.
>
> And so this life, almost *underprivileged*, if I dare say so, *by my austerity*, by my somber and solitary days, I bring it to you, oh young angel. And if you could only give me life and not death.
>
> Death or life, what does it matter! I will always thank God for having known you a day, for your having resuscitated my heart, for your returning to me even the experience of pain, the gift of tears which I had lost for such a long time.[7]

Athénaïs, Michelet hoped, could change his life of loving only France and the "great popular soul" or "the people," by giving him the love of an "individual attachment" that he had rarely experienced. In this way, he might end his "poor" and "underprivileged" emotional existence. Athénaïs could supply the harmony Michelet had alreays dreamt of, for, in their life, Michelet told her, "the work will be shared, like everything else, in a life fully united."[8]

## Woman, the Gentle Mediator Between Nature and Man

In a letter of January 27, 1849, Michelet informed Mickiewicz of his plans: "She has been formed by my books . . . I will marry her despite the age difference. She is my daughter in spirit."[9] On March 12, 1849, at the town hall of the twelfth district of Paris, Athénaïs and Michelet were married in a civil ceremony witnessed by Béranger and Mickiewicz for the bride and Quinet and Poret for the groom. In his diary in the following months and years, Michelet envisaged within "the new harmony" that Athénaïs would give him, his first happy home life.[10] Apparently recalling his unhappiness as a child and with Pauline, Michelet buoyantly exclaimed in his diary, that he now had "for the first time" what he had previously "ignored: the household."[11] The continuation of this new experience of domestic happiness and a long-lasting harmony between himself and another person, when his only memories of love and unity had been in his tragically fleeting relationships with Poinsot and Mme Dumesnil, were Michelet's ardent wishes in his marriage to Athénaïs Mialaret.

In his *Journal*, Michelet commented almost daily on his new wife. His autobiographical statements for the last twenty-five years of his life, manifest a complete obsession with Athénaïs. Contained within these hundreds of pages are references to problems of marriage consummation, ideas of incest, and passages on dreams, desires, and fantasies with sexual overtones.[12] This increasing erotic turn in Michelet's personal writings corresponded to long passages on incest and widespread sexual imagery in the last volumes of his *Histoire de France* and in *La Sorcière*.[13] Father-daughter feelings and incestuous ideas were shared between himself and his wife. He told of his wife's loving him and making love with him as if he were "her father."[14] Michelet gave a more historical perspective to these ideas in an entry of May 1857:

The most permitted of incestuous relations: Marriages in which there are age differences have a kind of gentleness when the older resembles the father or the mother of the younger and can be loved in that role.

Such was my first attachment. She seemed nice and desirable to me albeit older, because she resembled my mother.

And, in my happy marriage today, perhaps I resemble, being the age of her father, a much loved father.

*197*

Would it have happened, if they had survived alone on a deserted island with the loss of the human race? She would have married her father
and very willingly. Thus, this is what happened. I am indeed her
father.[15]

One of the appealing qualities of Michelet's writings, both public and
private, is the frankness and intimacy with which his emotions and those
of his historical personages are discussed. Michelet's unconscious appears
to be less hindered and more at the fore than most writers. Therefore,
although many of his sexual comments may be insignificant or typical of
middle-aged men, he, at least, gives voice to his feelings and allows his
inner desires to flow onto the printed page.

The majority of volumes 3 and 4 of his *Journal*—to the point of
monotony—revolve around the health and physical well-being of
Athénaïs. The diary can be picked up and read randomly, and almost
every page will speak of her health, her daily activities, her daily
feelings, or her daily eating habits—all of this in virtually the same
manner day after day and year after year. The slightest cold often worried
him for a week, at least, it comprised the majority of the diary for that
week. And she had these minor ailments frequently. Sleeping patterns
take up as much of the writing as any other single subject. If Athénaïs
did not sleep well, a common occurrence, Michelet would note only that
in his entry for the day.[16]

Michelet's engrossment with and idolatry of Athénaïs affected his
work and his relations with his family and friends. By the late 1860s
Michelet's relationship with his best friend, Quinet, and his closest
relative, Alfred, had deteriorated considerably. Since Alfred, Eugène
Noël, still a confidant of Michelet's, and, probably Quinet, did not like
Athénaïs, it might seem that she was behind her husband's increasing
isolation from his friends and relatives. Athénaïs's hatred of Alfred,
apparent in all of her writings, for example, *La Mort et les funérailles de J.
Michelet*, had some justification.[17] From the very beginning of her
romance with Michelet, Alfred and Adèle, who was only two years older
than Athénaïs, did not want them to marry. Alfred wrote Athénaïs on
December 13, 1848, and warned her bluntly that in becoming involved
with "a man of genius" she was risking to claim, alone, Michelet's love
and affection that hitherto had gone to the whole world.[18] Alfred, who

by this analysis seems to have understood his father-in-law better than most people did, condescendingly added, that if Athénaïs were more "worldly" and intelligent she would have grasped the situation, and he would not have been compelled to write this frank letter. Upset by the reaction of Adèle and Alfred, who still lived with him, Michelet complained about the "domestic tragedy," but was unable to change their viewpoints.[19] Neither of them attended his wedding.

Correspondence continued between Alfred and Michelet, but their previous close rapport never returned. Even with the death of Adèle in 1855 their relationship did not improve. By 1867, according to Quinet's wife, Michelet was nervous, ill, and sad because he no longer saw Alfred nor his grandchildren.[20] Athénaïs perhaps always saw in Alfred the representation of the person she most resented, Mme Dumesnil. Alfred and Athénaïs were forced together again during funeral arrangements for Michelet and they violently disagreed over his last wishes.[21]

Always more politically oriented than his fellow translator in the 1820s and comrade-in-arms in the 1840s, Quinet began an eighteen-year exile against Napoleon III in 1852. This geographical separation hampered his friendship with Michelet considerably. Michelet visited the Quinets with his wife several times in the 1860s, but not after his break with Quinet in 1868. For Quinet's wife, who compiled the correspondence between the two life-long friends, there was no permanent rupture.[22] However, the available evidence does not corroborate her interpretation.

The estrangement was initiated by Michelet probably in a letter of May 8, 1866, when he criticized Quinet's new work on the French Revolution. Quinet had committed two cardinal sins, in Michelet's opinion, which he never tolerated from anyone. Quantitatively, in terms of research, Quinet had only cited the *Histoire de la Révolution française* once in his two-volume work, despite relying heavily on it for the factual material. Qualitatively, Quinet had mistakenly reiterated his 1845 thesis that the French Revolution heralded the revival of the ideas and values of early Christianity. In 1845 Michelet had not written his history, but now, in 1866, he could not understand why his friend had insisted on this "other Christian form" when he had shown clearly that the Revolution itself "was a Church."[23] Quinet replied to these criticisms in a letter of November 18, 1867, protesting that their differences of interpretation were not very substantial. Imploringly, he added: "We are united, dear friend, and we must remain united."[24]

These and further exchanges of letters revealed that the two men attached different importance to their points of disagreement and viewed the essentials of their friendship from diverse perspectives. Unsatisfied with Quinet's responses, Michelet repeated that his political and religious ideas on the French Revolution, which for him also explained contemporary France, were significantly opposed to his friend's. Quinet's failure to follow his "Bible" on the French Revolution had contributed greatly to the tension of their relationship, which had reached the stage where it was no longer possible for them to discuss matters of importance, for example, present-day politics. After assailing every historian of the French Revolution for neither understanding the events nor researching them properly, as he had, Michelet concluded this letter by wishing that their "immutable" friendship might still be salvaged.[25]

Similar to the previous year, Quinet again wrote that their theoretical differences were not glaring but slight, and, regardless, these histories should not "sacrifice our present friendship."[26] Michelet was uncommunicative, and Quinet tried to discover the deeper, underlying causes of his friend's uncharacteristic behavior. Quinet wrote Alfred, telling him that he was mystified by Michelet's September letter of "quasi-rupture." Suspecting Athénaïs of interfering, Quinet added: "Someone wanted to separate us and they succeeded."[27] Athénaïs may have been behind this split, as Quinet suggested, since she did not like Quinet's wife. However, it also appears that Quinet did not comprehend the full force behind Michelet's serious denunciation of his book. These criticisms were not slight points of contention for Michelet. In their last six years, the two men corresponded little, and even after Quinet's return to Paris in 1870, they rarely saw each other. Quinet, like any other Frenchman, found out about Michelet's death while glancing through a newspaper.

According to Michelet, it was Athénaïs who "definitely led" him "to the sciences of nature."[28] Despite his writings on nature in the 1830s, particularly in the *Tableau de la France*, Michelet granted to his wife the merit of initially having interested him in nature and then having taught him the subject. In 1855, after already having begun his new field of inquiry, Michelet wrote Noël, informing him of his wife's role of "teacher" of natural history:

> And I am also occupying myself with natural history. I shall tell you all about the ideas and projects that my illustrious teacher and doctor has inspired in me by the long lessons she gives her insatiable disciple. I believe that, both of us together, are going to cause quite a stir this century.
> From her, I have learned all about birds.[29]

Athénaïs gathered the materials, kept abreast of the new literature in the area, took notes on the prominent secondary books, and then discussed the subject matter with her husband. She also wrote short chapters in several of Michelet's books on nature. In his first work on nature, *L'Oiseau*, Michelet posed the question: "How the Author was led to the Study of Nature," and then, after crediting Athénaïs with the influence, he added that his work was not really his own but the product of "two souls."[30]

In both *L'Oiseau* and *La Montagne* Michelet related that his change from history to natural history began while he was ill in November 1853, several months after the publication of his final volume of the *Histoire de la Révolution française*. Recuperating in Nervi, near Genoa, he temporarily lost interest in finishing his *Histoire de France*. "History, my grand occupation, claimed me, groaning that it could not complete its task. Nature claimed me."[31] The inspiration for his natural histories, in a touch of irony and with typical Michelet dramatization, had come in Italy, "just as thirty years before, it had lit for me, through Vico, the first spark of the historic fire."[32]

Michelet's four natural history works, *L'Oiseau, L'Insecte, La Mer,* and *La Montagne* were published in 1856, 1857, 1861, and 1868, respectively. Their success was instantaneous and tremendous. *L'Oiseau* went through seven editions in four years and nine in eleven years, totaling 33,000 copies, while *L'Insecte*, because of Michelet's popularity, had a huge 8,000-copy first edition, which sold out in two months, and Hachette, the publisher, printed 28,000 copies of the book in eleven years.[33] In 1861, 24,000 copies of *La Mer* were printed, while *La Montagne* went through seven editions in 1868 alone. Both cheaply printed and glossy, illustrated editions were avidly purchased. These works obviously appealed to the reading public more than did his histories.

During the years Michelet wrote these books he consciously kept them and their subject matter separate from his histories. Natural history encompassed rivers, mountains, and animals, but not man's creations. Cities, the arts, institutions, and personages belonged to "humanity, the times," the type of history Michelet preferred, whereas "the other history . . . eternal nature" contained none of these ingredients.[34] Michelet's diary entries showed that he often worked on both histories the same day, perhaps the morning for one and the afternoon for the other. Some days he was not in the mood for one type of history and skipped it altogether.

In his nature books, Michelet frequently paused to reflect on his motivations behind his spending time with this subject matter. In addition to Athénaïs, he set forth various other reasons for involving himself in nonhuman history. "Man makes his own history," after all, had been Michelet's guiding principle for thirty years, and he apparently needed to explain his deviation from this maxim. On one level, the motivational area relating to his wife, Michelet studied and wrote natural history as a pleasant diversion. These were Athénaïs's favorite topics, and the two of them could spend part of each day discussing books they had each read or mountains they had each seen. *L'Oiseau*, Michelet wrote, emanated "from our hours of relaxation, our afternoon conversations, our winter readings, our summer gossips."[35]

Escape, both from his personal situation in Paris and the unhappy political climate, was another prime reason Michelet suggested for his immersion in nature. The loss of his jobs in 1851 and 1852 had changed his whole pattern of living. Instead of passing part of each day at the Archives and at the Collège de France, he now remained home longer and more often. Despite writing once that "it was with much pleasure that, in the spring of 1852, I broke through all the ties of my old habits," the more prevalent reality was that the long arms of Napoleon III had slowly crushed his spirit.[36] Nature became Michelet's acknowledged refuge from the "present barbarism" of the Emperor and his fellow silencers of history.[37] Michelet had managed through his *Le Banquet* of early 1854 to maintain his interest, along with his multitude of ideas, in the building of modern society. By 1856, though, out of work for four years now, he allowed nature, as an escape or an "alibi" and for his own peace of mind, to consume part of his time every day. "Man! We have already met with him often enough in other places. Here, on the contrary, we have sought an alibi from the human world, from the miserable solitude and desolation of earlier days."[38]

Michelet maintained his sharp demarcation between history and natural history more fervently than ever in *La Montagne*. By the time of this 1868 work his gloom over human history had extended to contain the years prior to as well as those of the Second Empire. In *La Montagne* Michelet recalled his original decision to leave "the troubled history of humanity, so harsh in the past and still so harsh in the present."[39] The study of nature had provided the tranquil milieu he needed when history ran aground under Napoleon III. The sheer writing of *La Montagne* enabled him to preserve his intellectual acuity and emotional balance. "This book . . . prevented me from sinking, and held my head above waters. By a happy alternation between history and nature, I preserved my level. If I had followed man alone, and his savage records, melancholy would have enfeebled me."[40] Contemplating human history, Michelet added, was absolutely necessary for retaining a noble vision of justice and morality, but during the nadirs of history, such as this one, he had found the healthiest mental and emotional method to be the "frequent exchange of the two worlds."[41]

Michelet's "two worlds" of human and natural history in the 1850s and 1860s indicated that he had modified his 1830 idea of nature. In his *Introduction à l'histoire universelle* and his *Tableau de la France* nature was the central adversary of history. During that period, nature was the principle evil in Michelet's philosophy of history because all the hindrances to progress and unity—geography, climate, race—were associated with nature. By the 1850s, though, Michelet's 1830s idea that the obstacles of nature needed to be overcome for France to mirror oneness, had long been superseded by the human problems of social class, education, and religion. Man's harmful creations had replaced nature as the main detriment to French unity in Michelet's philosophy of history. Presently, Michelet had no difficulty distinguishing, without any ambiguity, human and natural history. This transformation of the role of nature in his thought permitted him to pleasurably escape from the harsh political climate in Paris and to please his wife through their enjoyment of mutual interests.

Michelet constructed, as he had with human history, an ideal of harmonious nature. Beginning with the generally held assumption that man changed whereas nature was unchangeable, Michelet formulated a natural-world paragon from basic elements opposite to those of the human world. Without the ever increasing variables of human history to contend with, the unity of nature became relatively simple for Michelet to describe. Natural history signified for him—in not an uncommon interpretation—infinity, immortality, timelessness, and the country. The history of man, on the contrary, was centered in the city, changed through time, while man and his creations were both finite and mortal. Man's insignificance and the absence of ongoing history at the seacoast did not bother Michelet in the 1850s and 1860s as it had in 1831 when he had to rush back to the center of *la patrie*, to the "only asylum," the city. Now, Michelet reveled in the delights of a utopia without man and without history. The contemplation of the inherent beauty of nature was as blissful and rewarding as the fulfillment of man and society through time and history. Society was "overworked" and "constantly agitated" in Napoleon III's France, prompting Michelet to recommend in *La Mer* that families follow his own actions and "go to the sea" for health, vigor, love, and harmony.[42]

In his 1858 *L'Amour* and 1859 *La Femme* Michelet added "the woman" and "the household" to his ahistorical utopia. These new elements not only became part of, but became central to his timeless, cityless, and historyless vision of nature. In one very important sense, this full-blown utopia of nature reflected and signified by 1858 far more than the results of a desire to escape from contemporary society and from sadness over the course of modern history. For, in creating an ideal world of the woman, family, and nature, Michelet had imprinted his unique vision onto a world he had always consciously avoided. Although unhappiness and neglect had characterized Michelet's attitude towards the home in the past, he now wrote a utopia of the home. The child, who through education had escaped from the world of his parents, the professor and historian who had shunned the world of Pauline, became, by 1858, a great celebrator of family life and family harmony. The key to the whole structure, and Michelet of course had Athénaïs in mind, was the woman, whose "natural tendencies" inclined her towards the eternal elements of nature. Man's duty, on the other hand, was to confront history—the world of the city, of society, of time, and of human conflict:

> For man, who is called to labor, to battle with the world, the great study is History, the story of this combat—history aided by languages, in each of which is the genius of a people—history prompted by Right, writing under and for it, constantly inspired, revised, and corrected by eternal Justice.
>
> For woman, the gentle mediator between nature and man, between father and child, the study, thoroughly practical, rejuvenating, and embellishing is Nature.
>
> The man passes from drama to drama, not one of which resembles another, from experience to experience, from battle to battle. History goes forth, ever far-reaching and continually crying to him: "Forward."
>
> The woman, on the contrary, follows the noble and serene epic that Nature charts in her harmonious cycles, repeating herself with a touching grace of constancy and fidelity. These refrains in her lofty song bestow peace, and, if I may say so, a relative changelessness. This is why the study of Nature never wearies, never jades; and woman can trustingly give herself up to it, for Nature is a woman. History, which we very foolishly put in the feminine gender, is a rough, savage male, a sun-burnt, dusty traveler.[43]

Fulfilling his duty as a man, Michelet had studied history and written his great dramas of justice and morality. In *L'Amour* he was also able to complete his historyless utopia, of the world he had previously not partaken of, by describing the ideal woman, "the gentle mediator between nature and man."

Michelet developed his ideas on the role of women and the ideal woman over a period of twenty years, with his fullest characterizations of women and their dominant position in his "other" utopia, presented in *L'Amour* and *La Femme*. In an address before the five principal academies of France on May 2, 1838, signifying his election to the Collège de France, Michelet described the ideal woman of the Middle Ages. His lecture, later published as *Fragment d'un mémoire sur l'éducation des femmes au Moyen Age*, praised the women, including the nuns, of the Middle Ages. According to Michelet, the Virgin was the ideal type which all good Christian women were taught to imitate. Dante's Beatrice was a medieval portrayal of this "high moral perfection."[44] However, despite the merits of the Christian doctrine on women during the Middle Ages, Michelet told his distinguished audience that the chief defect of this noble vision was in having neglected and "scorned marriage and the family."[45]

*Du prêtre, de la femme et de la famille*, published in 1845 after Michelet's dramatic break with the Middle Ages and Christianity, contained a vitriolic tirade against the medieval view of women and the harmful education of women by priests. The educational system begun in the Middle Ages had remained in effect. Priests taught and counseled women and girls on marriage and womanhood, but these celibates were, in truth, ignorant in these matters.[46] Michelet lamented that "our wives and our daughters are brought up and governed by our enemies."[47] To remedy this deleterious situation, Michelet emphatically suggested that the husbands wrest control of their wives and daughters from the destructive hands of priests. Through their entrapment by men of the past, women had remained intellectually inferior to their husbands, who were free from the influence of the old religion. The role of husbands should become, therefore, that of teacher and companion in order to raise their wives to their "own level."[48] "Marriage must once again become marriage; the husband must make his wife his companion in his intellectual development . . . In his impatience to make daily progress he has left his wife behind. He has hurried forwards and she has receded back. . . . This must happen no more."[49] Michelet did not characterize the ideal woman in this book, but he hoped that through her new mentor's aid and her innate love, she would strengthen the family and society.

In his works of the 1850s and 1860s Michelet continued his denunciation of the ideal woman of the Middle Ages. The "essential" trait of the Middle Ages, Michelet concluded in his 1862 *La Sorcière*, was the "anti-Nature" and anti-woman doctrine propagated by the Church.[50] The Virgin was no longer the symbol of a high moral ideal as she had been in 1838, but rather the reverse. "By a monstrous perversion of ideas, the Middle Ages regarded the flesh, in its representative, woman, as radically impure. The Virgin, exalted as virgin, and not as Our Lady, far from raising actual womanhood to a higher level, had degraded it."[51]

The sorceress, who arose in reaction against the perverse ideas of Christianity, represented the purity of nature and of the woman. Michelet also described ideal women in the centuries before Christianity. In *La Sorcière* he depicted the primitive women as creatures born of "enchantment" who reflected harmonious nature, while in his 1864 *Bible de l'humanité* Michelet located the origins of the perfect woman wedded to nature in India.[52] The sorceress of the Middle Ages revived the woman's natural role by "rehabilitating the flesh," as Michelet used a popular Saint-Simonian expression, and ending the Christian idea of impurity of body and sex.[53] By engaging in healing and consoling, the sorceress not only presaged ideas of modern science and the vocation of medicine, but she also initiated one key role of modern women, that of daily concern for the health of her husband.

The sorceress was not the prototype of the modern woman. No witch that Michelet ever discussed was married, and his ideal woman was always married. But, at least the sorceress afforded an example of rebellion against the highest values of the Middle Ages. As the sorceress was a product of the Middle Ages, engendered in reaction to Christianity, so, too, did she die out, in Michelet's world view, with Christianity and the old religion.

Some of the first modern women, coinciding with the new religion, emerged during the French Revolution. Michelet published in 1854 a novel work, *Les Femmes de la Révolution*. This book was primarily excerpts from his *Histoire de la Révolution française*, which included sketches of the famous women of the period such as Madame de Staël, Madame de Roland, and Charlotte Corday, and of the wives of leaders such as those of Danton and Desmoulins. It was in the role of wives that many of these women exhibited the characteristics of modern women. They "sacrificed" for their husbands and made their homes peaceful and free of tension. When Vergniaud and Danton wanted to escape from the pressure of public affairs, for example, "they shut themselves up at home and took refuge at their fireside, in love and nature."[54]

Michelet's ideal woman, characterized in *La Femme* and *L'Amour*, spent her time at home, belonged to her husband, and was the living embodiment of his ahistorical utopia. Ultimately, Michelet felt the reform of the family would change society. In *Du prêtre, de la femme, et de la famille* and his diary for the next five years, Michelet tied the stability

207

of the family to the decrease of class conflicts and the moral betterment of society. By 1858, though, having lost faith in history, having fallen in love, and having become involved in natural history, Michelet's utopia of the home had become as much a refuge from history as a potential cure. Exuberant over his marriage with Athénaïs, Michelet wrote in his diary in 1851: "Two harmonized souls, it is already a city. It is already a world."[55] In *L'Amour* and *La Femme* the borders of this world did not go beyond the home. While history went on more discordant than ever, Michelet wrote of his new found harmony.

Michelet's stated purpose for writing *L'Amour* and *La Femme*—the latter book being virtually identical in ideas and similar in content to the former—was to reverse the present trend of a decline in marriages by describing the ideal woman of a perfect marriage. In contrast to Balzac's diatribe against marriage in *Le Contrat de mariage* as "the most absurd of social customs," Michelet tried to show that marriage should be synonymous with love.[56]

The young wife in Michelet's books was childlike, docile, physically weak, and uneducated. She was inferior to her husband and, therefore, aided the marriage by being obedient and submissive. Women, as Michelet had elucidated already in *Du prêtre*, were far behind their husbands in all respects and needed to be educated by them. The husband in a harmonious marriage became the "tutor" of his wife, who was, after all, a virtual *tabula rasa* of historical knowledge. After many sessions, his wife would learn about history, society, culture, and politics solely through the ideas of her husband. Michelet, who wrote Mickiewicz in January 1849 that "she has been formed by my books," had experienced this process with Athénaïs.

The husband did not teach his wife about history and society in order for her to continue these subjects on her own or for her to pursue a career related to these matters. Instead, the husband was merely revealing this cultural and worldly knowledge to his wife, so that she would feel closer to him and be less inferior intellectually. The world of history, society, and government, even after her education, remained a man's world. It was his duty to work for her and to "make" history while she stayed at home. "It is the paradise of marriage that the man should work for the woman, that he alone shall support her, take pleasure in enduring fatigue for her sake and save her the hardships of labor and rough contact with the world."[57]

The role of the woman was to love her husband, to raise children, and to take care of the home. "To love and bear children" was the "sacred duty" of every woman.[58] The home was the woman's world. "Seeing her so obedient, so docile, and so attentive a pupil, following out her husband's ideas and treasuring up his words, you imagine that he is master in everything. It is exactly the contrary."[59] By "master" at home, Michelet meant, in this portrayal of a nineteenth-century bourgeois marriage, that the woman supervised the cleaning and cooking of the servants, or, if too poor, did the work herself. She did not dominate the relationship at home, but was forced to oversee the home since her husband, involved with "history," did not have any time for these affairs.

After many years of marriage, the wife became less like a child and more like a mother. There was never any sense of equality in Michelet's idea of a happy marriage, although he used the word "companionship." Seemingly overnight the docile child became a mother to her husband. This transformation was occasioned by the increasing physical frailty of the man. In her new role the wife had to be more attentive than ever to the duties of the home, paying particular attention to her husband's diet. Since her husband was probably working less in old age, the wife also had to plan appropriate recreational activities.

Michelet's ideal woman belonged to nature. She lived outside of history and had "a horror of the world, a distaste for society."[60] In return for security, happiness, and knowledge, she gave her husband the love and affection she had cultivated in the timeless world of nature. This harmonious marriage of the man of history and the woman of nature resembled the marriage Michelet felt he had with Athénaïs. By representing the timeless, historyless world of nature, the ideal woman gave man a "glimpse of the infinite."[61]

Michelet was extraordinarily concerned over the public response to *L'Amour*. He wrote Alfred on September 9, 1858, that the book would either be "an Austerlitz or a Waterloo."[62] As with his pamphlets and lectures of the 1840s, Michelet thought he could influence those who read him. "I hope for some results from this book," he jotted in his diary on January 1, 1859.[63] Although his "influence" cannot be measured,

Michelet's fears of failure with his new type of work proved unjustified. By the middle of January 1859 he informed Alfred that 22,000 copies had already been sold, while a new edition of 15,000 was coming out soon.[64] On February 1, 1859, he excitedly wrote that *L'Amour* had sold "30,000 copies in two months and soon 40,000. Nothing stops it, neither the stock exchange nor politics. Countless educated people have told me of its moral effect." [65] The reviews were generally favorable to the book, but as Michelet admitted, "everyone is for the *liberated woman*."[66]

Who read this Parisian best seller of 1859 and Michelet's other widely purchased books on the woman and nature? While probably not for "liberated women," not even in 1859, they did provide bedtime and vacation reading for thousands of people. Their appeal was bourgeois, both with his ideal bourgeois woman and marriage and his nature studies to be viewed first-hand by the traveling elite. During the 1850s and 1860s the literacy rate increased dramatically in France. In these two decades the number of secondary school students rose fifty per cent while the percentage of illiteracy decreased from 38.7 to 21.5.[67] Concurrently, despite the restrictive political atmosphere, but aided by financial innovations, some industrialization, and the economic effects from the railroad, the numbers of wealthy people rose significantly in the country. Might not the popularity of Michelet's nature and woman books have come through his expression of bourgeois sentiments for a new, leisured, literate class? Michelet was extremely gratified over his good fortune and was delighted to share his first years of family happiness with so many of his fellow Frenchmen.

# 15

## *The Decline of History*

Michelet's interest in natural history did not impede his continuous writing of histories. "History never releases its slave," he assured his admirers in *L'Oiseau*, "he who has once drunk of its sharp strong wine will drink from it till his death."[1] The fount of his dominant passion was France, and he completed between 1854 and 1867 the writing of the history of France from the Middle Ages until the Revolution. In the 1870s Michelet wrote three volumes of his *Histoire du XIX<sup>e</sup> siècle* before his death, bringing his history up to Waterloo. The last eleven volumes of the *Histoire de France* became essentially a prolegomenon to the source of justice, love, hope, and harmony of modern France, the first years of the Revolution. Everything central to the Revolution evolved from an embryonic stage to maturation between the sixteenth, seventeenth, and eighteenth centuries. During their incipiency, "the people," justice, right, and the true France, were represented by various individuals or groups. Partial and incomplete, these elements only became whole in 1789 and 1790. Concurrently, bearers of the spirit of the Middle Ages attempted to hinder this inevitable process. Michelet's *Histoire de France* related the development of the principles of the French Revolution and their incessant struggle with the principles of the Middle Ages. While France was progressing in these volumes towards the ripening of her utopian possibilities, Michelet, several years later in his *Histoire du XIX<sup>e</sup> siècle*, no longer as in the 1840s, perceived the lasting reemergence of this utopian moment, but rather described, in a major change in his philosophy of history, the moral decline of France.

## Jules Michelet

In the six original volumes of his *Histoire de France* Michelet emphasized the increasing centralization and unity of France; in these last eleven volumes, he stressed the increasing emergence of a truly harmonized France. However, aside from the biological imagery of development and the wish for a unified country, these two sets of histories contrasted strikingly. The obvious change, as it had been since the 1840s, was Michelet's Voltairian outrage against his *bête noire*, the Church and the Middle Ages. Not only, though, had Michelet's ideas and sympathies altered in the years between the two sets of histories, but the whole tone of his work had been transformed. His histories of the origins of France and of the Middle Ages flowed smoothly; the most famous sections were poetic and rhapsodic. The primary focus was on the actions of men and the events beneficial to the progress and centralization of France. Negative moments were discussed, but the high points for France under great monarchs or through the unique achievements of Joan of Arc gave the dominant tenor to these six volumes.

Contrary to the volumes on the Middle Ages, those written between 1854 and 1867 became more and more terse, sputtering instead of flowing. Despite Michelet's continued desire for a unified France and his frequent mentioning of the precursors of the spirit of the Revolution, the opposite tenor emerged. Enemies, evil acts, plots, and conspiracies protruded from these three centuries of French history. In the developing battle between the new and old principles of France, Michelet remained preoccupied with the old—hurling accusations of intrigue and collusion whenever possible. As the France of the Revolution formed gradually, so, too, did the conspiracy of the Church and the Middle Ages. Isolated evil acts of the sixteenth century became by the eighteenth, a vast network of plotting and conspiracy among all of the enemies of France, and by then the list was legion. With each side gathering momentum, partly in response to the other, the titanic struggle began to peak as the wheel of history turned towards 1789. The French Revolution, as seen through these volumes, not only brought to fruition the France of love and harmony, but it also prevented a great conflagration and the death of the true France.

The germs of the Revolution and of the Republic were contained primarily in such periods as the Renaissance, the Reformation, and the Regency; in such individuals as Rabelais, Calvin, Coligny, and even the

non-French Luther; in the Protestant minority and in eighteenth-
century thought. The major villains of history, on the other hand, who
continued the injurious morality of the Middle Ages through deceit and
naked power, included the Catholic League and the last three kings of
the *ancien régime*.

The Renaissance and Reformation were distinct and different movements, but, according to Michelet, they were united on the most
important issue, namely, a denial of the values of the Middle Ages. The
Renaissance restored the love of family, nature, and humanity—all
callously degraded during the Middle Ages. Rabelais epitomized the
essence of the Renaissance and he was, for Michelet, the greatest man of
the era. Owing "nothing" to non-Frenchmen such as Erasmus or More,
Rabelais mastered all of the dialects of the French language and was
thoroughly acquainted with all the arts and sciences.[2] In manifesting
universal wisdom in his writings, Rabelais represented the peace and
liberty of the future. He was the single most important man before
Voltaire to lead "the revolution of right" and of justice.[3]

Luther, Calvin, Coligny, and the Huguenots, as all Michelet forerun-
ners of the new religion, achieved their high distinction in his histories
by struggling against the power and morality of the Middle Ages. For
Luther and Calvin, successful confrontations with the Middle Ages
proved them to be harbingers of modern liberty. Despite their religious
views and contrary to what they may have believed, Michelet's Luther
and Calvin were "brothers of Rabelais and Copernicus, two branches
from the same tree. From the same trunk flourished the Renaissance and
the Reformation, the grandfathers of modern liberty."[4]

Prior to the French Revolution, the Huguenots were the main group
Michelet identified with "the people." Still "an enigma" in the sixteenth
century, "the people" were personified by the Huguenots in their
nascency by virtue of being primary opponents of the clergy and the
monarchy.[5] Because of their negation of the spirit of the Middle Ages,
these courageous Protestants were "born people" and presaged the
establishment of a republic in France.[6] Although the Huguenots advanced the developing traditions of justice and liberty, they began, in
their complete resistance to the monarchy, to build fortresses within
France. This attempt to separate themselves from the rest of France was a
cardinal Michelet mistake, since France was incapable of living and

growing divided. Therefore, Michelet applauded the crushing of Protestant fortresses under Richelieu, which preserved France's possibilities of organic unity.

In the last decades of the sixteenth century the Catholic League became the principal inheritor, for Michelet, of the ideas and values of the Middle Ages, and they tried to use this pernicious affiliation to destroy the Huguenots. The League, in alliance with the Church and Spain, attempted to usurp control of the French monarchy, but their plotting and scheming fortunately failed. Michelet scorned the League bitterly because they represented all of the evils thwarting the emergence of the French spirit. The League was for local rule and wanted "to destroy national unity."[7] Their secret dealings with Spain prompted the most vicious of all possible Michelet labels for an individual or a group: "Foreigners, forever foreigners; that is what all perceptive Frenchmen saw in the League."[8] At one point, Michelet characterized "the terror of the League" as more horrifying than those of the Jacobins, because of their close ties with the Church.[9]

The successive monarchical regimes of Louis XIV, Louis XV, and Louis XVI had far greater power than the League to use in their efforts to retard the growth of the true France. Louis XIV solidified the bonds of the increasingly authoritarian monarchy with the clergy. Louis XV and Louis XVI added Spain and Austria to complete the triumvirate of monarchy, clergy, and foreigners, and to bring the conspiracy to its pinnacle.

In his unremitting attack on Louis XIV, Michelet did not even pause to admire the accomplishments and achievements of the reign. The flowering of art and culture had led Voltaire to describe the Age of Louis XIV as one of the high points of civilization, despite the persecution of Huguenots. For Michelet, in contrast to Voltaire and also to his peers such as Henri Martin and Mignet, the Classical Age of Louis XIV was all "imitative." The art was borrowed from the Greeks, Romans, and the Italian and French Renaissance, and the drama "never reached the colossal heights of Greek drama, of Dante, Shakespeare, or Rabelais."[10]

The Revocation of the Edict of Nantes was Michelet's towering image for the reign of Louis XIV. This oppression of Frenchmen as well as disastrous wars and a licentious personal life, made Louis XIV the most detestable of French monarchs. In his 1833 *Tableau de la France* Michelet mentioned the tremendous advance of the centralization of the monarchy under Louis XIV as a positive step in the unification of the country. Twenty-five years later Michelet discerned no progress towards national harmony because of this centralization, but only a moral vacuum in leadership, blind to the sufferings of the hungry and to the harmful effects from exiling an integral part of France. The one positive aspect Michelet found in the forced emigration of Huguenots was the spread of the French language, a civilizing conduit, throughout Europe.

Michelet's single theme for the reign of Louis XV was "the conspiracy of the family," comprising the monarchy, clergy, and foreigners.[11] "Bourbon, Austria, Spain, holy trinity. A union eagerly desired by the clergy."[12] Even before Marie-Antoinette the "foreigner reigned at Versailles."[13] But under Louis XVI there was a greater and clearer dichotomy of the two opposing religions into the group of France or that of foreigners. Michelet's Louis XVI was not only tied with other countries through his wife, but he was not even French himself. Inheriting German blood through his mother, Louis XVI was "more German than Germany . . . A foreigner by race . . . and attached to a religion demanding obedience and resignation, suppression of *patrie* and of the noble instinct of liberty."[14] In these years before the Revolution there was no longer any middle ground, one was either for the true France or Francophobe. "The modern principle which I stated in 1846 at the beginning of my *Revolution* finds its decisive confirmation in this volume on Louis XV and Louis XVI."[15]

Sandwiched between the darkness of Louis XIV and Louis XV was the brightness of the Regency. Through an enlightened collective government, the Regency combated the spirit of the Middle Ages currently represented in Spain. This was the period when Voltaire and Montesquieu began to write and when the liberty and freedom of the future began to shine momentarily. The concern for humanity and openness of thought during the Regency propelled the spirit of the Revolution. "The friend is the future, progress and the new spirit, '89, that one sees rising already on the distant horizon; it is the Revolution, of which the Regency is the first act."[16] By mid-century, while the monarchy, clergy, and foreigners desperately conjured up new intrigues, "France," the real France, "invades Europe" through the works of the *philosophes* and the *Encyclopédie*.[17] The "sovereignty" of the France of 1789 was manifested in the eagerness with which Europe welcomed these ideas of the new "religion."[18]

In his 1869 preface to a new edition of the *Histoire de France* Michelet recalled that he had been the first historian "to pose France as a person" and to reveal her "soul."[19] While giving France an identity, he had, in turn, formed his own identity through this work, it had "created" him.[20] Like lovers, Michelet reminisced, he and France "spent forty years" together, and "what passionate hours . . . we have had together. . . . I worked, went, came, searched, and wrote for you."[21]

Having totally dedicated his life to France, it must have been personally horrifying for the seventy-two-year-old Michelet to live through the July 1870 to May 1871 shattering of France's "soul." The military victory by Prussia, the annexation of French territory, and the bloodiest civil war in French history destroyed in less than a year Michelet's forty-year dream of French superiority and of inevitable French harmony and unity. On July 19, 1870, France, militarily ill-prepared, declared war on Prussia. Michelet signed on August 5, an *Appel au peuple allemand et au people français*, calling for an immediate cessation of fighting. This declaration had been prepared in London and signed by Michelet's archenemy Louis Blanc as well as by two men whose writings he was unacquainted with, Karl Marx and Friedrich Engels. Battlefield defeats led to the fall of the Second Empire and the proclamation of another republic on September 4, 1870. Michelet, having left Paris two days earlier, wrote in his diary on September 5 that he would follow his "line of abstention, as in 1830 and 1848."[22] Fleeing Paris and then France, Michelet and Athénaïs arrived in Florence in October.

While in Florence during December and January, Michelet wrote a short patriotic tract, *La France devant l'Europe*. In this book Michelet characterized a limping giant besieged by savage neighbors banded together and bent on destroying her mighty achievements. France, of course, was the giant, and, as always, at the forefront of history leading humanity towards the paradise of the future. However, in the past when Michelet laid out the hierarchy of nations, if he deigned to mention another country harming France, it was England, whereas, in 1870 and 1871 the war with Prussia had changed the problems of the world. The new threat to civilization was coming from the East. Both Prussia—or the expanded Germany as of January 18, 1871—and Russia were the nineteenth-century version of the barbarians invading the West. France, synonymous in Michelet's world view with progress, enlightenment, and civilization, was now fighting alone on French territory these modern-day Huns who were threatening to darken the landscape of Western civilization. With the ominous advance of Moltke's army, Michelet called on the European nations and even America to combat the "barbarian invasion." "I speak for the world even more than for France. France will save herself. But will the world be saved while it hesitates and is divided? At this supreme moment I call on all to unite for defense and to arm. The enemy is on us."[23]

Naturally, Michelet proceeded to attack Bismarck and Prussian militarism. To justify his accusations, Michelet attempted to show historically that Prussia always started wars and France was always the innocent defender. A quarter century of war during the French Revolution and Napoleonic Empire, Michelet now blamed on Prussia and Europe, because of Prussia's 1792 invasion of Poland and Europe's invasion of France the same year. These aggressive actions started a twenty-five-year chain reaction of wars, whereby Napoleon, in an atypical Michelet analysis, was not the primary perpetrator of evil.

Russia, although not involved in the Franco-Prussian war, was maligned by Michelet as vehemently as Prussia. This colossus to the East was a "giant beggar" inhabited by poor, uneducated people.[24] Since the Russian peasants produced less food and earned less money than their European counterparts, they were inferior human beings. In any future war, Michelet warned, Russia could fight recklessly and lose millions of men, because the majority of her citizens were of "such slight individual value."[25]

Michelet wondered why France, "the nation which hates least is hated most?" Frenchmen were totally trustworthy, and Michelet, as an example, recalled the extraordinary hospitality evinced by his loving countrymen when they hosted the Great Exhibition in 1867. Foreigners were given everything imaginable, even homes temporarily, as Frenchmen graciously stayed with other families. Yet, these Europeans of all nationalities remained "livid with envy."[27] Answering his own question, Michelet reiterated his forty-year-old image of France as the center of the arts, sciences, and culture. All nations hated and were jealous of France, because of her undeniable leadership in all forms of creativity and knowledge.

Five months before the Paris Commune, in his *La France devant l'Europe*, Michelet scoffed at contemporary analyses forecasting social turmoil. While acknowledging social conflicts, Michelet claimed that the limited clash of contending classes and forces in France fostered creativity and strength rather than internal weakness. Furthermore, he noted that the urban workers, whom he never identified with, had, through the decades, become more cooperative and fraternal. The Frenchmen, according to Michelet, who were "preoccupied" with internal antagonisms were unaware of their easy solvability.[28] He maintained, as he always had, that France inherently tended towards equilibrium, harmony, and unity. It was France's very equilibrium of all forces, Michelet asserted, that would enable her to defend the light of civilization against the forces of darkness crossing the Rhine. "She alone, by her singular strength of equilibrium, . . . can await the tempest, and, organizing the world of labor, defend even her enemies, by stopping the march of yonder giant masses which are darkening the horizon."[29]

While Michelet was writing *La France devant l'Europe* in Florence, only Paris, amidst famine and epidemics, was holding out from Prussia. Yet Michelet, in a letter to Noël, thought his book would have some influence. "The events are shattering me. Here I hope to publish before very long a work which will be useful even in the present crisis."[30] Even in these worst of circumstances for France the old historian revealed again his tremendous belief in his own importance and in the power of the word. In a diary entry of January 29, 1871, four days after the publication of his book and the day after the signing of the armistice agreement, Michelet noted that even if he did not influence these particular events through his book, at least he showed that he alone understood the situation because of his immense vision:

> My liberty permits me to follow and embrace the general situation: I am stating clearly from the beginning: the judge of events must remain free. Thanks to this liberty, I, alone, spoke when no one else was speaking up, except for the very confusing newspapers; I was the only voice of the times. I spoke for France, to reestablish enlightenment.[31]

Michelet, old, residing in Italy, and removed from the dire situation in Paris, could scarcely have imagined the calamitous series of events during the next four months. On February 8, 1871, in a hastily arranged election, a National Assembly with monarchical rather than republican sentiments was chosen in France. In the peace terms with Germany negotiated the same month by the Provisional Government, most of Alsace and Lorraine were annexed by the new Empire. The perfect hexagonal unity of France which, for Michelet, helped explain the equilibrating and harmonizing tendencies of the country, was mutilated.

The sixty-two-day Paris Commune and the attempted Parisian repudiation of the authority of the new Thiers government began in March 1871. On May 22, 1871, during the second day of the week-long siege of Paris by the government of France, in which some twenty thousand people would lose their lives, Michelet received news of the events, and shortly thereafter had a stroke, temporarily losing his speech and the use of his right hand.

Michelet recuperated from his mild stroke, and he now spent all of his winters in the southern coastal city of Hyères. However, he did not recuperate from the shock of another French civil war and the humiliation of French military defeat and loss of territory. He attempted, in a letter written February 20, 1872, and published June 5, 1872, in the Belfort newspaper *Libéral de l'Est*, to reassert France's privileged position in the world. Michelet chastized the Germans for not realizing that France was "less dismemberable than any other country of the world, because she possessed the most perfect organic unity."[32] Despite this defense of France, Michelet, by 1872, had lost most of his faith in the future prospects for France and the world.

In the preface of Michelet's last work, volume three of *Histoire du XIXᵉ siècle*, dated January 1874, one month before his death, he set forth a transformed philosophy of history and morality. In this "Glance at the whole century and its rapid decline," Michelet indicated his deep pessimism concerning the past, present, and future course of humanity.[33] His last reflections on mankind were the consequence of a twenty-year evolution of his world view, a process accelerated in the 1870s by catastrophic events, and perhaps also, by old age. In the 1830s and 1840s Michelet had accepted unquestioningly and had been a great proponent of the idea of progress. By the 1850s, though, after the loss of his positions at the Collège de France and the Archives, the return of another Napoleon, and his retreat into natural history, Michelet began to examine this previously held a priori truth. His conclusion to *Les Femmes de la Révolution* suggested that fifty years of reaction after the happy days of the Revolution had prevented progress in France. In *L'Oiseau* Michelet, venting his rage on Napoleon III, repeatedly bewailed man's present "plunge into barbarism."[34]

Michelet's most serious doubts about progress before the events of 1870 and 1871 were expressed in his 1868 *La Montagne*. In his last chapter, "Will our era succeed in regenerating itself?" Michelet acknowledged the stagnation and silence of history under Napoleon III as it had been under his uncle. However, Michelet's great knowledge of history, his "experience" of having "traversed . . . many ages," and having suffered during other historical epochs, reaffirmed his faith that the causes of the present "melancholy" were temporary and that a "downward movement" was not "our definitive law."[35] The two decades of Napoleonic rule and the current battlefield debacle prompted Michelet to exclaim in *La France devant l'Europe* that the hopes for eternal justice aroused in the events of 1789 and 1848 "seems lost forever."[36]

In Michelet's "Glance" at nineteenth-century France and Europe, his previous suggestions of past, present, and future decline have become more pronounced and more broadly stated. Reversing completely his 1830 "perception of France" and the prospects of unlimited progress, Michelet now perceived a steady decline of France and the world since the first years of the French Revolution. The reign of Napoleon I, one of the great periods of the silence of history, had become for Michelet in 1874 the imprinter of the whole history of France and of Europe for the nineteenth century. No longer was this historyless era a temporary aberration before the inevitable revival of the Federation spirit and of the principles of 1789. The Napoleonic Empire had wiped out the great "moments" of the past and had become the beginning of the decline of Western civilization. Now, the Festival of the Federation, the momentary example of the ineluctable harmony and bliss of a future France, appeared to have become the unrecoverable pinnacle of French and world history.

The three major causes inducing nineteenth-century decay, Michelet explained in the preface to this first volume of *Histoire du XIX<sup>e</sup> siècle*, were socialism, militarism, and industrialism. "I was born in the midst of the great territorial revolution and I shall have lived to see the dawning of the great industrial revolution. Born under the terror of Babeuf, I shall have lived to see the terror of the International."[37] Industrialism and the creation of a working class had begun in England and had spread to the continent. The factory system had engendered "regimentation" as a way of existence among the masses, who in turn followed false theories of socialism which threatened the established order of society.[38] Michelet had not evinced sympathy for these workers in 1848 nor 1871, and presently lamented the increasing movement of peasants from the country to the city. Since Michelet's "people" had always been predominantly peasants or the dwindling artisan class, the proliferation of industrialism and the working class eroded in reality his conception of the ideal social composition for France.

Militarism, the third "ism" of Michelet's nineteenth century, endangered the future survival of mankind. Associating this evil with Napoleon again, rather than with Prussia as in 1870, Michelet blamed the Emperor for beginning the century by "ruining Europe and leaving France worn out and withered."[39] With wars becoming more and more destructive through new, dangerous inventions, Michelet began to question the value of science and technology. He had always accepted the accomplishments in these fields, because they had led to increased communications between peoples, as with the railroad, and to less suffering for the poor, as with mass-produced clothing. The building of bridges, railroads, and canals had facilitated, in a Saint-Simonian sense, the civilizing spread of French culture and ideas. However, in *La France devant l'Europe* and again in the third volume of *Histoire du XIXᵉ siècle*, Michelet posed the problem of science having the capacity for as much evil as good. Machinery "for the last thirty years has served war and has transformed it. The various arts which were combined in machinery have been more and more applied to purposes of destruction."[40] Constant wars were destroying France and civilization. Furthermore, new weapons such as fast-repeating pistols and more refined cannon, would inevitably lead nations "like a mathematical progression" to a new round of producing more fatal weapons.[41]

The continual moral and historical decline of the nineteenth century since the early years of the French Revolution was certain. Socialism, industrialism, militarism, and the luxuries of alcohol, meat, coffee, and tobacco had increasingly regimented and corrupted man while loosening the moral fibers of society. "Several people . . . have asked me," related Michelet at the conclusion of his "Glance at the whole century and its rapid decline," "What do you think of the future? Will this century be able to rise again?"[42] In responding, Michelet observed the other nations of the world and wondered whether they would be capable of leading humanity onto the paths of progress again. Everyone was currently looking to America, but Michelet noted earlier in his preface that the United States would decline in the future, because they were allowing the "lower classes of Europe" to immigrate.[43] Moreover, all American art and culture was "imitative" of France and Europe.[44] If the world was to revive again it had to occur in France, still the dominant nation. France had brought hope to the world three times within one hundred years—1789, 1830, 1848—and therefore was capable of rejuvenating the world a fourth time.[45] Seventy-five years of personal observation had deeply scarred Michelet's belief in progress, but he still felt, with some hesitancy, that brief periods of revival, further great "moments," were quite probable.

In his final forward to his *Histoire du XIX⁺ siècle*, written in January 1874, Michelet consciously correlated the approaching end of his own life cycle and his idea of the decline of history. "I am declining and the decline of the century, too, has been so rapid during the past twenty years that one could say that it is literally rushing to its end."[46] A month later the great historian had a fatal heart attack, dying at Hyères on February 9, 1874. Following his only request, his body was exposed for two days to the light and sun of the Mediterranean Sea before being lowered into darkness. Alfred arrived immediately and, adhering to the sentence in Michelet's will, "I will be taken to the nearest cemetery," had his former father-in-law buried in Hyères.[47] In her book *La Mort et les funérailles de J. Michelet*, Athénaïs bitterly attacked Alfred for intervening at all. Contrary to any stated wishes by her husband, Athénaïs pressed government authorities for more than a year to allow her to have him reburied in his native Paris. On August 11, 1875, a Paris court granted her request. Exhumed on May 13, 1876, Michelet's coffin arrived in Paris on May 16, exactly one year before the *seize mai* crisis which has since symbolized the solidification of republicanism in France.

Before thousands of public officials, academicians, students, and friends, Michelet was buried a second and final time at Père Lachaise, where, alone, he had spent his happiest childhood moments.

# Epilogue

# I Have Exhumed Them
# for a Second Life

While preparations were being made to commemorate the centenary of Michelet's birth, highlighted by the ceremony at the Panthéon on July 13, 1898, presided over by the President of France, Félix Faure, an article appeared in the *Revue politique et littéraire* entitled: "Pourquoi on ne lit plus Michelet." Georges Meunier, the author, suggested that Michelet was no longer read because his emotive, imprecise, and personal method of history writing was not "understood" by the new generation. Michelet was out of fashion and even difficult to read, because people preferred more exacting scientific histories. Positivism had made Michelet anachronistic. He was "too emotional" for the youth, who reacted to him "with astonishing irreverence," while the Church and the political right still detested him because of the incessant attacks on priests and religion.[1] With Michelet unread, mocked, or scorned, it was likely, concluded Meunier, that Frenchmen would "remain indifferent to this great patriotic demonstration."[2]

Reacting to this same centenary celebration, Charles Maurras, founder several months later of the Action Française to combat Dreyfusards, bemoaned the popularity of Michelet. "Modern France accepts Michelet for master but she is wrong."[3] Acknowledging Michelet for what he was, the near official historian of France during the Third Republic (in the last third of the century nine editions of the *Histoire de la Révolution française*

224

and eleven of the *Histoire de France* appeared), Maurras derided the action of the ministry of education to distribute excerpts of Michelet to all schoolchildren gratis, and implored the future generations of France not to read Michelet. Whereas Alphonse Aulard and Jean Jaurès were inspired in their writings by the passionate, humanistic method of Michelet, Maurras was repulsed and minced no words in expressing his feelings. For Maurras, Michelet "ignored reason," had "no method," and managed to think "without a brain."[4] Michelet was illogical, irrational, and absurd for this reactionary intellectual who claimed Auguste Comte as his philosophical master. "He thinks he knows by heart the causes of facts, their reasons, and their divine or human sense," Maurras sarcastically wrote, "he even trained his heart to play chess and to reduce fractions."[5] Condescendingly, Maurras referred to Michelet as "the little Parisian apprentice," and complained that "if our children appear stupider than us" it can be attributed "to the lessons of Michelet which they were forced to learn."[6]

Michelet's stature and popularity declined in the first decades of the twentieth century. One of the few groups by the early 1920s still maintaining that Michelet's influence was significant were the rightist political and literary writers. Léon Daudet, a Michelet detractor, was an ally of Maurras's at the Action Française, and, when elected to the Chamber of Deputies in 1919, became a spokesman for the group in the tangled political arena of the Third Republic. Expanding Maurras's critique, Daudet accused Michelet as well as Victor Hugo of having been "two perverters of men's minds, and . . . almost as pernicious as Rousseau."[7] Daudet had been imbued with the Maistrian and then official Catholic philosophy of history that the thirteenth century was the high water mark of civilization. Whereas Maistre charged Bacon as the culprit who polluted men's minds with false notions of science, reason, and progress, Daudet now upbraided Michelet for injecting the evil idea of progress into the veins of French society. This fraud of progress was pure self-deception on Michelet's part, according to Daudet, but more than that, this idea had caused workers to fight for unattainable goals through uprisings and strikes, and had led to the middle and lower classes wiping out cultivated, elite society. The destruction of high society signified the demise of true culture and true religion.

## Jules Michelet

Michelet's scholarly importance had fallen remarkably by the 1920s. Aulard's assessment that Michelet's influence in the last half of the nineteenth century was comparable to Rousseau's in the eighteenth, failed to take account of the rising tide of positivistic and scientific histories. By the twentieth century these more sober histories had replaced, in scholarly circles, the frenzied, unfootnoted histories of Michelet. These largely political analyses, along with some economic and social history, were far more factually accurate than Michelet's works. Leftist historians, aware of the weaknesses in Michelet's social and educational thought, began to chide his ideas and to bring them under closer scrutiny. Albert Mathiez, a former student of Aulard's, generally mentioned Michelet only to attack him, especially on his one-sided interpretation of Danton. Among historians Mathiez had one of the most highly unfavorable opinions of the historian of "the people":

> Michelet, all imbued with mysticism, invoked a vague Providence; for all the evils of society, whose causes he understood poorly, there was only one remedy which he could propose: education. He was undoubtedly concerned about the miseries of the people, but his response was only a series of protests and pleas which sometimes bordered on the ridiculous. At the same time that Marx was writing the *Communist Manifesto*, he was bleating for the union of the classes. Far from having nourished the democratic opposition, he had probably exhausted it and certainly led it astray. Because he had lived his first years in the midst of the printing business of his father, he boasted of being from the people. An unbearable pretension. . . . He was in reality one of the beautiful fruits of the classical education that the sons of the bourgeoisie received in the private schools; fruits of dazzling colors, but frequently hollow inside. I am struck by the incoherence and by the frequent banality of his thought. This amateur of philosophy was not a philosopher.[8]

At his nadir of popularity and scholarly impact, Michelet was revived and put into twentieth-century clothing by one of the founders of the Annales School, Lucien Febvre. Symbolically, Febvre viewed his 1933 election to the chair of modern civilization at the Collège de France as a restoration of the Michelet spirit to a dominant position in historical methodology. Aware of the criticisms of Michelet by positivistic historians, Febvre parroted their complaints in his jesting style:

## Epilogue: I Have Exhumed Them for a Second Life

Do you know Michelet? . . . Between you and me he wasn't that good at history! He didn't get to the bottom of his sources. Far better scholars than he . . . have proved it. His bibliography . . . not worth speaking of: he didn't even keep his notes in a filing box. And his history, rotted through with errors and mistakes: one can't trust it. Besides, an old fogey, a humanitarian, a professional patriot, a liberal.[9]

Despite these flagrant weaknesses as a historian, Febvre called Michelet "the father of history."[10]

Febvre found in Michelet a method of history writing that had been buried beneath the avalanche of specialized, dry, scientific histories of the previous generation. Michelet's "resurrection of the fullness of life" had great appeal as an answer to Febvre's distaste for historical works that had become more and more specialized and impersonal and less and less humanistic. Febvre's terminology of *mentalité, sensibilité*, mental equipment, psychological history, and *histoire totale*, expressed his desire for full resurrections of past periods of history. As Michelet had criticized in his 1869 preface to the *Histoire de France* all other historians for their "partial" histories, so did Febvre hope to counteract the recent trend of incomplete histories through the use and acceptance of his methodological ideas.

General, humanistic histories of a region or a nation, including all possible physical, mental, and emotional factors of the area and of the inhabitants, could reveal, according to Febvre, the *mentalité* and *sensibilité* of those people. Febvre's ideas for discovering the mental and emotional limits of a historical group or period resembled Michelet's beliefs in the possibilities inherent in his own approach for reviving the past:

> If archeology can decide from the shape of such and such a Gothic arch that a building is of such and such a date, with how much more certainty can historical psychology demonstrate that a particular moral circumstance belongs to a particular century and to no other, that a particular idea, a particular passion, equally impossible in more ancient ages and in more modern epochs, was precisely what was to be expected at a particular date?[11]

In his desire to write *histoire totale* Febvre continued to suggest physical factors and emotions, such as love and fear, that, although

*227*

hitherto largely neglected, could shed light on the *mentalité* of other eras. Michelet's ideas on geographical influences and the need for a history of hunger or for a history of alimentation became standard topics for Febvre and the Annales School. Febvre, however, was only one of the leaders of this presently dominant historical group in France. While his plans for full histories of the mental equipment of the past are basically followed, the emphases and priorities have altered. Along with general histories Febvre attempted to revive the psychological and humanistic side of history which has lately been superseded in stress by structural and quantified social and economic studies of societies. Most of the various streams of the Annales School today reflect somewhat less of the human ingredient in history than Febvre desired and Michelet insisted upon, but these historians still refer to Michelet as one of the greatest French historians. Febvre gave another reason for his love of Michelet, in addition to his methodological importance, with which most French historians would probably concur. "Michelet, a Frenchman to the highest degree, carried in him not only the France of the present, but the France of twenty-five centuries . . . translating in his magnificent language and with all of his emotion, the sentiment of eternal France."[12]

What is Michelet's enduring value, those magnetic factors that continue to make his works objects of fascination and marvel? Although Michelet is the great French national historian, his patriotic sentiments are certainly insufficient reason for his appeal today. His belief in the importance of history and of the historian seems to belong squarely in the nineteenth century. His philosophical, social, and patronizing educational ideas were mediocre for his own day and appear even more superficial in the twentieth century. His historical works were full of bombast, nonsense, mistakes, misquoting, and blatant prejudices. His "resurrection of the fullness of life" neglected or reflected his unawareness of entire fields of knowledge that are essential for complete historical inquiries today. Yet, despite all of his undistinguished philosophizing, fallacious notions, and supposed deficiencies as a historian, his *Histoire de la Révolution française* remains the monumental history of that event. As *histoire totale* Michelet's work was a full social and emotive re-creation of the period. But more than that, Michelet also gave the reader a sense of active participation in the French Revolution. The fantastic combination of the excitement generated by his writing as a living witness, nourished by the oral tradition; by the inspiration from his basic idea that man makes history, that "man is his own Prometheus"; and by his fertile and insightful imagination—all these give this work a unique and eternal quality.

Michelet's manner of "resurrecting the fullness of life" cannot be imitated, and his "mind and sensibilities" reflected different values, assumptions, and beliefs than historians possess more than a century after his death. But his humanistic history can be continued with knowledge and language appropriate to our own social and emotive world. Michelet's enduring value is contained in the novel, romantic way he made the dead bones live again. As an old man he worried that "individuals and peoples were forgetting themselves because they were ungrateful and blind to their fathers and to their great moments of history."[13] But he knew that he had fulfilled his function as a historian and hoped that others would follow him and revive more epochs, more "great moments," and more men "for a second life," including himself. "Never in my career have I lost from view this duty of a historian. I have given to many of the too long forgotten dead the assistance that I will need myself. I have exhumed them for a second life."[14]

# Notes

## Introduction

1. Jules Michelet, *Journal*, ed. and introduction by Paul Viallaneix, 2 vols. (Paris: Gallimard, 1959, 1962), 1:11-25.

2. Michelet never entitled these documents, but, apparently, Monod, with the prior agreement of Mme Michelet, gave the labels *Journal* and *Journal intime*. *Journal* referred to any personal paper, primarily travel journals, while the *Journal intime* contained the papers Monod and Mme Michelet considered to be the most private and intimate statements of Michelet.

3. Jules Michelet, *Ecrits de jeunesse*, ed. and introduction by Paul Viallaneix (Paris: Gallimard, 1959).

4. With the depositing of the papers in 1911 both the *Journal* and *Journal intime* were thereafter referred to only as the *Journal*.

5. Michelet, *Journal*, ed. Paul Viallaneix covers the period 1828 to 1860. For the rest of Michelet's life—1861-1874—see: *Journal*, vols. 3 and 4 ed. and introduction by Claude Digeon (Paris: Gallimard, 1976).

6. Gabriel Monod, *La Vie et la pensée de Jules Michelet*, ed. Charles Bémont and Henri Hauser, 2 vols. (Paris: Champion, Bibliothèque de l'Ecole des hautes études, 1923).

7. Monod's magisterial study only went through the year 1848, with the years 1849-52 only sketched and nothing on the last twenty-two years. Subsequent biographies were written by Jean Guéhenno, *L'Evangile éternel* (Paris: Grasset, 1927); Daniel Halévy, *Jules Michelet* (Paris: Hachette, 1929). Since 1951 and with the appearance of the *Journal*, a number of works have appeared. Literary perspectives have been given by Oscar Haac, *Les Principes inspirateurs de Michelet* (Paris: Presses Universitaires de France, 1951); Roland Barthes, *Michelet par lui-même* (Paris: Editions du Seuil, 1954); Linda Orr, *Jules Michelet: Nature, History, and Language* (Ithaca and London: Cornell University Press, 1976); and Edward K. Kaplan, *Michelet's Poetic Vision: A Romantic Philosophy of Nature, Man and Woman*. (Amherst: University of Massachusetts Press, 1977). Religious perspectives have been given by Mary Elisabeth Johnson, *Michelet et le christianisme* (Paris: Nizet, 1955); Jean-Louis Cornuz, *Jules Michelet: Un aspect de la pensée religieuse au XIX$^e$ siècle* (Geneva: Droz et Lille, Giard, 1955); and José Cabanis, *Michelet, le prêtre et la femme* (Paris: Gallimard, 1978). For Michelet and women see: Jeanne Calo, *La création de la femme chez Michelet* (Paris: Nizet, 1975). For Michelet as seminal thinker in historical

method see: Lucien Febvre, *Michelet* (Geneva: Editions des Trois Collines, 1946). For Michelet and "the people" see: Paul Viallaneix, *La Voie royale* (Paris: Delagrave, 1959; reprint ed., Paris: Flammarion, 1971).

8. For a variety of samplings see: Viallaneix, *La Voie royale*; Pieter Geyl, *Debates with Historians* (Cleveland: World Publishing Company, 1958), pp. 70-108; Hans Kohn, *Prophets and Peoples* (New York: Macmillan Company, 1946), pp. 43-76; Maxime Leroy, *Histoire des idées sociales en France*, 3 vols. (Paris: Gallimard, N.R.F., 1946-54); Roger Soltau, *French Political Thought in the Nineteenth Century* (New Haven: Yale University Press, 1931); J. L. Talmon, *Political Messianism: The Romantic Phase* (New York: Ferderick A. Praeger, 1960, pp. 242-55; Edmund Wilson, *To The Finland Station* (New York: Doubleday and Company, Inc., Anchor Books, 1953, pp. 1-34.

## Chapter 1

1. Jules Michelet, *Le Peuple*, ed. and introduction by Lucien Refort (Paris: Didier, 1946), p. 19.

2. Bibliothèque historique de la ville de Paris, MS. Histoire Religieuse 3, A3827, fol. 113, May 14, 1868.

3. Jules Michelet, *Journal*, ed. and introduction by Paul Viallaneix, 2 vols. (Paris: Gallimard, 1959, 1963), 1:290. February 1839.

4. Bibliothèque historique de la ville de Paris, MS. Biographie 1, A3744, fol. 254, April 20, 1872.

5. Michelet, *Journal*, 2:61. August 16, 1849.

6. According to Michelet's cousin, Félicie Lefebvre Guyot, there were sixteen children. Bibliothèque historique de la ville de Paris, MS. Correspondance 6, A4733, fol. 252, Félicie Guyot to Michelet, February 18, 1846.

7. Michelet, *Le Peuple*, pp. 13-14.

8. Quoted in Paul Viallaneix, *La Voie royale* (Paris: Delagrave, 1959; reprint ed., Paris: Flammarion, 1971), p. 56.

9. Ibid.

10. Noted by Paul Viallaneix in Jules Michelet, *Ecrits de jeunesse*, ed. and introduction by Paul Viallaneix (Paris: Gallimard, 1959), p. 396. According to Félicie Lefebvre Guyot 120,000 francs were left. Bibliothèque historique de la ville de Paris, MS. Correspondance 6, A4733, fol. 252, Félicie Guyot to Michelet, February 18, 1846.

11. Quoted in Viallaneix, *La Voie royale*, p. 57.

12. Jules Michelet, *Histoire de la Révolution française*, ed. Gérard Walter, 2 vols. (Paris: Gallimard, N.R.F., Bibliothèque de la Pléiade, 1939, 1952), 1:1150.

13. Michelet, *Ecrits de jeunesse*, p. 187.

14. Michelet, *Histoire de la Révolution française*, 1:1151.

15. Bibliothèque historique de la ville de Paris, MS. Biographie 1, A3744, fols. 257, 259. A similar version is found in Jules Michelet *Œuvres complètes*, vol. 24: *Histoire du XIX<sup>e</sup> siècle* (Paris: Flammarion, 1898), p. 333.

16. Archives Nationales, MS. F⁷4774, n° 45, dossier 4.

17. Michelet, *Le Peuple*, p. 4.

18. Ibid., p. 15.

19. Michelet, *Ecrits de jeunesse*, p. 198.

20. Michelet, *Le Peuple*, p. 15.

21. Archives Nationales, MS. F¹⁸2371.

22. Michelet, *Œuvres complètes*, 24:333-35.

23. Michelet, *Journal*, 1:621-22. August 23, 1845.

24. The manuscript of the *Mémorial* at the Bibliothèque historique de la ville de Paris has parts of pages cut out while phrases and sentences are crossed out with a pen similar in ink and done with the same technique as that used on Michelet's *Journal* of later decades. Since Athénaïs, Michelet's widow, possessed these documents after his death, it was probably her work, although some of the work may have been done by Michelet. There are many references by Michelet in the 1850s and 1860s to his destruction of his personal papers; see for example, Michelet, *Journal*, 2:714. February 2, 1852.

25. Michelet, *Ecrits de jeunesse*, p. 182.

26. Ibid., p. 184.

27. Ibid., p. 212.

28. Michelet, *Journal*, 2:245. April 18, 1854.

29. Ibid., 1:622. August 23, 1845.

30. Michelet, *Œuvres complètes*, vol. 1: *Histoire de France* (1893), p. xviii.

31. Michelet, *Ecrits de jeunesse*, pp. 185, 191.

32. Bibliothèque historique de la ville de Paris, MS. Biographie 1, A3744, fol. 262, [1850s.].

33. Michelet, *Ecrits de jeunesse*, p. 201.

34. Bibliothèque historique de la ville de Paris, MS. Biographie 1, A3744, fol. 258.

35. Ibid.

36. Michelet, *Ecrits de jeunesse*, p. 212.

37. Ibid., pp. 184-85. The recitation which made his mother cry, "Mortals are equal, it is not at all a question of birth," was from Voltaire's 1732 *Eriphyle*. Voltaire, *Œuvres complètes*, vol. 2: *Théâtre* (Paris: Baudouin frères, 1828), act 2, sc. 1, p. 449. This first line is nearly illegible in the manuscript as someone attempted to cross it out. The second verse was, "It is virtue alone by which people differ." These lines in Voltaire's attempt at a Shakespearean tragedy were part of soliloquy by Alcméon. Unaware in the second act of his princely origins, Alcméon was bemoaning the situation in Argos whereby Hermogide, a prince of royal blood, would become the next king merely on account of his birth, since he had no virtue. Virtuous Alcméon was determined to convert value systems in order for character and morality to be preferred over noble ancestry.

38. Jules Michelet, "Sur le livre *Du prêtre et de la femme*: Réponse aux critiques," *Revue indépendante*, ser. 1, 19 (March 25, 1845):202. A similar version is also found in Michelet, *Œuvres complètes*, vol. 32: *Du prêtre, de la femme, de la famille*, (1895), pp. 32-33.

39. Michelet, *Ecrits de jeunesse*, p. 186.

40. Bibliothèque historique de la ville de Paris, MS. Biographie 1, A3744, fol. 263, [1850s.].

41. Michelet, *Ecrits de jeunesse*, p. 183.

42. Ibid., p. 186.

43. Ibid., p. 183.

44. Ibid.

## Chapter 2

1. Jules Michelet, *Œuvres complètes*, vol. 24: *Histoire du XIX<sup>e</sup> siècle* (Paris: Flammarion, 1898), pp. 147-48.
2. Jules Michelet, *Le Peuple*, ed. and introduction by Lucien Refort (Paris: Didier, 1946), pp. 16-17.
3. Ibid., p. 20.
4. Jules Michelet, *Ecrits de jeunesse*, ed. and introduction by Paul Viallaneix (Paris: Gallimard, 1959), p. 189.
5. Ibid., p. 190.
6. Jules Michelet, *Journal*, ed. and introduction by Paul Viallaneix, 2 vols. (Paris: Gallimard, 1959, 1962), 1:656-57. November 21, 1846.
7. Jules Michelet, *Lettres inédites de Jules Michelet*, ed. Paul Sirven (Paris: Presses Universitaires de France, 1924), Furcy to Xavier-Félix Millet, January 17, 1820, p. 327.
8. Quoted in Michelet, *Ecrits de jeunesse*, Furcy Xavier-Félix Millet, January 22, 1822, p. 378.
9. Bibliothèque historique de la ville de Paris, MS. Biographie 2, A3756, fol. 311, Victor Duruy to Athénaïs Michelet, May 2, 1884.
10. Michelet, *Ecrits de jeunesse*, p. 202.
11. Ibid.
12. Ibid.
13. Ibid.
14. Ibid., p. 203.
15. Ibid.
16. *Désintéressé*, similar to the English word "unselfish," and used frequently by Michelet has an especially positive meaning in all of his writings.
17. Michelet, *Ecrits de jeunesse*, p. 210.
18. Ibid., p. 207.
19. Ibid., p. 79. May 18, 1820.
20. Ibid., p. 191.
21. Ibid., p. 192.
22. Ibid., p. 198.
23. Ibid., Michelet to Poinsot, May 25, 1820, p. 256.
24. Ibid., p. 168. September 27, 1821.
25. Ibid., p. 187.
26. Ibid.
27. Ibid.
28. Ibid., p. 75. May 4, 1820.
29. Ibid., p. 165. September 20, 1821.
30. Quoted in Gabriel Monod, *La Vie et la pensée de Jules Michelet*, ed. Charles Bémont and Henry Hauser, 2 vols. (Paris: Champion, Bibliothèque de l'Ecole des hautes études, 1923), 1:36.
31. Michelet, *Ecrits de jeunesse*, Michelet to Poinsot, June 9, 1820, p. 263.
32. Ibid., p. 342.
33. Ibid., p. 105. August 18, 1820.
34. Ibid., pp. 105-6.

34. Ibid., pp. 105-6.
35. Ibid., Michelet to Poinsot, May 31, 1820, p. 259.
36. Bibliothèque historique de la ville de Paris, MS. Biographie 1, A3743, fol. 169. Michelet to his aunts in Renwez, March 8, 1824.
37. Ibid.
38. For letters, see: Michelet, *Journal*, 1:707-799 passim.
39. Ibid., 1:306. July 24, 1839.
40. Ibid.
41. Ibid., 1:330. June 23, 1840.
42. Ibid., 1:290. February 1839.
43. Michelet, *Le Peuple*, p. 18.
44. Quoted in Michelet, *Ecrits de jeunesse*, Furcy to Xavier-Félix Millet, November 10, 1821, p. 376.
45. Michelet, *Ecrits de jeunesse*, p. 93. July 3, 1820.
46. Ibid., p. 121. November 5, 1820.
47. Michelet, *Le Peuple*, p. 21.
48. Bibliothèque historique de la ville de Paris, MS. Biographie 1, A3742, fol. 161, Michelet to Monseigneur Frayssinous, [1826.].
49. Michelet, *Journal*, 1:488. December 10, 1842.
50. Dugald Stewart, *Histoire abrégée des sciences métaphysiques, morales et politiques depuis la Renaissance des lettres*, trans. and ed. J. A. Buchon, 3 vols. (Paris: F. G. Levrault, 1820-23), 3: 369-72.

## *Chapter 3*

1. Jules Michelet, *Tableau chronologique de l'histoire moderne* (Paris: L. Colas, 1825); *Tableaux synchroniques de l'histoire moderne* (Paris: L. Colas, 1826); *Précis de l'histoire moderne* (Paris: L. Colas, L. Hachette, 1827).
2. Jules Michelet, *Ecrits de jeunesse*, ed. and introduction by Paul Viallaneix (Paris: Gallimard, 1959), Michelet to Cousin, [1824,] p. 410.
3. Ibid., p. 227. December 1823.
4. Ibid., p. 235. September 21, 1825.
5. Their meeting was arranged by Hector Poret. Michelet and Poret had gone through school together; receiving their secondary school diplomas, their bachelor degrees, and passing their doctoral examinations at the same time. Now they were colleagues at the Collège Sainte-Barbe, where Poret was a professor of Greek. Poret knew Cousin, because he was helping him with some translations of Plato in 1824, and, at that time, he was able to set up an appointment for Michelet.
6. Michelet, *Ecrits de jeunesse*, p. 409.
7. Ibid.
8. Ibid., p. 231. April 19, 1824.
9. Ibid., p. 409.
10. Ibid., p. 293.
11. Ibid.
12. Ibid., p. 297.
13. Ibid., p. 299.

14. Ibid., Michelet to Cousin, June 14, 1824, p. 410.
15. Victor Cousin, *Cours de philosophie*, vol. 1: *Introduction à l'histoire de la philosophie* (Paris: Pichon et Didier, 1828), lesson 11, pp. 34-35. Cousin told his students: "I congratulate myself for having encouraged my two young friends MM. Michelet and Quinet for having given France Vico and Herder."
16. Jules Michelet, *Œuvres complètes*, vol. 1: *Histoire de France* (Paris: Flammarion, 1893), p. xi.
17. Jules Michelet, *Œuvres complètes*, ed. Paul Viallaneix, vol. 1: *1798-1827* (Paris: Flammarion, 1971), pp. 283-301.
18. Ibid., 1:287-88.
19. Michelet, *Œuvres complètes*, vol. 2: *1828-1831*, (1972), p. 342.
20. For example, see: Michelet, *Œuvres complètes* (1971-72), 1:288, 299; 2:341.
21. Ibid., 2:297.
22. Johann Gottfried von Herder, *Idées sur la philosophie de l'histoire de l'humanité*, trans. Edgar Quinet, 3 vols. (Paris: Levrault, 1827-28).
23. Henri Tronchon, *Le Jeune Edgar Quinet* (Paris: Les Belles Lettres, 1937), pp. 289-351 passim.
24. Ibid., pp. 344-51.
25. Herder, *Idées sur la philosophie de l'histoire*, 1:7.
26. Bibliothèque historique de la ville de Paris, MS. Correspondance 3, A4291, fol. 243, Michelet to Quinet, May 27, 1827.
27. Quoted in Henri Tronchon, *Etudes* (Paris: Champion, 1935), p. 86.
28. Jules Michelet, *Journal*, ed. and introduction by Paul Viallaneix, 2 vols. (Paris: Gallimard, 1959, 1962), Michelet to family, September 4, 1828, 1:713-14.
29. Cousin, *Cours de philosophie*, vol. 1: *Introduction à l'histoire de la philosophie*. Cousin had his 1828 and 1829 courses published together soon after the conclusion of the second term.
30. Ibid., 1, lecture 4:6.
31. Ibid., 1, lecture 6:34.
32. Ibid., 1, lecture 11:23.
33. Ibid., 1, lecture 11:27.
34. Michelet, *Ecrits de jeunesse*, p. 237. February 5, 1826.
35. Bibliothèque historique de la ville de Paris, MS. Correspondance 3, A4291, fol. 243, Michelet to Quinet, May 27, 1827.

## Chapter 4

1. Bibliothèque historique de la ville de Paris, MS. Biographie 1, A3742, fol. 161, Michelet to Monseigneur Frayssinous, [1826.].
2. Bibliothèque historique de la ville de Paris, MS. Correspondance 3, A4291, fol. 243, Michelet to Quinet, May 27, 1827.
3. Ibid.
4. Centre de recherches révolutionnaires et romantiques, Université de Clermont, Clermont-Ferrand, typescripts of Michelet's courses at the Ecole Normale, 1828-29, lecture 1, p. 1.
5. Ibid., p. 2.

6. Jules Michelet, *Ecrits de jeunesse*, ed. and introduction by Paul Viallaneix (Paris: Gallimard, 1959), p. 248. September 22, 1829.

7. Centre de recherches révolutionnaires et romantiques, course of 1829-30.

8. Unfortunately most of Michelet's diary for the years 1829-30 was apparently destroyed in the 1850s and 1860s. See, for example: Jules Michelet, *Journal*, ed. and introduction by Paul Viallaneix, 2 vols. (Paris: Gallimard, 1959, 1962), 2:714.

9. Ibid., 1:76. April 28, 1830.

10. Bibliothèque historique de la ville de Paris, MS. Correspondance 3, A4300, fol. 260, Michelet to Quinet, August 10, 1830.

11. Jules Michelet, *Œuvres complètes*, ed. Paul Viallaneix, vol. 2: *1828-1831* (Paris: Flammarion, 1972), pp. 254-55.

12. Jules Michelet, *Œuvres complètes*, vol. 1: *Histoire de France* (Paris: Flammarion, 1893), p. xii.

13. Ibid., 1:i.

14. Centre de recherches révolutionnaires et romantiques, course of 1828-29, lecture 9, p. 51.

15. Ibid.

16. Michelet, *Œuvres complètes*, (1972), 2:249.

17. Ibid., 2:258.

18. Michelet, *Journal*, 1:83. August 7, 1831.

19. Ibid.

## Chapter 5

1. Jules Michelet, *Œuvres complètes*, ed. Paul Viallaneix, vol. 3: *1832-1839* (Paris: Flammarion, 1973), pp. 217-23.

2. Ibid., 3:217.

3. Ibid. Michelet was referring to two 1750 lectures, the *Sorboniques*, found in Anne Robert Jacques Turgot, *Œuvres*, ed. Pierre Samuel Dupont de Nemours, 9 vols. (Paris: A. Belin, 1808-11), 2:19-92.

4. Ibid.

5. Ibid., 3:217-18.

6. Ibid., 3:218.

7. Ibid.

8. Ibid., 3:223.

9. Ibid.

10. Jules Michelet, *History of France*, trans. G. H. Smith, 2 vols. (New York: D. Appleton and Company, 1845, 1848), 1:479.

11. Ibid., 1:480.

12. Ibid., 1:479.

13. Jules Michelet, *Œuvres complètes*, vol. 1: *Histoire de France* (Paris: Flammarion, 1893), pp. xxxvii-xxxviii.

14. Jules Michelet, *Histoire de la Révolution française*, ed. Gérard Walter, 2 vols. (Paris: Gallimard, N.R.F., Bibliothèque de la Pléiade, 1939, 1972), 1:13.

15. Bibliothèque historique de la ville de Paris, MS. Correspondance 5, A4687, fol. 171, Michelet to Charles, December 28, 1851.

16. Michelet, *Histoire de la Révolution française*, 1:17.

17. The majority of these documents are at: Archives Nationales, ABIX$_I$ and ABVF$_I$; Bibliothèque historique de la ville de Paris, Fonds Baudoüin-Dumesnil, Michelet aux Archives.

18. Michelet, *History of France*, 1:479.

19. Archives Nationales, MS. ABIX$_I$, report of November 8, 1830.

20. Archives Nationales, MS. ABIX$_I$, report of December 31, 1830.

21. Archives Nationales, MS. ABIS$_I$, reports of January 1833, February 1838, and April 1840.

22. Quoted in Carlo Pellegrini, "Sismondi e Michelet," *Studi Francesi* (1965), Michelet to Sismondi, January 9, 1833, p. 34.

23. For example, see: Jules Michelet, *Journal*, ed. and introduction by Paul Viallaneix, 2 vols. (Paris: Gallimard, 1959, 1962), 1:252. July 11, 1838.

24. Michelet, *Œuvres complètes* (1973), 3:545-63.

25. Guizot's questions are preserved at: Bibliothèque historique de la ville de Paris, MS. Fonds Baudoüin-Dumesnil, Michelet aux Archives, fol. 1,1, Guizot to Michelet, August 11, 1835.

26. For these letters, see: Michelet, *Journal*, 1:777-79, 783-84.

27. Archives Nationales, MS. ABVF$_I$, report of July 28, 1838, *Renseignements sur les archives de Besançon, de Berne, de Lucerne, de Venise*.

28. Michelet, *History of France*, 1:480.

29. Michelet's most complete reports advocating this method of classification are: Archives Nationales, MS. ABVF$_I$, report of July 3, 1850; Bibliothèque historique de la ville de Paris, MS. Fonds Baudoüin-Dumesnil, Michelet aux Archives, fol. 17, 49-50, report of September 11, 1850.

30. Michelet, *History of France*, 1:480.

31. Ibid.


## Chapter 6


1. Augustin Thierry, "Première lettre sur l'histoire de France," *Dix ans d'études historiques* (bound with *Lettres sur l'histoire de France*) (Paris: Furne, Jouvet et Cie., 1866), p. 502.

2. Ibid., p. 501.

3. Ibid., p. 502.

4. Jules Michelet, *History of France*, trans. G.H. Smith, 2 vols. (New York: D. Appleton and Company, 1845, 1848), 1:479.

5. Thierry, *Dix ans d'études historiques*, pp. 310-11.

6. For example see: Thierry, "Première lettre sur l'histoire de France," pp. 501-3.

7. Amédée Thierry, *Histoire des Gaulois*, 3 vols. (Paris. A. Sautelet et Cie., 1828; Augustin Thierry, *Lettres sur l'histoire de France*, pp. 18-25.

8. Amédée Thierry, *Histoire des Gaulois*, 1:ii.

9. Henri Martin, *Histoire de France*, 4th ed., 17 vols. (Paris: Furne, 1860-62), 1:xii.

10. Augustin Thierry, *Dix ans d'études historiques*, p. 314.

11. Ibid., "Sur l'antipathie de race qui divise la nation française," p. 486.

12. François Guizot, *The History of Civilization*, trans. William Hazlitt, 2 vols. (London: H. G. Bohn, 1856), 1, 1829-30 course lecture 2:289.

13. Ibid., 1, 1828-29 course, lecture 8:147.

14. Ibid., 2, 1829-30 course, lecture 24:288-90.

15. Ibid., 2, 1829-30 course, lecture 25:308.

16. Jules Michelet, *Ecrits de jeunesse*, ed. and introduction by Paul Viallaneix (Paris: Gallimard, 1959), p.. 316-30.

17. Jules Michelet, *Histoire de France*, 2 vols. (Paris: Hachette, 1833), 1:5.

18. Ibid.

19. Jules Michelet, *Journal*, ed. and introduction by Paul Viallaneix, 2 vols. (Paris: Gallimard 1959, 1962), 1:358. March 10, 1841.

20. Jules Michelet, "L'Héroïsme de l'esprit," *L'Arc* 52 (1973):17. He wrote: "Cousin and Guizot had no influence on me. I like these outstanding men . . . but too great were the differences of ideas, personalities, temperament, and method."

21. Jules Michelet, *Œuvres complètes*, vol. 1: *Histoire de France* (Paris: Flammarion, 1893), p. ii.

22. Ibid.

23. Ibid.

24. Ibid., 1:i.

25. Ibid.

26. Ibid.

27. Jules Michelet, *Le Peuple*, ed. and introduction by Lucien Refort (Paris: Didier, 1946), p. 25.

28. Michelet, *Œuvres complètes*, 1:iv.

29. Ibid., 1:135.

30. Michelet, *History of France*, 1:67.

31. Ibid., 1:148.

32. Ibid.

33. Michelet, *Œuvres complètes*, 1:vi.

34. Anne Robert Jacques Turgot, *Œuvres*, ed. Pierre Samuel Dupont de Nemours, 9 vols. (Paris: A. Belin, 1808-11), 2:166-208.

35. Michelet, "L'Héroïsme de l'esprit," p. 11.

36. Michelet, *History of France*, 1:149.

37. Ibid.

38. Ibid.

39. Ibid., 1:150.

40. Ibid., 1:151.

41. Ibid., 1:148.

42. Ibid., 1:168.

43. Ibid., 1:148.

44. Jules Michelet, *Œuvres complètes*, ed. Paul Viallaneix, vol. 2: *1828-1831* (Paris: Flammarion, 1972), p. 229. In this instance I have translated *fatalité* as fate, but most other uses of the word have been left in the original, since the English "fatality" has lost its nineteenth-century equivalence, and no other word seems to capture the spirit of both determinism and negativity implied by Michelet.

45. Ibid., 2:247.

46. William Frédéric Edwards, *Des caractères philosophiques des races humaines considérées dans leurs rapports avec l'histoire: Lettre à M. Amédée Thierry* (Paris: Compère jeune, 1829).

47. Michelet, *Ecrits de jeunesse*, p. 244. March 12, 1829.
48. Ibid., p. 247. May 15, 1829.
49. Bibliothèque historique de la ville de Paris, MS. Biographie 2, A3754.
50. Edwards, *Des caractères philosophiques*, p. 29.
51. Ibid., p. 37.
52. Michelet, *Œuvres complètes* (1972), 2:290.
53. Michelet, *History of France*, 2:392.
54. Ibid., 2:395.
55. Michelet, *Œuvres complètes* (1972), 2:247.
56. Michelet, *History of France*, 1:179.
57. Ibid., 1:181.
58. Ibid.
59. Ibid.
60. Ibid.
61. Ibid.
62. Ibid., 1:182.
63. Michelet, *Journal*, 1:76. April 28, 1830.
64. Michelet, *Œuvres complètes* (1972), 2:290-91.
65. Michelet, *Journal*, 1:290-91. February 1839.
66. Michelet, *History of France*, 1:438.
67. Michelet, *Œuvres complètes* (1972), 2:247.
68. Michelet, *Journal*, 1:501. March 25, 1843.
69. Ibid., 1:164. August 15, 1835.
70. Ibid., 1:80. August 2, 1831.
71. Jules Michelet, *Histoire de la Révolution française*, ed. Gérard Walter, 2 vols. (Paris: Gallimard, N.R.F., Bibliothèque de la Pléiade, 1939, 1952), 2:627.

*Chapter 7*

1. François Guizot, *The History of Civilization*, trans. William Hazlitt, 2 vols. (London: H.G. Bohn, 1856), 1, 1828-29 course, lecture 1:2.
2. Quoted in François Guizot, *Historical Essays and Lectures*, ed. and introduction by Stanley Mellon (Chicago: University of Chicago Press, 1972), p. xliv.
3. Augustin Thierry, "Sur l'antipathie de race qui divise la nation française," *Dix ans d'études historiques* (bound with *Lettres sur l'histoire de France*) (Paris: Furne, Jouvet et Cie., 1866), p. 486.
4. Henri Martin, *Histoire de France*, 4th ed., 17 vols. (Paris: Furne, 1860-62), 1:xi.
5. Jules Michelet, *History of France*, trans. G.H. Smith, 2 vols. (New York: D. Appleton and Company, 1845, 1848), 1:182.
6. Ibid., 1:72.
7. Ibid., 1:183.
8. Ibid.
9. Ibid.
10. Jules Michelet, *Ecrits de jeunesse*, ed. and introduction by Paul Viallaneix (Paris: Gallimard, 1959), p. 319, July 1824.
11. Michelet, *History of France*, 1:179.

12. Ibid., 2:205.

13. Jules Michelet, *Œuvres complètes*, ed. Paul Viallaneix, vol. 3: *1832-1839* (Paris: Flammarion, 1973), p. 222.

14. Michelet, *Œuvres complètes*, vol. 2: *1828-1831* (1972), p. 249.

15. Ibid., 2:252.

16. Ibid.

17. Ibid., 2:253.

18. Ibid., 2:252.

19. Jules Michelet, *Journal*, ed. and introduction by Paul Viallaneix, 2 vols. (Paris: Gallimard, 1959, 1962), 1:123. August 8, 1834.

20. Ibid., 1:152. August 26, 1834.

21. Ibid., Michelet to Pauline, August 10, 1834, 1:750.

22. Ibid., 1:160. September 3, 1834.

23. Ibid., 1:126. August 10, 1834.

24. Ibid., 1:160. September 3, 1834.

25. Ibid.

26. Jules Michelet, *Histoire de la Révolution française*, ed. Gérard Walter, 2 vols. (Paris: Gallimard, N.R.F., Bibliothèque de la Pléiade, 1939, 1952), 1:233.

27. Jules Michelet, *Œuvres complètes*, vol. 1: *Histoire de France* (Paris: Flammarion, 1893), p. viii.

28. Centre de recherches révolutionnaires et romantiques, Université de Clermont, Clermont-Ferrand, typescripts of Michelet's courses at the Ecole Normale, 1828-29, lecture 18, p. 124.

29. Michelet, *Œuvres complètes* (1972), 2:229.

30. Ibid.

31. Ibid., 2:253.

32. Bibliothèque historique de la ville de Paris, MS. Correspondance 22, A4834, fols. 124-25, Sismondi to Michelet, April 5, 1840.

33. Michelet, *History of France*, 1:148.

34. Ibid.

35. Ibid., 1:191.

36. Ibid., 1:311.

37. J. C. L. Simonde de Sismondi, *Histoire des Français*, 31 vols. (Paris: Treuttel et Würtz, 1821-44), 5:67.

38. Michelet, *History of France*, 1:311.

39. Ibid., 1:395.

40. Ibid., 1:477.

41. Michelet, *Œuvres complètes* (1893), 3:413.

42. Ibid.

43. See Guizot, *The History of Civilization*, 1, 1828-29 course, lecture 11:197-98; Martin, *Histoire de France*, 6:139-463, follows Michelet's interpretation closely.

44. Gustave Rudler, *Michelet, historien de Jeanne d'Arc*, 2 vols. (Paris: Presses Universitaires de France, 1926).

45. Ibid., 1:162.

46. Michelet, *History of France*, 2:129.

47. Ibid., 2:141.

48. Jules Michelet, *Lettres inédites de Jules Michelet*, ed. Paul Sirven (Paris: Presses Universitaires de France, 1924), Michelet to Mme Dumesnil, April 1841, p. 5.

49. Michelet, *History of France*, 2:372.
50. Michelet, *Ecrits de jeunesse*, pp. 315-22, passim.
51. Walter Scott, *Quentin Durward* (Oxford: Clarendon, 1920), p. xi.
52. Michelet, *History of France*, 1:183.
53. Ibid.
54. Michelet, *Journal*, 1:469. August 11, 1842.
55. Michelet, *Œuvres complètes* (1972), 2:255.

## Chapter 8

1. Centre de recherches révolutionnaires et romantiques, Université de Clermont, Clermont-Ferrand, typescripts of Michelet's courses at the Collège de France, 1846, p. 17.
2. Jules Michelet, *Journal*, ed. and introduction by Paul Viallaneix, 2 vols. (Paris: Gallimard, 1959, 1962), 1:353. August 1840.
3. Ibid., 1:364. August 13, 1841.
4. Ibid., 1:491. 1843.
5. There are dozens of examples of this outlook in Michelet's *Journal*. Among them are 1:399. May 9, 1842; 1:400. May 10, 1842; 1:622-23. August 23, 1845; 1:654. November 20, 1846.
6. Ibid., 1:516-17. August 5, 1843.
7. Ibid., 1:307. July 24, 1839.
8. Ibid.
9. Quoted in Eugène Noël, *J. Michelet et ses enfants* (Paris: Maurice Dreyfous, 1878), Alfred Dumesnil to Eugène Noël, 1840, pp. 9-10.
10. Jules Michelet, *Lettres inédites de Jules Michelet*, ed. Paul Sirven (Paris: Presses Universitaires de France, 1924), Michelet to Mme Dumesnil, April 1841, p. 7.
11. This moment of creativity is the subject of Lucien Febvre, "How Jules Michelet invented the Renaissance," *A New Kind of History*, ed. Peter Burke, trans. K. Folca (New York: Harper and Row, 1973), pp. 258-67.
12. Michelet, *Lettres inédites*, Michelet to Alfred, May 15, 1841, pp. 12-13.
13. Ibid.
14. Michelet, *Journal*, 1:367. August 21, 1841.
15. Ibid., 1:379. February 22, 1842.
16. Archives du Collège de France, MS. Michelet dossier fol. 9.
17. Michelet, *Journal*, 1:405. May 30, 1842.
18. Ibid., 1:406. June 2, 1842.
19. Ibid.
20. Ibid., 1:407.
21. Michelet, *Lettres inédites*, Michelet to Alfred, August 10, 1842, p. 30.
22. Ibid., Michelet to Alfred, September 1, 1842, p. 34.
23. Ibid., Michelet to Alfred, September 4, 1842, p. 35.
24. Michelet, *Journal*, Michelet to Alfred, September 9, 1842, 1:836.
25. Quoted in Noël, *J. Michelet et ses enfants*, Alfred to Eugène Noël, September 17, 1842, p. 113.
26. Michelet, *Lettres inédites*, Michelet to Alfred, October 13, 1842, p. 40.

27. Ibid., Michelet to Alfred, December 2, 1842, p. 53.

28. Ibid., Michelet to Alfred, December 7, 1842, p. 55.

29. Ibid., Michelet to Alfred, December 9, 1842, p. 56.

30. Michelet, *Journal*, Michelet to Alfred, December 11, 1842, 1:841; *Journal*, 1:488. December 10, 1842.

31. Joseph Moody, "The French Catholic Press in the Education Conflict of the 1840s," *French Historical Studies* 7 (Spring 1972):398.

32. Quoted in Jean Gaulmier, *Michelet* (Paris: Desclée de Brouwer, 1968), p. 62.

33. Nicolas Desgarets [pseud.], *Monopole Universitaire* (Lyon: n.p., 1843), pp. 395, 398.

34. See April 1, 1848 lecture for this interpretation in Jules Michelet, *L'Etudiant*, in introduction by Gaëtan Picon (Paris: Editions du Seuil, 1970), p. 175.

35. This plaque reads: "To the memory of Mickiewicz, Michelet, and Quinet / In gratitude from their former students / April 12, 1884."

36. Quoted in Edouard Krakowski, *Adam Mickiewicz: philosophe mystique* (Paris: Mercure de France, 1935), Prefect of Police Delessert to Minister of Public Education Villemain, August 16, 1842, p. 296.

37. Quoted in Wiktor Weintraub, *Literature as Prophecy: Scholarship and Martinist Poetics in Mickiewicz's Parisian Lectures* (The Hague: Mouton and Co., 1959), p. 74.

38. Quoted in Krakowski, *Adam Mickiewicz*, minister of interior to minister of public education, March 24, 1844, p. 302.

39. Weintraub, *Literature as Prophecy*, p. 75.

40. Michelet, *Lettres inédites*, Michelet to Alfred, July 31, 1843, p. 69.

41. Jules Michelet, *Des jésuites*, introduction by Paul Viallaneix (Paris: Jean-Jacques Pauvert, 1966), p. 41.

42. Ibid., p. 44.

43. Ibid., p. 48.

44. Ibid., p. 47.

45. Ibid., p. 51.

46. Ibid., p. 63.

47. Ibid., p. 84.

48. Ibid., p. 85.

49. Ibid.

50. Ibid., p. 86.

51. Edgar Quinet, *Des jésuites*, introduction by Paul Viallaneix (Paris: Jean-Jacques Pauvert, 1966), p. 187.

52. Michelet, *Des jésuites*, p. 87.

53. Ibid., p. 112.

54. Quoted in Michelet, *Journal*, 1:850.

55. The author was E. Merminier, a former professor at the Collège de France. Quinet was furious over the attack, but Michelet wrote Alfred on October 21, 1843, quoted in *Journal*, 1:866, "I think nothing is more popular than to be attacked in an article signed by that name."

56. Michelet, *Journal*, 1:519. August 11, 1843.

57. Nicolas Desgarets [pseud.], *L'Université jugée par elle-même* (Lyon: n.p., September 1843), pp. 165-66.

58. Ibid., p. 179.

59. Quoted in Mme Edgar Quinet, *Cinquante années d'amitié: 1825-1875* (Paris: Armand Colin et Cie., 1899), Michelet to Quinet, June 5, 1843, p. 120.

60. Michelet, *Lettres inédites*, Michelet to Alfred, October 19, 1844, p. 82.

61. Bibliothèque historique de la ville de Paris, MS. Correspondance 6, A4718, fol. 183, September 6, 1845; MS. Correspondance 11, A4747, fol. 102, Charles Cocks to Michelet, May 25, 1846.

62. Jules Michelet, *Œuvres complètes*, vol. 32: *Du prêtre, de la femme, de la famille* (Paris: Flammarion, 1895), p. 106.

63. Archives Nationales, MS. BB$^{18}$1428 (d$^r$9741), fol. 187, prosecuting attorney to minister of justice.

64. Ibid.

65. Archives Nationales, MS. CC469.

66. Ibid.

67. Archives du Collège de France, MS. Michelet dossier, fol. 86, copy of *Le Moniteur universel* of April 15, 1845.

68. Bibliothèque de l'Arsenal, MS. 7631, Enfantin to Michelet, February 25, 1845.

69. Ibid.

70. Quoted in Gabriel Monod, *Jules Michelet* (Paris: Hachette, 1905), George Sand to Michelet, April 1, 1845, pp. 353-54.

71. Michelet, *Journal*, 1:546. January 25, 1844.

## Chapter 9

1. Jules Michelet, *Journal*, ed. and introduction by Paul Viallaneix, 2 vols. (Paris: Gallimard, 1959, 1962), 1:296-302, passim.

2. Bibliothèque historique de la ville de Paris, MS. Correspondance 6, A4728, fol. 206, Michelet to his aunts in Renwez, February 2, 1846.

3. Bibliothèque historique de la ville de Paris, MS. Correspondance 6, A4729, fol. 208, Michelet to his aunts in Renwez, February 23, 1846.

4. Félicité Robert de Lamennais, *Paroles d'un croyant* (Paris: Armand Colin, 1949), p. 73.

5. Quoted in Gabriel Monod, *La Vie et la pensée de Jules Michelet*, ed. Charles Bémont and Henri Hauser, 2 vols. (Paris: Champion, Bibliothèque de l'Ecole des hautes études, 1923), 2:98.

6. Louis Chevalier, *Laboring Classes and Dangerous Classes: In Paris During the First Half of the Nineteenth Century*, trans. Frank Jellinek (New York: Howard Fertig, 1973), pp. 93-98.

7. Jules Michelet, *The People*, trans. and introduction by John P. McKay (Chicago: University of Illinois Press, 1973), p. 3.

8. Ibid.

9. Ibid., p. 7.

10. Ibid., p. 9.

11. Ibid., p. 10.

12. Ibid., p. 16.

13. Ibid., p. 18.

14. Ibid., p. 7.

15. Ibid., p. 26.
16. Ibid., p. 32
17. Ibid., pp. 32-33.
18. Ibid., p. 39.
19. Ibid., p. 40.
20. Ibid., p. 45.
21. Ibid., p. 47.
22. Ibid., p. 50.
23. Ibid., p. 15.
24. Ibid., p. 65.
25. Ibid., p. 67.
26. Ibid., p. 69.
27. Ibid., p. 70.
28. Ibid., p. 76.
29. Ibid., pp. 77-78.
30. Ibid., p. 83.
31. For example, see: Michelet, *Journal*, 1:592. February 20, 1845.
32. Michelet, *The People*, p. 83.
33. Ibid., p. 87.
34. Ibid.
35. Ibid.
36. Ibid., p. 89.
37. Ibid., p. 93.
38. Ibid., p. 99.
39. Ibid., p. 98.
40. Ibid.
41. Ibid.
42. Ibid., pp. 4-5.
43. Ibid., p. 99.
44. Ibid., p. 106.
45. Ibid., p. 109.
46. Ibid., p. 103.
47. Ibid., p. 104.
48. Ibid., p. 115.
49. Ibid., p. 117.
50. Ibid., p. 118.
51. Ibid., p. 99.
52. Lamennais, *Paroles d'un croyant*, p. 150.
53. Michelet, *The People*, p. 90.
54. Ibid., p. 159.
55. Ibid., p. 161.
56. Lamennais, *Paroles d'un croyant*, p. 150.
57. Félicité Robert de Lamennais, *Le Livre du peuple*, 4th ed. (Paris: Pagnerre, 1838), p. 139.
58. Michelet, *The People*, p. 179.
59. Ibid., p. 190.
60. Ibid., p. 200.
61. Ibid., p. 201.

62. Ibid., p. 21.
63. Ibid., pp. 204-5.
64. Ibid., pp. 205-6.
65. Ibid., p. 205.
66. Ibid., p. 204.
67. Ibid., pp. 141-42.
68. Ibid., p. 143.
69. Ibid., p. 90.

## Chapter 10

1. Gustave Flaubert, *Sentimental Education*, trans. and introduction by Robert Baldick (Baltimore: Penguin Books, 1964), pp. 157-59.
2. Jules Michelet, *The People*, trans. and introduction by John P. McKay (Chicago: University of Illinois Press, (1973), p. 11.
3. Mme Edgar Quinet, *Cinquante années d'amitié: 1825-1875* (Paris: Armand Colin et Cie., 1899), p. 6.
4. Quoted in Jules Michelet, *Journal*, ed. and introduction by Paul Viallaneix, 2 vols. (Paris: Gallimard, 1959, 1962), Eugène Noël to his parents, January 29, 1846, 1:902.
5. Jules Michelet, *L'Etudiant*, introduction by Gaëtan Picon (Paris: Editions du Seuil, 1970), lecture 1, p. 58.
6. Ibid., lecture 1, p. 59.
7. Ibid.
8. Ibid., lecture 1, p. 60.
9. Ibid., lecture 2, p. 65.
10. Ibid., lecture 2, p. 62.
11. Ibid., lecture 2, p. 65.
12. Michelet, *The People*, p. 90.
13. Jules Michelet, *Lettres inédites de Jules Michelet*, ed. Paul Sirven (Paris: Presses Universitaires de France, 1924), Michelet to Noël, December 9, 1847, p. 114.
14. Michelet, *L'Etudiant*, lecture 1, p. 63.
15. Ibid., lecture 1, p. 57.
16. Ibid., Michelet to Letronne, January 3, 1848, pp. 91-92.
17. Michelet kept the letters of protest. Bibliothèque historique de la ville de Paris, MS. Collège de France 1, A3779, fol. 90.
18. Bibliothèque historique de la ville de Paris, MS. Correspondance 6, A4712, fol. 171, Michelet to his aunts in Renwez, January 15, 1848.
19. Michelet, *L'Etudiant*, lecture 8, p. 140.
20. Michelet, *Journal*, Michelet to Lamartine, February 22, 1848, 1:921.
21. Quoted in Michelet, *Journal*, Alfred to Noël, February 25, 1848, 1:921.
22. Ibid., Alfred to Noël, March 2, 1848, 1:921-22.
23. Ibid., Alfred to Noël, March 4, 1848, 1:922.
24. Ibid., Alfred to Noël, March 3, 1848.
25. Bibliothèque historique de la ville de Paris, MS. Correspondance 6, A4741, fol. 169, Michelet to his Aunt Hyacinthe, 1848.

26. Bibliothèque historique de la ville de Paris, MS. Correspondance 6, A4710, fol. 167, Michelet to his aunts in Renwez, 1848.

27. Quoted in J. M. Carré, *Michelet et son temps* (Paris: Perrin, 1926), Michelet to representatives in the Ardennes, March 10, 1848, p. 31.

28. Michelet, *L'Etudiant*, p. 183.

29. Ibid., p. 181.

30. Ibid., p. 175.

31. Ibid., p. 178.

32. Ibid., p. 174.

33. Michelet, *Journal*, 1:685. April 4, 1848.

34. Michelet, *Lettres inédites*, Michelet to Alfred, April 21, 1848, p. 117.

35. Michelet, *Journal*, 1:925. April 23, 1848 copy of his voting choices.

36. Ibid., 1:688. May 18, 1848.

37. Ibid., Michelet to Béranger, June 16, 1848, 1:928-29.

38. Quoted in Jean Touchard, *La Gloire de Béranger* (Paris: Armand Colin, 1968), Béranger to Michelet, June 19, 1848, p. 245.

39. Michelet, *Journal*, 1:929.

40. Eugène Noël, *J. Michelet et ses enfants* (Paris: Maurice Dreyfous, 1878), p. 220.

41. Michelet, *Journal*, 1:693. June 27, 1848.

42. Ibid., 1:693-94. June 28, 1848.

43. Ibid., Michelet to Noël, July 21, 1848, 1:932. On the same day Michelet wrote virtually the same thing to his future wife, Athénaïs, 2:606. "It is [the June Days] the act of an *imperceptible minority* in comparison with the total population."

44. Quoted in Michelet, *Journal*, Alfred to Félicie Lefebvre Guyot, July 14, 1848, 1:931.

45. Michelet, *Lettres inédites*, Michelet to Alfred and Adèle, July 16, 1848, p. 119; Michelet to Alfred, October 10, 1848, p. 124.

46. Noël, *J. Michelet et ses enfants*, Noël to Alfred, January 3, 1849, pp. 227-28.

47. Michelet, *Journal*, 2:31. March 11, 1849.

48. Jules Michelet, *Nouvelles lettres inédites de Michelet*, ed. Paul Desachy (Monaco: Edition de l'Acanthe, 1955), Michelet to Charles Alexandre, September 22, 1848, p. 7.

49. Michelet, *Lettres inédites*, Michelet to Noël, January 1, 1850, p. 145.

50. Michelet, *Journal*, 2:23. February 27, 1849.

51. Ibid., 2:8. January 21, 1849.

52. Ibid., 2:11. January 22, 1849.

53. Ibid., 2:12. January 23, 1849.

54. Ibid., 2:16. January 29, 1849.

55. Ibid., 2:43. April 24, 1849.

56. Ibid., 2:101. May 16, 1850.

57. Ibid., 2:45. April 26, 1849.

58. Centre de recherches révolutionnaires et romantiques, Université de Clermont, Clermont-Ferrand, typescripts of Michelet's courses at the Collège de France, April 26, 1849, p. 64; Cf. Maistre who wrote: "During my life, I have seen Frenchmen, Italians, Russians, and so on; thanks to Montesquieu, I even know that one can be Persian; but I must say, as for man, I have never come across him anywhere; if he exists, he is completely unknown to me." Joseph de Maistre, *The Works of Joseph de Maistre*, trans. and introduction by Jack Lively (New York: Macmillan Company, 1965), p. 80.

59. Centre de recherches révolutionnaires et romantiques, 1849 course at the Collège de France, April 26, 1849, p. 62.

60. Quoted in Gabriel Monod, *Jules Michelet* (Paris: Hachette, 1905), Michelet to Sand, April 2, 1850, p. 358.

61. Centre de recherches révolutionnaires et romantiques, 1851 course at the Collège de France, December 26, 1850, p. 18.

62. Archives du Collège de France, MS. Michelet dossier, fol. 11, Barthélemy Saint-Hilaire to Michelet, February 3, 1849; fol. 13A, posted warning, February 17, 1849.

63. Archives du Collège de France, MS. Michelet dossier, fol. 14A, posted warning, March 6, 1849.

64. Archives du Collège de France, MS. Michelet dossier, fol. 15, prefect of police to Barthélemy Saint-Hilaire, March 6, 1849.

65. Archives du Collège de France, MS. Michelet dossier, fol. 17, Barthélemy Saint-Hilaire to Michelet, March 14, 1849.

66. Michelet, *Lettres inédites*, Michelet to Noël, March 1849, p. 128.

67. Archives du Collège de France, MS. Michelet dossier, fol. 20, minister of public education to Barthélemy Saint-Hilaire, February 8, 1850.

68. Archives du Collège de France, MS. Michelet dossier, fol. 27, minister of public education to Barthélemy Saint-Hilaire, February 5, 1851.

69. Archives du Collège France, MS. Michelet dossier, fol. 35, Barthélemy Saint-Hilaire to Michelet, March 5, 1851.

70. Archives du Collège de France, MS. Michelet dossier, fol. 37A, minister of public education to Barthélemy Saint-Hilaire, March 5, 1851.

71. Archives du Collège de France, MS. Michelet dossier, fol. 37B, minister of public education to Barthélemy Saint-Hilaire, March 5, 1851.

72. Archives du Collège de France, MS. Michelet dossier, fol. 38, Barthélemy Saint-Hilaire to prefect of police, March 6, 1851.

73. Archives du Collège de France, MS. Michelet dossier, fol. 45 B, Barthélemy Saint-Hilaire to each professor, March 8, 1851.

74. Archives du Collège de France, MS. Michelet dossier, fol. 52, Quinet to Barthélemy Saint-Hilaire, n.d.

75. Quoted in Oscar Haac, *Les Principes inspirateurs de Michelet* (Paris: Presses Universitaires de France, 1951), p. 129.

76. Archives du Collège de France, MS. Michelet dossier, fol. 74A, copy of decree of April 12, 1852.

77. Bibliothèque historique de la ville de Paris, MS. Fonds Baudoüin-Dumesnil, Michelet aux Archives, fol. 3, 7, Chabrier to Michelet, March 10, 1849.

78. Quoted in Emile Campardon, *Souvenirs d'un vieil archiviste* (Paris: n.p., 1906), p. 102.

79. Bibliothèque historique de la ville de Paris, MS. Fonds Baudoüin-Dumesnil, Michelet aux Archives, fol. 6, 16.

80. Michelet, *Journal*, 2:191-92. May 19, 1852.

81. Michelet, *Lettres inédites*, Michelet to Alfred, December 6, 1852, p. 193.

82. Michelet, *Journal*, 2:243. April 13, 1854.

83. Jules Michelet, *Le Banquet* (Paris: Marpon et Flammarion, 1879), p. 197.

84. Ibid., p. 208.

85. Ibid., p. 210.

86. Ibid., p. 233.
87. Michelet, *Journal*, 2:248. May 30, 1854.
88. Bibliothèque historique de la ville de Paris, MS. Correspondance 3, A4238, fol. 135, Michelet to Quinet, April 24, 1854.
89. Michelet, *Journal*, 2:254. May 6, 1854.
90. Ibid.
91. Michelet, *Le Banquet*, p. 173.
92. Ibid.
93. Quoted in Paul Viallaneix, "En marge du *Banquet*: deux inédits de Michelet," *Revue d'histoire littéraire de la France* 53 (July-September 1953):308.
94. Ibid., p. 307.

## Chapter 11

1. Jules Michelet, *Lettres inédites de Jules Michelet*, ed. Paul Sirven (Paris: Presses Universitaires de France, 1924), Michelet to Alfred, October 1852, p. 186.
2. Bibliothèque historique de la ville de Paris, MS. Fonds Baudoüin-Dumesnil, Michelet et ses éditeurs, Cote 5716, February 2, 1847.
3. Bibliothèque historique de la ville de Paris, MS. Fonds Baudoüin-Dumesnil, Michelet et ses éditeurs, Cote 5716, June 29, 1851.
4. Gustave Planche, "Histoire de la Révolution française: par M. Michelet," *Revue des Deux Mondes* 20 (January 15, 1850):352-54.
5. Bibliothèque historique de la ville de Paris, MS. Fonds Baudoüin-Dumesnil, Michelet et ses éditeurs, Cote 5716, June 18, 1849.
6. Alphonse Aulard, "Michelet: Historien de la Révolution française," *La Révolution française* 81 (1928):136.
7. Jean Jaurès, *Histoire socialiste de la Révolution française*, 8 vols. (Paris: Editions de la librairie de l'humanité, 1922-24), 1:26.
8. George Rudé, *The Crowd in the French Revolution* (London, Oxford, and New York: Oxford University Press, 1967), pp. 59, 232.
9. Albert Soboul, *The Sans-Culottes*, trans. Remy Inglis Hall (New York: Doubleday and Company, Inc., Anchor Books, 1972), p. xxiii.
10. Jules Michelet, *Histoire de la Révolution française*, ed. Gérard Walter, 2 vols. (Paris: Gallimard, N.R.F., Bibliothèque de la Pléiade, 1939, 1952), 1:13.
11. Ibid., 1:13-14.
12. Quoted in Paul Viallaneix, "En marge du *Banquet*: deux inédits de Michelet," *Revue d'histoire littéraire de la France* 53 (July-September 1953):309.
13. Michelet, *Histoire de la Révolution française*, 1:13.
14. Ibid., 1:14.
15. Jules Michelet, *Œuvres complètes*, vol. 4: *Histoire de France* (Paris: Flammarion, 1894), p. 348.
16. Jules Michelet, *Journal*, ed. and introduction by Paul Viallaneix, 2 vols. (Paris: Gallimard, 1959, 1962), 1:657. November 21, 1846.
17. Jules Michelet, *History of the French Revolution*, ed. and indroduction by Gordon Wright, trans. Charles Cocks (Chicago: University of Chicago Press, 1967), pp. 13-14.
18. Michelet, *Histoire de la Révolution française*, 1:283.

19. Ibid.
20. Ibid., 1:286.
21. Ibid., 1:967.
22. Ibid., 2:1018-19.
23. Ibid., 1:282.
24. Ibid., 2:991.
25. Ibid., 1:608.
26. Michelet, *History of the French Revolution*, pp. 12-13.
27. François Mignet, *Histoire de la Révolution française*, 2 vols. (Paris: Firmin Didot frères, 1837), 2:366.
28. Adolphe Thiers, *History of the French Revolution*, trans. Frederick Shoberl, 4 vols. (Philadelphia: Carey and Hart, 1842), 1:68.
29. Ibid., 4:430.
30. Ibid., 4:429.
31. Mignet, *Histoire de la Révolution française*, 1:4.
32. Ibid., 1:290.
33. Thomas Carlyle, *The French Revolution*, 3 vols. (New York: Frederick A. Stokes Company, 1893), 1:243-44.
34. Ph. Buchez and P. C. Roux, *Histoire parlementaire de la Révolution française*, 40 vols. (Paris: Paulin, 1834-40), 1:1.
35. Edgar Quinet, *Œuvres complètes*, 10 vols. (Paris: Pagnerre, 1857-58), 3:224.
36. Alphonse de Lamartine, *History of the Girondists*, trans. H. T. Ryde, 3 vols. (New York: Harper and Brothers, 1854-59), 1:38.
37. Ibid., 1:249.
38. Ibid., 1:19.
39. Louis Blanc, *History of the French Revolution*, trans. from the French (Philadelphia: Lea and Blanchard, 1848), p. 567.
40. Ibid.
41. Alexis de Tocqueville, *The Old Régime and the French Revolution*. trans. Stuart Gilbert (New York: Doubleday and Company, Inc., Anchor Books, 1955), p. 19.
42. Ibid., p. vii.
43. Ibid., p. 209.
44. Michelet, *Histoire de la Révolution française*, 1:vii.
45. Michelet, *History of the French Revolution*, p. 3.
46. Ibid.
47. Ibid., p. 5.
48. Ibid., p. 18.
49. Ibid., p. 17.
50. Ibid.
51. Ibid.
52. Ibid., p. 22.
53. Ibid.
54. Ibid.
55. Ibid., p. 27.
56. Ibid.
57. Bibliothèque historique de la ville de Paris, MS. Correspondance 3, A4237, fol. 132, Michelet to Quinet, February 10, 1854.
58. Michelet, *History of the French Revolution*, p. 21.

## Jules Michelet

59. Michelet, *Histoire de la Révolution française*, 1:294.
60. Quoted in J. M. Carré, *Michelet et son temps* (Paris: Perrin, 1926), Michelet to Lamartine, November 1847, pp. 26-27.
61. Michelet, *History of the French Revolution*, p. 29.
62. Ibid., p. 34.
63. Ibid., p. 35.
64. Ibid., p. 36.
65. Ibid., pp. 57-59.
66. Jaurès, *Histoire socialiste de la Révolution française*, attacked Michelet's interperation of economic decline prior to the French Revolution. He showed the increasing prosperity of France and the bourgeoisie during these pre-Revolutionary years and has been followed in his interpretation, for example, by Georges Lefebvre, *The French Revolution*, vol. 1: *From Its Orgins to 1793*, trans. Elizabeth Moss Evanson (New York: Columbia Univeristy Press, 1962), p. 117.
67. Michelet, *History of the French Revolution*, p. 80.
68. Ibid., p. 83.
69. Ibid., p. 121.
70. Ibid., p. 122.
71. Ibid., p. 161.
72. Ibid.
73. Rudé, *The Crowd in the French Revolution*, p. 59.
74. Michelet, *History of the French Revolution*, p. 231.
75. Ibid., p. 232.
76. Ibid., p. 233.
77. Ibid., p. 240.
78. Ibid., p. 245.
79. Ibid., 246.
80. Ibid., p. 279.
81. Ibid., p. 323.
82. Ibid., p. 325.
83. Ibid., p. 366.
84. Ibid., pp. 390-91.
85. Ibid., p. 430.
86. Ibid., p. 431.
87. Ibid., p. 432.
88. Ibid., p. 444.
89. Ibid.
90. Ibid., p. 452.
91. Ibid., p. 13.
92. Michelet, *Histoire de la Révolution française*, 1:430.

## Chapter 12

1. Jules Michelet, *Histoire de la Révolution française*, ed. Gérard Walter, 2 vols. (Paris: Gallimard, N.R.F., Bibliothèque de la Pléiade, 1939, 1952), 2:1019.

2. Jules Michelet, *Lettres inédites de Jules Michelet*, ed. Paul Sirven (Paris: Presses Universitaires de France, 1924), Michelet to Alfred, September 13, 1847, p. 109.

3. Michelet, *Histoire de la Révolution française*, 2:995.

4. Ibid., 1:14.

5. Ibid., 1:290-91.

6. Ibid., 1:14.

7. Ibid., 2:991.

8. Ibid., 1:287.

9. Ibid., 1:283.

10. Ibid., 1:291.

11. Ibid., 1:293.

12. Ibid., 1:761, 967; Jules Michelet, *History of the French Revolution*, ed. and introduction by Gordon Wright, trans. Charles Cocks (Chicago: University of Chicago Press, 1967), p. 281.

13. Michelet, *History of the French Revolution*, p. 12.

14. Michelet, *Histoire de la Révolution française*, 1:1093.

15. Ibid., 1:1451.

16. For example, see: Alphonse de Lamartine, *History of the Girondists*, trans. H. T. Ryde, 3 vols. (New York: Harper and Brothers, 1854-59), 1:19.

17. Michelet, *History of the French Revolution*, pp. 338-39.

18. Michelet, *Histoire de la Révolution française*, 2:142.

19. Thomas Carlyle, *The French Revolution*, 3 vols. (New York: Frederick A. Stokes Company, 1893), 2:164.

20. Ibid., 2:167.

21. Louis Blanc, *History of the French Revolution*, trans. from the French (Philadelphia: Lea and Blanchard, 1848), p. 451.

22. Michelet, *Histoire de la Révolution française*, 1:555.

23. Michelet, *History of the French Revolution*, p. 266.

24. Ibid., pp. 376-77.

25. Ibid., p. 267.

26. Ibid., p. 265.

27. Ibid., p. 433.

28. Michelet, *Histoire de la Révolution française*, 1:443.

29. Ibid., 1:1142-43.

30. Ibid., 1:1165-66.

31. Ibid., 2:14.

32. Ibid., 2:201.

33. Ibid., 2:195.

34. Ibid., 2:203.

35. Ibid., 2:201.

36. Ibid., 2:202.

37. Ibid.

38. Louis Blanc, *Histoire de la Révolution française*, 12 vols. (Paris: Langlois et Leclercq, 1847-62), 7:207.

39. Ibid., 7:35.

40. Michelet, *Histoire de la Révolution française*, 1:475.

41. Ibid., 2:38.

42. Ibid., 1:491.

43. Ibid., 1:733.
44. For example, see: Ibid., 1:850, 865.
45. Ibid., 1:869.
46. Ibid., 1:1177.
47. Ibid., 1:835.
48. Blanc, *Histoire de la Révolution française*, 6:263.
49. Michelet, *Histoire de la Révolution françasie*, 2:35.
50. Ibid., 2:348.
51. Ibid., 2:869.
52. Ibid., 2:671.
53. Blanc, *Histoire de la Révolution française*, 6:354-56.
54. Michelet, *Histoire de la Révolution française*, 2:1016.
55. Ibid.
56. Ibid., 1:494.
57. Ibid., 1:495.
58. Ibid., 1:505.
59. Ibid., 1:1178.
60. Ibid., 1:534.
61. Lamartine, *History of the Girondists*, 1:138-40.
62. Michelet, *Histoire de la Révolution française*, 1:844.
63. Ibid., 1:968.
64. Lamartine, *History of the Girondists*, 2:152.
65. Michelet, *Histoire de la Révolution française*, 1:908.
66. Ibid., 1:908.
67. Ibid., 2:161.
68. Ibid., 1:1287.
69. Ibid., 1:1025.
70. Ibid., 2:309.
71. Ibid., 2:310.
72. Ibid., 2:580.
73. Ibid., 2:796.
74. Blanc, *Histoire de la Révolution française*, 10:409.
75. Lamartine, *History of the Girondists*, 3:385.
76. Carlyle, *The French Revolution*, 3:296.
77. Michelet, *Histoire de la Révolution française*, 2:807.
78. Ibid.
79. Ibid., 2:809.

## *Chapter 13*

1. Jules Michelet, *Journal*, ed. and introduction by Paul Viallaneix, 2 vols. (Paris: Gallimard, 1959, 1962), 1:604. June 3, 1845.
2. Bibliothèque historique de la ville de Paris, MS. Correspondance 5, A4673, fol. 149, Michelet to Charles Michelet, April 29, 1850.
3. Michelet, *Journal*, 1:604. June 3, 1845.
4. Ibid., 1:610. July 19, 1845.

5. Jules Michelet, *Lettres inédites de Jules Michelet*, ed. Paul Sirven (Paris: Presses Universitaires de France, 1924), Michelet to Noël, July 2, 1852, pp. 178-79.

6. Michelet, *Journal*, 1:621. August 23, 1845.

7. Ibid., 1:622.

8. Jules Michelet, *L'Etudiant*, introduction by Gaëtan Picon (Paris: Editions du Seuil, 1970), lecture 3, p. 83.

9. Michelet, *Journal*, 1:622. August 23, 1845.

10. Ibid., 1:679. November 20, 1847.

11. Jules Michelet, *History of the French Revolution*, ed. and introduction by Gordon Wright, trans. Charles Cocks, (Chicago: University of Chicago Press, 1967), p. 20.

12. Michelet, *Journal*, 1:685. March 21, 1848.

13. Michelet, *L'Etudiant*, p. 173.

14. Michelet, *Journal*, 2:147-48. January 22, 1851.

15. Ibid., 1:678. November 20, 1847.

16. Jules Michelet, *Nouvelles lettres inédites de Michelet*, ed. Paul Desachy (Monaco: Edition de l'Acanthe 1955), Guillaume Le Jean to Charles Alexandre, 1848, pp. 5-6.

17. Michelet, *Journal*, 2:116. August 11, 1850.

18. Bibliothèque historique de la ville de Paris, MS. Correspondance 37, A4997, fol. 130, Augustin Thierry to Michelet, December 20, 1848.

19. Michelet, *Journal*, 2:128. September 5, 1850.

20. Ibid., 2:37. March 26, 1849.

21. Ibid., Michelet to Alexandre Laya, July 20, 1852, 2:748.

22. Ibid., 1:590. February 14, 1845.

23. Ibid., 1:684. February 23, 1848.

24. Centre de recherches révolutionnaires et romantiques, Université de Clermont, Clermont-Ferrand, typescripts of Michelet's courses at the Collège de France, June 11, 1848, p. 76.

## Chapter 14

1. Jules Michelet, *Journal*, ed. and introduction by Paul Vaillaneix, 2 vols. (Paris: Gallimard, 1959, 1962), 2:595.

2. Ibid., 2:575.

3. Quoted in Michelet, *Journal*, Athénaïs to Michelet, October 23, 1847, 2:602.

4. Ibid., Michelet to Athénaïs, October 30, 1847, 2:603.

5. Ibid., Athénaïs to Michelet, December 2, 1848, 2:609.

6. Ibid., Athénaïs to Michelet, December 13, 1848, 2:614.

7. Ibid., Michelet to Athénaïs, January 3, 1849, 2:628.

8. Ibid., Michelet to Athénaïs, January 9, 1849, 2:635.

9. Quoted in Ladislas Mickiewicz, "Jules Michelet et Adam Mickiewicz," *Revue des Deux Mondes* 20 (1924), Michelet to Mickiewicz, January 27, 1849, p. 179.

10. Michelet, *Journal*, 2:12. January 23, 1849.

11. Ibid., 2:214. February 11, 1853.

12. For example, see: Michelet, *Journal*, 2:32, 75, March 13, 1849, November 1, 1849; *Journal*, vols. 3 and 4, ed. and introduction by Claude Digeon (Paris: Gallimard, 1967), 3:315-6, 407, 470. August 12, 1865, August 7, 1866, May 29, 1867.

13. A psychological examination of *La Sorcière* was begun by Alain Besançon, "Le Premier Livre de *La Sorcière*," *Annales* 26 (January-Februray 1971):186-204.

14. Michelet, *Journal*, 3:273, 322, 343, 370. December 25, 1864, August 18, 1865, September 10, 1865, January 25, 1866.

15. Michelet, *Journal*, 2:323-24. May 1857.

16. See ibid., 2:21, 22, 33, 37, 38, 49, 66, for typical examples of this kind of entry, found throughout volumes 3 and 4.

17. Athénaïs Michelet, *La Mort et les funérailles de J. Michelet* (Paris: Sandoz et Fischbacher, 1876).

18. Bibliothèque historique de la ville de Paris, MS. Correspondance 7, A4735, fol. 40, Alfred to Athénaïs, December 13, 1848.

19. Michelet, *Journal*, Michelet to Athénaïs, January 1, 1849, 2:626.

20. Mme Edgar Quinet, *Cinquante années d'amitié: 1825-1875* (Paris: Armand Colin et Cie., 1899), p. 307.

21. Most of Michelet's personal papers from the two years he knew Mme Dumesnil were destroyed. Athénaïs wanted any expression of feeling and concern for Mme Dumesnil by her husand thrown away.

22. Mme Quinet, *Cinquante années d'amitié*, p. 324.

23. Ibid., Michelet to Quinet, May 8, 1866, p. 302.

24. Ibid., Quinet to Michelet, November 18, 1867, p. 314.

25. Ibid., Michelet to Quinet, September 9, 1868, pp. 321-22.

26. Ibid., Quinet to Michelet, September 18, 1868, pp. 322-23.

27. Eugène Noël, *J. Michelet et ses enfants* (Paris: Maurice Dreyfous, 1878), Quinet to Alfred, December 28, 1868, pp. 358-59.

28. Bibliothèque historique de la ville de Paris, MS. Histoire du XIX$^e$ siècle marginalia, A3855, fol. 35.

29. Jules Michelet, *Lettres inédites de Jules Michelet*, ed. Paul Sirven (Paris: Presses Universitaires de France, 1924), Michelet to Noël, September 11, 1855, pp. 230-31.

30. Jules Michelet, *The Bird*, trans. W. H. Davenport Adams (London: T. Nelson and Sons, 1869), pp. 13-15.

31. Jules Michelet, *The Mountain*, trans. W. H. Davenport Adams (London: T. Nelson and Sons, 1872), p. 104.

32. Michelet, *The Bird*, p. 53.

33. Bibliothèque historique de la ville de Paris, MS. Fonds Baudoüin-Dumesnil, Michelet et ses éditeurs, Cote 5716. In this box are contained Hachette's publication records for each edition of these works.

34. Michelet, *Journal*, 2:313. September 16, 1856.

35. Michelet, *The Bird*, p. 13.

36. Ibid., p. 42.

37. Ibid., p. 312.

38. Ibid., p. 17.

39. Michelet, *The Mountain*, p. 213.

40. Ibid., p. 300.

41. Ibid.

42. Jules Michelet, *The Sea*, trans. from the French (New York: Follett, Foster and Co., 1864), pp. 393, 398.

43. Jules Michelet, *The Woman*, trans. J. W. Palmer (New York: Rudd and Carleton, 1860), pp. 104-5.

44. Jules Michelet, *Œuvres complètes*, ed. Paul Viallaneix, vol. 3: *1832-1839* (Paris: Flammarion 1973), p. 887.

45. Ibid., 3:890.

46. Jules Michelet, *Œuvres complètes*, vol. 32: *Du prêtre, de la femme, de la famille* (Paris: Flammarion 1895), p. 13.

47. Ibid., 32:4.

48. Ibid., 32:9.

49. Ibid.

50. Jules Michelet, *Satanism and Witchcraft*, trans. A. R. Allinson (New York: Citadel Press, 1939), p. 86.

51. Ibid., p. 87.

52. Ibid., p. viii; Jules Michelet, *Bible de l'humanité* (Paris: Chamerot, 1864), pp. 1-9.

53. Michelet, *Satanism and Witchcraft*, p. 86.

54. Jules Michelet, *Women of the French Revolution*, trans. M. Roberts Penington (Philadelphia: Henry Carey Baird, 1855), p. 281.

55. Michelet, *Journal*, 2:154. March 25, 1851.

56. Honoré de Balzac, *Le Contrat de mariage* (Paris: Paul Ollendorf, Société d'éditions littéraires et artistiques, 1902), p. 8.

57. Jules Michelet, *Love*, trans. J. W. Palmer (New York: Rudd and Carleton, 1859), p. 53.

58. Michelet, *Woman*, p. 81.

59. Michelet, *Love*, p. 277.

60. Ibid., p. 197.

61. Ibid., p. 295.

62. Michelet, *Lettres inédites*, Michelet to Alfred, September 9, 1858, p. 255.

63. Michelet, *Journal*, 2:453. January 1, 1859.

64. Michelet, *Lettres inédites*, Michelet to Alfred, January 12, 1859, p. 265.

65. Ibid., Michelet to Alfred, February 1, 1859, p. 266.

66. Ibid., Michelet to Alfred, December 1, 1858, p. 261.

67. Alain Plessis. *De la fête impériale au mur des fédérés: 1852-1871*, Nouvelle histoire de la France contemporaine, vol. 9 (Pairs: Editions du Seuil, 1973), pp. 134. 170.

## Chapter 15

1. Jules Michelet, *The Bird*, trans. W. H. Davenport Adams (London: T. Nelson and Sons, 1869), p. 15.

2. Jules Michelet, *Œuvres complètes*, vols. 1-16: *Histoire de France* (Paris: Flammarion, 1893-97), 8:362-64. The original edition was seventeen volumes, but in this edition vols. 10-12 are contained in two volumes.

3. Ibid., 7:171.

4. Ibid., 10:200.

5. Ibid., 8:7.

6. Ibid., 9:443.

7. Ibid., 9:496.

8. Ibid., 9:581.

9. Ibid., 10:94-95.

10. Ibid., 12:7.

11. Ibid., 16:3.

12. Ibid., 15:81.

13. Ibid., 16:3.

14. Ibid., 16:9.

15. Ibid., 16:2

16. Ibid., 14:9.

17. Ibid., 15:380.

18. Ibid.

19. Ibid., 1:xvi, xxiii.

20. Ibid., 1:x.

21. Ibid., 1:xliv-xlv.

22. Jules Michelet, *Journal*, ed. and introduction by Claude Digeon, vols, 3 and 4 (Paris: Gallimard, 1976), 4:240, September 5, 1870.

23. Jules Michelet, *France before Europe*, trans. from the French (Boston: Roberts Brothers, 1871), p. xix.

24. Ibid., p. xii.

25. Ibid., p. xvii.

26. Ibid., p. 17.

27. Ibid., p. 13.

28. Ibid., p. 111.

29. Ibid.

30. Jules Michelet, *Lettres inédites de Jules Michelet*, ed. Paul Sirven (Paris: Presses Universitaires de France, 1924), Michelet to Noël, 1870, pp. 314-15.

31. Michelet, *Journal*, 4:268. January 29, 1871.

32. Bibliothèque historique de la ville de Paris, MS. Biographie 3, A3774, vol. 151. letter to *Libéral de l'Est*, February 20, 1872.

33. Michelet, *Œuvres complètes*, vols. 24-26: *Histoire du XIXᵉ siècle*, (1898), 26:3-14.

34. Michelet, *The Bird*, p. 312.

35. Jules Michelet, *The Mountain*, trans. W. H. Davenport Adams (London: T. Nelson and Sons, 1872), pp. 286-87.

36. Michelet, *France before Europe*, p. 18.

37. Michelet, *Œuvres complètes*, 24:9.

38. Ibid., 24:12.

39. Ibid., 26:5.

40. Michelet, *France before Europe*. p. 41.

41. Ibid., p. 42.

42. Michelet, *Œuvres complètes*, 26:13.

43. Ibid., 26:3-4.

44. Ibid., 26:13.

45. Ibid., 26:14.

46. Ibid., 26:1.

47. Quoted in Athénaïs Michelet, *La Mort et les funérailles de J. Michelet* (Paris: Sandoz et Fischbacher, 1876), p. 6.

## Epilogue

1. Georges Meunier, "Pourquoi on ne lit plus Michelet." *Revue politique et littéraire*, ser. 4, 9 (1898):786-88.

2. Ibid., p. 786.

3. Charles Maurras, *"Trois idées politiques"* in *Romantisme et révolution* (Versailles; Bibliothèque des oeuvres politiques, 1928), p. 243.

4. Ibid., pp. 250, 253.

5. Ibid., p. 252.

6. Ibid., p. 254.

7. Léon Daudet, *The Stupid 19th Century*, trans. Lewis Galantière (New York: Payson and Clarke, 1928), p. 102.

8. Quoted in Alfred Chabaud, *Jules Michelet: son oeuvre* (Paris: Nouvelle Revue critique, 1929), p. 54.

9. Quoted in H. Stuart Hughes, *The Obstructed Path* (New York: Harper and Row, Harper Torchbooks, 1969), pp. 21-22.

10. Lucien Febvre, *Michelet* (Geneva: Editions des Trois Collines, 1946), p. 58.

11. Jules Michelet, *Satanism and Witchcraft*, trans. A. R. Allinson (New York: Citadel Press, 1939), pp. 316-17.

12. Febvre, *Michelet*, pp. 82-83.

13. Jules Michelet, *Œuvres complètes*, vol. 25: *Histoire du XIXᵉ siècle* (Paris: Flammarion, 1898), pp. 4-5.

14. Ibid., 25:3.

# Bibliography

## I. Manuscripts

A. Bibliothèque historique de la ville de Paris. This library houses most of Michelet's papers.

1. a) Forty books with various titles such as Biographie I or Voyage I, averaging four hundred folio pages each, contain: Notes for all of his lectures and books; diaries for his travels; large segments of his *Journal*, expecially for the early years; marginalia for his works; official documents relating to his life; and hundreds of other items, since he apparently kept everything he wrote or that was sent to him.

   b) Thirty-seven numbered volumes of correspondence averaging some three hundred letters each. These are letters to and from members of his family and hundreds of intellectuals and artists in Paris and beyond. The most substantial single correspondence is with Quinet, Correspondance 3, A4171-A4383.

   c) Manuscripts of most of his works, which I examined but did not footnote.

2. Fonds Baudoüin-Dumesnil. This deposit, given in 1948 by the descendants of Alfred Dumesnil, contains:

   a) Four books of correspondence from Michelet to Alfred.

   b) Two books of correspondence from Michelet to Noël.

   c) One book on Michelet and the Archives, with notes from many of his reports, copies of his final reports, and correspondence relating to his work.

   d) One carton of correspondence and notes between Michelet and his publishers.

   e) Some fifty-one other cartons, mostly relating to Alfred and his work, but some of them with material relating to his father-in-law.

B. Bibliothèque de l'Institut

1. Letters of Michelet to Athénaïs, to his son, and friends. Cotes 2198 and 3687.

C. Archives Nationales

1. Michelet's reports as head of the historical section, mostly grouped in cartons AB VF$_I$ and AB IX$_I$.

2. Government correspondence and other documents relating to controversies over Michelet's books, especially *Du prêtre* and *La Sorcière*. BB[18]1662; BB[18]1428, dr9741; and CC 469.

D. Bibliothèque de l'Arsenal

1. Correspondence between Michelet, Enfantin, Thoré, and d'Eichthal. Cotes 7757, 7913, 13749, and 7631.

E. Archives du Collège de France
  1. Michelet's dossier contains everything pertaining to his thirteen years at the Collège de France. The most interesting documents are the correspondence between Michelet and the administration, and between the administration, government, and police department.
F. Centre de recherches romantiques et révolutionnaries, Université de Clermont, Clermont-Ferrand
  1. This is the center for M. Paul Viallaneix's current preparation of a new edition of Michelet's *Œuvres complètes*. I read typescripts, which will appear in a future volume, of Michelet's courses at the Ecole Normale from 1827 to 1836, except for 1834 and 1835. Notes were taken by students in these courses, but Michelet edited and approved the copies. The manuscripts of these notes are at the Bibliothèque de l'Ecole Normale in Paris. I also read manuscripts of Michelet's courses at the Collège de France from 1839 to 1851. These courses have been only partially preserved. The manuscripts are at the Bibliothèque historique de la valle de Paris.

## *II. Books, articles, and letters of Michelet*

*Œuvres complètes*. 40 vols. Paris: Flammarion, 1893-98.
*Œuvres complètes*. 46 vols. Paris: Calmann-Lévy, 1898-1903.
*Œuvres complètes*. Edited by Paul Viallaneix. 20 vols. Paris: Flammarion, 1971-.
*L'Amour*. Paris: Hachette, 1858.
*Le Banquet*. Paris: Marpon et Flammarion, 1879.
*Bible de l'humanité*. Paris: Chamerot, 1864.
*The Bird*. Translated by W. H. Davenport Adams. London: T. Nelson and Sons, 1869.
*Ecrits de jeunesse*. Edited and Introduction by Paul Viallaneix. Paris: Gallimard, 1959.
*L'Etudiant*. Introduction by Gaëtan Picon. Paris: Editions du Seuil, 1970.
*Examen des vies des hommes illustres de Plutarque*. Paris: Fain, 1819.
*La Femme*. Paris: Hachette, 1860.
*Les Femmes de la Révolution*. Paris: A. Delahays, 1854.
*France before Europe*. Translated from the French. Boston: Roberts Brothers, 1871.
*La France devant l'Europe*. Florence: Le Monnier, 1871.
"L'Héroïsme de l'esprit." *L'Arc* 52 (1973): 3-17.
*Histoire de France*. 2 vols. Paris: Hachette, 1833.
*Histoire de France*. 17 vols. Paris: A. Lacroix. 1871-74.
*Histoire de la République romaine*. 2 vols. Paris: Hachette, 1831.
*Histoire de la Révolution française*. Edited by Gérard Walter. 2 vols. Paris: Gallimard, N.R.F., Bibliothèque de la Pléiade, 1939, 1952.
*Histoire du XIX^e siècle*. 3 vols. Paris: Lévy frères, 1875-76.
*History of France*. Translated by G. H. Smith. 2 vols. New York: D. Appleton and Company, 1845, 1848.
*History of the French Revolution*. Edited and Introduction by Gordon Wright. Translated by Charles Cocks. Chicago: University of Chicago Press, 1967.
*L'Insecte*. Paris: Hachette, 1858.
*Introduction à l'histoire universelle*. Paris: Hachette, 1831.

*Des jésuites*. Introduction by Paul Viallaneix. Paris: Jean-Jacques Pauvert, 1966.

*Journal*. Edited and Introduction by Paul Viallaneix, 2 vols. Paris: Gallimard, 1959, 1962; Vols. 3 and 4 edited and introduction by Claude Digeon, Paris: Gallimard, 1976.

*Légendes démocratiques du Nord*. Edited by Michel Cadot. Paris: Presses Universitaires de France, 1968.

*Lettres inédites de Jules Michelet*. Edited by Paul Sirven. Paris: Presses Universitaires de France, 1924.

*Love*. Translated by J. W. Palmer. New York: Rudd and Carleton, 1859.

*La Mer*. Paris: Hachette, 1861.

*La Montagne*. Paris: A. Lacroix, Verboeckhoven et Cie., 1868.

*The Mountain*. Translated by W. H. Davenport Adams. London: T. Nelson and Sons, 1872.

*Nos Fils*. Paris: A. Lacroix, Verboeckhoven et Cie., 1870.

*Nouvelles lettres inédites de Michelet*. Edited by Paul Desachy. Monaco: Edition de l'Acanthe, 1955.

*L'Oiseau*. Paris: Hachette, 1856.

*Origines du droit français*. Paris: Hachette, 1837.

*The People*. Translated and Introduction by John P. McKay. Chicago: University of Illinois Press, 1973.

*De percipienda infinitate secundum Lockium*. Paris: Fain, 1819.

*Le Peuple*. Edited and Introduction by Lucien Refort. Paris: Didier, 1946.

*Précis de l'histoire de France jusqu'à la Révolution française*. Paris: Hachette, 1833.

*Précis de l'histoire moderne*. Paris: L. Colas, L. Hachette, 1827.

*Du prêtre, de la femme, de la famille*. Paris: Hachette, 1845.

*Satanism and Witchcraft*. Translated by A. R. Allinson. New York: Citadel Press, 1939.

*The Sea*. Translated from the French. New York: Follet, Foster and Co., 1864.

*La Sorcière*. Introduction by Paul Viallaneix. Paris: Garnier-Flammarion, 1966.

"Sur le livre *Du prêtre et de la femme*: Réponse aux critiques." *Revue indépendante*, Ser. 1, 19 (March 25, 1845):188-202.

*Sylvine*. Paris: René Debresse, 1940.

*Tableau chronologique de l'histoire moderne*. Paris: L. Colas, 1825.

*Tableau de la France*. Edited by Lucien Refort. Paris: Société des Belles Lettres, 1949.

*Tableaux synchroniques de l'histoire moderne*. Paris: L. Colas, 1826.

*The Woman*. Translated by J. W. Plamer. New York: Rudd and Charleton, 1860.

*Women of the French Revolution*. Translated by M. Roberts Penington. Philadelphia: Henry Carey Baird, 1855.

## III. Secondary sources on Michelet and related works and articles

Agulhon, Maurice. *1848 ou l'apprentissage de la république*. Nouvelle histoire de la France contemporaine, vol. 8. Paris: Editions du Seuil, 1973.

Albitreccia, A. *Jules Michelet et les leçons de son œuvre*. Mulhouse: Société générale d'imprimerie, 1926.

Atherton, John. "The Function of Space in Michelet's Writings." *Modern Language Notes* 80 (1965):336-46.

# Bibliography

Aulard, Alphonse: "Michelet: historien de la Révolution française." *La Révolution française* 81 (1928):136-50.

Balzac, Honoré de. *Le Contrat de mariage*. Paris: Société d'éditions littéraires et artistiques, Paul Ollendorff, 1902.

———. *Les Paysans*. Paris: Garnier frères, 1964.

Barante, Prosper Brugière, Baron de. *Histoire des Ducs de Bourgogne*. 12 vols. Paris: Delloye, 1839.

Barthes, Roland. *Michelet par lui-même*. Paris: Editions du Seuil, 1954.

Bellanger, Claude; Godechot, Jacques; Guiral, Pierre; and Terrou, Fernand. *Histoire générale de la presse française*. Vol. 2: *De 1815 à 1871*. Paris: Presses Universitaires de France, 1969.

Besançon, Alain. "Le premier livre de *La Sorcière*." *Annales* 26 *(January-February 1971):186-204.*

Blanc, Louis. *Histoire de la Révloution française*. 12 vols. Paris: Langlois et Leclercq, 1847-62.

———. *History of the French Revolution*. Translated from the French. Philadelphia: Lea and Blanchard, 1848.

Bonald, L. A., Vicomte de. *Théorie du pouvoir politique et religieux*. Paris: union générale d'éditions, 1966.

Borzeix, Jean-Marie. "L'Unité et l'union du 'Peuple' à 'La Bible de l'humanité.'" *Romantisme* 1-2 (October 1971):111-16.

Brahm, Alcanter de. *Michelet inconnu*. Paris: Debresse, 1937.

Brunhes, Jean. *Michelet*. Paris: Perrin, 1898.

Buchez, Ph., and Roux, P.C. *Histoire parlementaire de la Révolution française*. 40 vols. Paris: Paulin, 1834-40.

Bury, R. de. "Michelet, sa veuve et Jules Claretie." *Mercure de France* 38 (1901):107-19.

Cabanis, José. *Michelet, le prêtre et la femme*. Paris: Gallimard, 1978.

Calo, Jeanne. *La Création de la femme chez Michelet*. Paris: Nizet, 1975.

Campardon, Emile. *Souvenirs d'un vieil archiviste*. Paris: n. p., 1906.

Carlyle, Thomas. *The French Revolution*. 3 vols. New York: Frederick A. Stokes Company, 1893.

Carré, Jean-Marie. *Les Ardennes et leurs écrivains*. Charleville: Ruben, 1922.

Carré, Jean-Marie. *Michelet et son temps*. Paris: Perrin, 1926.

———. "Michelet et les travaux récents." *Revue des cours et conférences* 26 (1926):274-87.

Cavanaugh, Gerald L. "The Present State of French Revolutionary Historiography: Alfred Cobban and Beyond." *French Historical Studies* 7 (Fall 1972):587-606.

Chabaud, Alfred. *Jules Michelet: son œuvre*. Paris: Nouvelle Revue Critique, 1929.

Charléty, Sébastien. *Histoire du Saint-Simonisme*. Paris: Editions Gonthier, 1931.

Chatelain, B. *Michelet: ses idées sur l'histoire*. Paris: Cahiers des études littéraires françaises, 1930.

Chevalier, Louis. *Laboring Classes and Dangerous Classes: In Paris during the First Half of the Nineteenth Century*. Translated by Frank Jellinek. New York: Howard Fertig, 1973.

Claretie, Jules. "La Jeunesse de Michelet." *Le Temps*, March 19, 1901.

Cobban, Alfred. *Aspects of the French Revolution*. New York: W. W. Norton and Company, Inc., 1970.

Collins, Irene. *The Government and the Newspaper Press in France, 1814-1881*. London: Oxford University Press, 1959.

## Jules Michelet

Condorcet, J. A., Marquis de. *Esquisse d'un tableau historique des progrès de l'esprit humain*. Paris: Editions sociales, 1966.

Cornuz, Jean-Louis. *Jules Michelet: un aspect de la pensée religieuse au XIX^e siècle*. Geneva: Droz et Lille, Giard, 1955.

Cousin, Victor. *Cours de philosophie*. Vol. 1: *Introduction à l'histoire de la philosophie*. Paris: Pichon et Didier, 1828.

————. *Œuvres*. 16 vols. Paris: Ladrange, 1846-51.

Daménie, Louis. "La Révolution phénomène divin, mécanisme social ou complot diabolique? Michelet: romancier, prêtre et prophète de la révolution." *L'Ordre français* 116 (1967): 14-42.

Dansette, Adrien. *Religious History of Modern France*. Translated by John Dingle. Vol. 1. New York: Herder and Herder, 1961.

Daudet, Léon. *The Stupid 19th Century*. Translated by Lewis Galantière. New York: Payson and Clarke, 1928.

Daumard, Adeline. *Les Bourgeois de Paris au XIX^e siècle*. Paris: Flammarion, 1970.

Derré, Jean-René. *Le Renouvellement de la pensée religieuse en France de 1824 à 1834*. Paris: C. Klincksieck, 1962.

Desachy, Paul. "Lettres de Michelet." *Europe* 38 (May-August 1935):333-55.

Desgarets, Nicolas. [pseud.] *Monopole Universitaire*. Lyon: n. p., 1843.

————. *L'Université jugée par elle-même*. Lyon: n. p., September 1843.

Digeon, Claude. *Note sur le "Journal" de Michelet: 1870-1874*. Saarbrücken: Universität des Saarlandes, 1959.

*The Doctrine of Saint-Simon: An Exposition*. Translated and Introduction by George G. Iggers. New York: Schocken Books, 1972.

Dolléans, Edouard. *Histoire du mouvement ouvrier*. 2 vols. Paris: Armand Colin, 1936-39.

Dupouy, Auguste. *Michelet en Bretagne*. Paris: Editions des Horizons de France, 1948.

Edwards, William Frédéric. *Des caractères philosophiques des races humaines considérées dans leurs rapports avec l'histoire: Lettre à M. Amédée Thierry*. Paris: Compère jeune, 1829.

Evans, David Owen. *Le socialisme romantique: Pierre Leroux et ses contemporains*. Paris: M. Rivière, 1948.

Evans, Serge. *Leur jeunesse: Michelet, Renan, Taine*. Paris: Revue Moderne des Arts et de la Vie, 1934.

Favret, Jeanne. "Sorcières et lumières." *Critique* 24 (1971): 351-76.

Febvre, Lucien. "How Jules Michelet invented the Renaissance." *A New Kind of History*. Edited by Peter Burke. Translated by K. Folca. New York: Harper and Row, 1973.

————. *Michelet*. Geneva: Editions des Trois Collines, 1946.

————. *La Terre et l'évolution humaine*. L'Evolution de l'Humanité. Paris: Editions Albin Michel, 1970.

Flaubert, Gustave. *Sentimental Education*. Translated and Introduction by Robert Baldick. Baltimore: Penguin Books, 1964.

Fourier, Charles. *The Utopian Vision of Charles Fourier: Selected Texts on Work, Love, and Passionate Attraction*. Translated, Edited, and Introduction by Jonathan Beecher and Richard Bienvenu. Boston: Beacon Press, 1971.

Furet, François and Richet, Denis. *La Révolution française*. Paris: Fayard, 1973.

Gualmier, Jean. *Michelet*. Paris: Desclée de Brouwer, 1968.

Gérard, Alice. *La Révolution française, mythes et interprétations: 1789-1870*. Paris: Flammarion, 1970.

Geyl, Pieter. *Debates with Historians*. Cleveland: World Publishing Company, 1958.

————. *Napoleon: For and Against*. Translated by Olive Renier. New Haven: Yale University Press, 1949.

Giraud, Victor. "L'évolution spirituelle de Michelet." *Revue des Deux Mondes* 41 (1927):218-30.

Godechot, Jacques. *Les Révolutions*. Nouvelle Clio, vol. 36. Paris: Presses Universitaires de France, 1970.

Gooch, G. P. *History and Historians in the Nineteenth Century*. London: Longmans, Green and Co., Ltd., 1952.

Grimaud, Louis. *Histoire de la liberté d'enseignement en France*. Vol. 6. Paris: B. Arthaud, 1954.

Guéhenno, Jean. *L'Evangile éternel*. Paris: Gresset, 1927.

Guizot, François. *Essais sur l'histoire de France*. 4th ed. Paris: Ladrange, 1836.

————. *Historical Essays and Lectures*. Edited and Introduction by Stanley Mellon. Chicago: University of Chicago Press, 1972.

————. *The History of Civilization*. Translated by William Hazlitt. 2 vols. London: H. G. Bohn, 1856.

Haac, Oscar. "Jules Michelet: cours professé au Collège de France dans le second semestre 1839, d'après les notes d'Alfred Dumesnil." *Revue d'histoire littéraire de la France* 54 (July-September 1954):1-139.

————. *Les principes inspirateurs de Michelet*. Paris: Presses Universitaires de France, 1951.

Halévy, Daniel. *Histoire d'une histoire*. Paris: Bernard Grasset, 1939.

————. *Jules Michelet*. Paris: Hachette, 1928.

————. "Le Mariage de Michelet." *Revue de Paris* 4 (1902):557-79.

Halévy, Elie. *Sismondi*. Paris: Librairie Félix Alcan, 1933.

Hauser, Henri. "Lettres inédites sur la mort de Charles Michelet." *Revue Bleue* 1 (1914):421-23.

————. "Michelet et Sismondi." *La Semaine littéraire de Genève* 23 (July 3, 1915):328-32.

Hegel, Georg Wilhelm Friedrich. *The Philosophy of History*. Translated by J. Sibree. New York: Dover Publications, Inc., 1956.

Herder, Johann Gottfried von. *Idées sur la philosophie de l'histoire de l'humanité*. Translated by Edgar Quinet. 3 vols. Paris: Levrault, 1827-28.

————. *Reflections on the Philosophy of the History of Mankind*. Translated by T. O. Churchill. Edited and Introduction by Frank E. Manuel. Chicago: Univeristy of Chicago Press, 1968.

Hughes, H. Stuart. *The Obstructed Path*. New York: Harper and Row, Harper Torchbooks, 1969.

Jardin, André and Tudesq, André-Jean. *La France des notables: 1815-1845*. Nouvelle histoire de la France contemporaine, vols. 6, 7. Paris: Editions du Seuil, 1973.

Jaurès, Jean. *Histoire socialiste de la Révolution française*. 8 vols. Paris: Editions de la librairie de l'humanité, 1922-24.

Jeannin, Pierre. *Ecole Normale Supérieure*. Brussels: Gregg Associates, 1963.

Johnson, Douglas. *Guizot: Aspects of French History, 1787-1874*. London: Routledge and K. Paul, 1963.

Johnson, Mary-Elisabeth. *Michelet et le christianisme*. Paris: Nizet, 1955.

# Jules Michelet

Kaegi, Werner. *Michelet und Deutschland*. Basel: Schwabe, 1936.

Kaplan, Edward K., *Michelet's Poetic Vision: A Romantic Philosophy of Nature, Man and Woman*. Amherst: University of Massachusetts Press, 1977.

Kohn, Hans. *Prophets and Peoples*. New York: Macmillan Company, 1946.

Krakowski, Edouard. *Adam Mickiewicz: philosophe mystique*. Paris: Mercure de France, 1935.

Labrousse, Camille Ernest. *Le Mouvement ouvrier et les théories sociales en France de 1815 à 1848*. Paris: Centre de documentation universitaire, 1964.

Lamartine, Alphonse de. *History of the Girondists*. Translated by H. T. Ryde. 3 vols. New York: Harper and Brothers, 1854-59.

Lamennais, Félicité Robert de. *Le livre du peuple*. 4th ed. Paris: Pagnerre, 1838.

————. *Paroles d'un croyant*. Paris: Armand Colin, 1949.

Lanson, Gustave. "La Formation de la méthode historique de Michelet." *Revue d'histoire moderne et contemporaine* 7 (1905):5-31.

Lavisse, Ernest. "L'Etudiant de Michelet." *Revue de Paris* 6 (January 15, 1899):326-42.

Lefebvre, Georges. *The French Revolution*. Vol. 1: *From Its Origins to 1793*. Translated by Elizabeth Moss Evanson. New York: Columbia University Press, 1962.

Ledré, Charles. *Histoire de la presse*. Paris: Librairie Arthème Fayard, 1958.

Leroux, Pierre. *De l'humanité*. 2 vols. Paris: Perrotin, 1840.

Leroy, Maxime. *Histoire des idées sociales en France*. 3 vols. Paris: Gallimard, N.R.F., 1946-54.

Mahieu, Bernard. "Michelet aux Archives Nationales." *Bulletin de la Société de l'histoire de France* 82 (1946-47):71-86.

Maistre, Joseph de. *The Works of Joseph de Maistre*. Translated and Introduction by Jack Lively. New York: Macmillan Company, 1965.

Manuel, Frank E. *The New World of Henri Saint-Simon*. Notre Dame: University of Notre Dame Press, 1963.

————. *The Prophets of Paris*. New York: Harper and Row, Harper Torchbooks, 1965.

Martin, Henri. *Histoire de France*. 4th ed. 17 vols. Paris: Furne, 1860-62.

Mathiez, Albert. *The French Revolution*. Translated by Catherine Alison Phillips. New York: Grosset and Dunlap, 1964.

Maurras, Charles. "Trois Idées politiques" in *Romantisme et révolution*. Versailles: Bibliothèque des œuvres politiques, 1928.

Mellon, Stanley. *The Political Uses of History*. Stanford: Stanford University Press, 1958.

Meunier, Georges. "Pourquoi on ne lit plus Michelet." *Revue politique et littéraire*, Ser. 4, 9 (1898):786-90.

Meyerhoff, Hans. *Time in Literature*. Berkeley and Los Angeles: University of California Press, 1955.

Michelet, Athénaïs. *Le centenaire de Michelet*. Paris: Flammarion, 1898.

————. *Ma collaboration à "L'Oiseau," "L'Insecte," "La Mer," "La Montagne"; mes droits à la moitié de leur produit*. Paris: Chamerot, 1876.

————. *La Mort et les funérailles de J. Michelet*. Paris. Sandoz et Fischbacher, 1876.

————. *La Tombe de Michelet*. Paris: S. Raçon, 1875.

Mickiewicz, Adam. *Selected Poems*. Edited by Clark Mills. New York: Noonday Press, 1956.

Mickiewicz, Ladislas. "Jules Michelet et Adam Mickiewicz." *Revue des Deux Mondes* 20 (1924):168-87.

Mignet, François. *Histoire de la Révolution française.* 2 vols. Paris: Firmin Didot frères, 1837.

Monin, H. "La Rupture de Michelet et de Quinet." *Revue d'histoire littéraire de la France* 19 (1912):818-41.

Monod, Gabriel. *Jules Michelet.* Paris: Hachette, 1905.

———. "Jules Michelet et Alexandre Herzen d'après leur correspondance intime." *La Revue* 68 (May 15, 1907): 145-64.

———. *Les Maîtres de l'histoire: Renan, Taine, Michelet.* Paris: Calmann-Lévy, 1894.

———. "Michelet à l'Ecole Normale." *Revue des Deux Mondes* 126 (Demember 15, 1894):894-917.

———. "M. et Mme Michelet en 1870-1871." *Revue Bleue,* Ser. 5, 4 (1905):582-84.

———. "Michelet et Béranger." *La Revue* 93 (1911):14-34.

———. "Michelet et l'histoire de la Révolution française." *Revue internationale de l'enseignement* 59 (January-June 1910):414-37.

———. "Michelet et son *Journal intime.*" *Revue Bleue* 41 (March 3, 1888):272-76.

———. "Michelet et son père." *Revue Bleue* 3 (1905):225-27; 260-63.

———. *La Vie et la pensée de Jules Michelet.* Edited by Charles Bémont and Henri Hauser. 2 vols. Paris: Champion, Bibliothèque de l'Ecole des hautes études, 1923.

Moody, Joseph. "The French Catholic Press in the Education Conflict of the 1840s." *French Historical Studies* 7 (Spring 1972):394-415.

Noël, Eugène. *J. Michelet et ses enfants.* Paris: Maurice Dreyfous. 1878.

Orr, Linda. *Jules Michelet: Nature, History, and Language.* Ithaca and London: Cornell University Press, 1976.

Pellegrini, Carlo. "Sismondi e Michelet." *Studi Francesi* (1965):25-40.

Pinkney, David H. *The French Revolution of 1830.* Princeton: Princeton University Press, 1972.

Plamenatz, John. *Man and Society.* 2 vols. New York: McGraw-Hill, 1963.

Planche, Gustave. "Histoire de la Révolution française; par M. Michelet." *Revue des Deux Mondes* 20 (January 15, 1850): 343-55.

Plessis, Alain. *De la fête impériale au mur des fédérés: 1852-1871.* Nouvelle histoire de la France contemporaine, vol. 9. Paris: Editions du Seuil, 1973.

Pochon, Jacques. "Edgar Quinet et les luttes du Collège de France." *Revue d'histoire littéraire de la France* 70 (July-August 1970):619-27.

Pommier, Jean. "Les idées de Michelet et de Renan sur la confession en 1845." *Journal de Psychologie normale et pathologique* 33 (1936):514-44.

———. *Michelet interprète de la figure humaine.* London: Athlone Press, 1961.

Poulet, Georges. "Michelet et le moment d'eros." *La Nouvelle Revue Française* 15 (1967):610-35.

———. *Studies in Human Time.* Translated by Elliott Coleman. Baltimore: Johns Hopkins Press, 1956.

Powers, Richard. *Edgar Quinet: A Study in French Patriotism.* Dallas: Southern Methodist University Press, 1957.

Proudhon, Pierre. *General Idea of the Revolution in the Nineteenth Century.* Translated by John Beverley Robinson. New York: Haskell House, 1969.

———. *What is Property?* Translated by Benjamin R. Tucker. New York: Howard Fertig, 1966.

Pugh, Anne R. *Michelet and His Ideas on Social Reform.* New York: Columbia University Press, 1923.

Quinet, Edgar. *Des jésuites*. Introduction by Paul Viallaneix. Paris: Jean-Jacques Pauvert, 1966.

———. *Œurves complètes*. 10 vols. Paris: Pagnerre, 1857-58.

Quinet, Mme Edgar. *Cinquante années d'amitié: 1825-1875*. Paris: Armand Colin et Cie., 1899.

Rearick, Charles. "Symbol, Legend and History: Michelet as Folklorist-Historian." *French Historical Studies* 7 (1971):72-92.

Refort, Lucien. *L'Art de Michelet dans son œuvre historique*. Paris: Champion, 1923.

Renan, Ernest. *L'Avenir de la science*. Paris: Calmann-Lévy, 1890.

Rocquain, Félix. "Michelet aux Archives Nationales" in *Notes et fragments d'histoire*. Paris: Plon, 1906.

Rousseau, Jean-Jacques. *Œuvres complètes*. 3rd ed. 25 vols. Paris: Baudouin frères, 1827-30.

Rudé, George. *The Crowd in the French Revolution*. London, Oxford, and New York: Oxford University Press, 1967.

Rudler, Gustave. *Michelet, historien de Jeanne d'Arc*. 2 vols. Paris: Presses Universitaires de France, 1926.

Ruggiero, Guido de. *The History of European Liberalism*. Translated by R. G. Collingwood. Boston: Beacon Press, 1959.

Salis, Adolphe de. *Sismondi*. Paris: Champion, 1932.

Scharten, Théodora. *Les voyages et séjours de Michelet en Italie*. Paris: Droz. 1934.

Schwab, Raymond. *La Renaissance orientale*. Paris: Payot, 1950.

Scott, Walter. *Quentin Durward*. Oxford: Clarendon, 1920.

Sée, Henri. "Michelet et l'histoire: résurrection." *Mercure de France* 189 (August 1, 1826):570-81.

Seebacher, Jacques. "L'attitude politique de Michelet." *Revue des Travaux de l'Académie des sciences morales*. Ser. 4, 120 (1967):107-22.

Seznec, Jean. "Michelet humaniste et les symboles de l'histoire." *Saggi e ricerchi de litteratura francese* 3 (1963):105-19.

Shafer, Boyd. *Faces of Nationalism*. New York: Harcourt, Brace, Jovanovich, Inc., 1972.

Simon, Jules. *Mignet, Michelet, Henri Martin*. Paris: Calmann-Lévy, 1890.

Sismondi, J. C. L. Simonde de. *Histoire des français*. 31 vols. Paris: Treuttel et Würtz, 1821-44.

Soboul, Albert. *Précis d'histoire de la Révolution française*. Paris: Editions sociales, 1972.

———. *The Sans-Culottes*. Translated by Remy Inglis Hall. New York: Doubleday and Company, Inc., Anchor Books, 1972.

Soltau, Roger. *French Political Thought in the Nineteenth Century*. New Haven: Yale University Press, 1931.

Stearns, Peter. *Priest and Revolutionary: Lamennais and the Dilemma of French Catholicism*. New York: Harper and Row, 1967.

Stewart, Dugald. *Histoire abrégée des sciences métaphysiques, morales et politiques depuis la Renaissance des lettres*. Translated and edited by J. A. Buchon. 3 vols. Paris: F. G. Levrault, 1820-23.

Sullerot, Evelyne. *Histoire de la presse feminine en France*. Paris: Armand Colin, 1966.

Talmon, J. L. *Political Messianism: The Romantic Phase*. New York: Frederick A. Praeger, 1960.

Theau, Jean. *La Conscience de la durée et le concept de temps*. Toulouse: Edouard Privat, 1969.

Thierry, Amédée. *Histoire des Gaulois*. 3 vols. Paris: A. Sautelet et Cie., 1828.

Thierry, Augustine. *Dix ans d'études historiques*. Paris: Furne, Jouvet et Cie., 1866.

―――. *Histoire de la conquête de l'Angleterre*. 2 vols. Paris: Furne, 1851.

―――. *Lettres sur l'histoire de France*. Paris: Furne, Jouvet et Cie., 1866.

Thiers, Adolphe. *History of the French Revolution*. Translated by Frederick Shoberl. 4 vols. Philadelphia: Carey and Hart, 1842.

Thompson, J. W. *A History of Historical Writing*. New York: Macmillan Company, 1942.

Tocqueville, Alexis de. *The Old Régime and the French Revolution*. Translated by Stuart Gilbert. New York: Doubleday and Company, Inc., Anchor Books, 1955.

―――. *Recollections*. Translated by George Lawrence. Edited by J. P. Mayer and A. P. Kerr. New York: Doubleday and Company, Inc., Anchor Books, 1971.

Touchard, Jean. *La Gloire de Béranger*. Paris: Armand Colin, 1968.

Tronchon, Henri. *Etudes*. Paris: Champion, 1935.

―――. *Le Jeune Edgar Quinet*. Paris: Les Belles Lettres, 1937.

Turgot, Anne Robert Jacques. *Œuvres*. Edited by Pierre Samuel Dupont de Nemours. 9 vols. Paris: A. Belin, 1808-11.

Valès, Albert. *Edgar Quinet*. Vienna: E. Aubinet fils, 1936.

Viallaneix, Paul. "En marge du *Banquet*: deux inédits de Michelet." *Revue d'histoire littéraire de la France* 53 (July-September 1953):306-18.

―――. "Le héros selon Michelet." *Romantisme* 1-2 (October 1971):102-10.

―――. "Michelet devant Dieu." *Revue d'histoire littéraire de la France* 70 (1970):667-73.

―――. *La Voie royale*. Paris: Delagrave, 1959; reprint ed., Paris: Flammarion, 1971.

Vico, Giambattista. *The New Science*. Translated by Thomas Bergin and Max Harold Fisch. Cornell: Cornell University Press, 1968.

Vigny, Alfred de. *Œuvres complètes*. 2 vols. Paris: Gallimard, N.R.F., Bibliothèque de la Pléiade, 1948.

Voltaire. *Œuvres complètes*. 2nd ed. 75 vols. Paris: Baudouin frères, 1825-28.

Weintraub, Wiktor. *Literature as Prophecy: Scholarship and Martinist Poetics in Mickiewicz's Parisian Lectures*. The Hauge: Mouton and Co., 1959.

―――. *The Poetry of Adam Mickiewicz*. The Hague: Mouton and Co., 1954.

Wilson, Edmund. *To The Finland Station*. New York: Doubleday and Company, Inc., Anchor Books, 1953.

Zaleski, Z. L. "Une amitié franco-polonaise: Mickiewicz, Michelet, Quinet." *Séances et travaux de l'Académie des Sciences morales et politiques* 204 (1925):97-114.

―――. "La légende de Kosciusko: Mickiewicz et Michelet." *Revue des études Slaves* 6 (1926):99-105.

# Index